Get the eBook FREE!

(PDF, ePub, Kindle, and liveBook all included)

We believe that once you buy a book from us, you should be able to read it in any format we have available. To get electronic versions of this book at no additional cost to you, purchase and then register this book at the Manning website.

Go to https://www.manning.com/freebook and follow the instructions to complete your pBook registration.

That's it!
Thanks from Manning!

Feature Engineering Bookcamp

Feature Engineering Bookcamp

SINAN OZDEMIR

MANNING
SHELTER ISLAND

For online information and ordering of this and other Manning books, please visit www.manning.com. The publisher offers discounts on this book when ordered in quantity. For more information, please contact

> Special Sales Department
> Manning Publications Co.
> 20 Baldwin Road
> PO Box 761
> Shelter Island, NY 11964
> Email: orders@manning.com

Manning Publications Co.
20 Baldwin Road
PO Box 761
Shelter Island, NY 11964

Development editor:	Toni Arritola
Technical development editor:	Al Krinker
Review editor:	Adriana Sabo
Production editor:	Andy Marinkovich
Copy editor:	Christian Berk
Proofreader:	Katie Tennant
Technical proofreader:	Ninoslav Čerkez
Typesetter:	Gordan Salinovic
Cover designer:	Marija Tudor

ISBN 9781617299797
Printed in the United States of America

brief contents

contents

3 Healthcare: Diagnosing COVID-19 34

4 Bias and fairness: Modeling recidivism 72

preface

Like many data scientists and machine learning engineers out there, most of my professional training and education came from real-world experiences, rather than classical education. I got all my degrees from Johns Hopkins in theoretical mathematics and never once learned about regressions and classification models. Once I received my master's degree, I decided to make the switch from pursuing my PhD to going into startups in Silicon Valley and teaching myself the basics of ML and AI.

I used free online resources and read reference books to begin my data science education and started a company focusing on creating enterprise AIs for large corporations. Nearly all of the material I picked up focused on the types of models and algorithms used to model data and make predictions. I used books to learn the theory and read online posts on sites like Medium to see how people would apply that theory to real-life applications.

It wasn't until a few years later that I started to realize that I could only go so far learning about topics like models, training, and parameter tuning. I was working with raw text data at the time, building enterprise-grade chatbots, and I noticed a big difference in the tone of the books and articles about natural language processing (NLP). They focused a lot on the classification and regression models I could use, but they focused equally, if not even more, on how to process the raw text for the models to use. They talked about tuning parameters for the data more than tuning parameters for the models themselves.

I wondered why this wasn't the case for other branches of ML and AI. Why weren't people transforming tabular data with the same rigor as text data? It couldn't be that it wasn't necessary or helpful because pretty much every survey asking about time spent in the data science process revealed that people spent a majority of time getting and cleaning data. I decided to take this gap and turn it into a book.

Funny enough, that wasn't this book. I wrote another book on feature engineering a few years prior to this one. My first book on feature engineering focused on the basics of feature engineering with an emphasis on explaining the tools and algorithms over showcasing how to use them day to day. This book takes a more practical approach. Every chapter in this book is dedicated to a use case in a particular field with a dataset that invites different feature engineering techniques to be used.

I tried to outline my own thinking process when it came to feature engineering in an easy-to-follow and concise format. I've made a career out of data science and machine learning, and feature engineering has been a huge part of that. I hope that this book will open your eyes and your conversations with colleagues about working with data and give you the tools and tricks to know which feature engineering techniques to apply and when.

acknowledgments

This book required a lot of work, but I believe that all the time and effort resulted in a great book. I sure hope that you think so as well! There are many people I'd like to thank for encouraging me and helping me along the way.

First and foremost, I want to thank my partner, Elizabeth. You've supported me, listened to me as I paced around our kitchen trying to figure out the best analogy for a complex topic, and walked the dog when it was my turn, but I was so engrossed in my writing that it totally slipped my mind. I love you more than anything.

Next, I'd like to acknowledge everyone at Manning who made this text possible. I know it took a while, but your constant support and belief in the topic kept me going when things were rough. Your commitment to the quality of this book has made it better for everyone who will read it.

I'd also like to thank all the reviewers, who took the time to read my manuscript at various stages during its development. To Aleksei Agarkov, Alexander Klyanchin, Amaresh Rajasekharan, Bhagvan Kommadi, Bob Quintus, Harveen Singh, Igor Dudchenko, Jim Amrhein, Jiri Pik, John Williams, Joshua A. McAdams, Krzysztof Jędrzejewski, Krzysztof Kamyczek, Lavanya Mysuru Krishnamurthy, Lokesh Kumar, Maria Ana, Maxim Volgin, Mikael Dautrey, Oliver Korten, Prashant Nair, Richard Vaughan, Sadhana Ganapathiraju, Satej Kumar Sahu, Seongjin Kim, Sergio Govoni, Shaksham Kapoor, Shweta Mohan Joshi, Subhash Talluri, Swapna Yeleswarapu, and Vishwesh Ravi Shrimaland: your suggestions helped make this a better book.

Finally, a special thank you goes to my technical proofreaders, who made sure that I crossed my t's, dotted my i's, and commented on my code!

All in all, many people made this book possible. Thank you all so much!

about this book

Feature Engineering Bookcamp was written both to give the reader an overview of popular feature engineering techniques and to provide a framework for thinking about when and how to use certain techniques. I have found that books that focus on one or the other can sometimes fall a bit flat. The book that focuses only on overviews tends to ignore the practical application side of things, whereas the book that focuses on the frameworks can leave readers asking themselves, "Sure, but why does it work?" I want readers to walk away confident in both understanding and applying these techniques.

Who should read this book?

Feature Engineering Bookcamp is for machine learning engineers and data scientists who have already entered the space and are looking for a boost in their abilities and skill sets. I assume that the reader already has functional knowledge of machine learning, cross-validation, parameter tuning, and model training using Python and scikit-learn. This book builds on that knowledge by incorporating feature engineering pipelines directly into existing machine learning frameworks.

How this book is organized: A roadmap

This book has two introductory chapters that cover the basics of feature engineering, including how to recognize different types of data and the different categories of feature engineering. Each of chapters 3 through 8 focuses on a specific case study with a different dataset and a different goal. Each chapter gives the reader a new perspective, a new dataset, and new feature engineering techniques that are specific to the type of data we are working with. The goal is to provide a broad and comprehensive view of the types of feature engineering techniques, while showcasing a variety of datasets and data types.

About the code

This book contains many examples of source code both in numbered listings and in line with normal text. In both cases, source code is formatted in a `fixed-width font` `like this` to separate it from ordinary text. Sometimes code is also **in bold** to highlight code that has changed from previous steps in the chapter, such as when a new feature adds to an existing line of code.

In many cases, the original source code has been reformatted; we've added line breaks and reworked indentation to accommodate the available page space in the book. In some cases, even this was not enough, and listings include line-continuation markers (➥). Additionally, comments in the source code have often been removed from the listings when the code is described in the text. Code annotations accompany many of the listings, highlighting important concepts.

You can get executable snippets of code from the liveBook (online) version of this book at https://livebook.manning.com/book/feature-engineering-bookcamp. The complete code for the examples in the book is available for download from my personal GitHub at https://github.com/sinanuozdemir/feature_engineering_bookcamp.

liveBook discussion forum

Purchase of *Feature Engineering Bookcamp* includes free access to liveBook, Manning's online reading platform. Using liveBook's exclusive discussion features, you can attach comments to the book globally or to specific sections or paragraphs. It's a snap to make notes for yourself, ask and answer technical questions, and receive help from the author and other users. To access the forum, go to https://livebook.manning .com/book/feature-engineering-bookcamp/discussion. You can also learn more about Manning's forums and the rules of conduct at https://livebook.manning.com/ discussion.

Manning's commitment to our readers is to provide a venue where a meaningful dialogue between individual readers and between readers and the author can take place. It is not a commitment to any specific amount of participation on the part of the author, whose contribution to the forum remains voluntary (and unpaid). We suggest you try asking the author some challenging questions lest his interest stray! The forum and the archives of previous discussions will be accessible from the publisher's website for as long as the book is in print.

about the author

 **SINAN OZDEMIR** is the founder and CTO of Shiba and is currently managing the Web3 components and machine learning models that power the company's social commerce platform. Sinan is a former lecturer of data science at Johns Hopkins University and the author of multiple textbooks on data science and machine learning. Additionally, he is the founder of the acquired Kylie.ai, an enterprise-grade conversational AI platform with robotic process automation (RPA) capabilities. He holds a master's degree in pure mathematics from Johns Hopkins University and is based in San Francisco, CA.

about the cover illustration

The figure on the cover of *Feature Engineering Bookcamp* is captioned "Homme du Thibet," or "Man from Tibet," taken from a collection by Jacques Grasset de Saint-Sauveur, published in 1797. Each illustration is finely drawn and colored by hand.

In those days, it was easy to identify where people lived and what their trade or station in life was just by their dress. Manning celebrates the inventiveness and initiative of the computer business with book covers based on the rich diversity of regional culture centuries ago, brought back to life by pictures from collections such as this one.

Introduction to feature engineering

This chapter covers
- Understanding the feature engineering and machine learning pipeline
- Examining why feature engineering is important to the machine learning process
- Taking a look at the types of feature engineering
- Understanding how this book is structured and the types of case studies we will focus on

Much of the current discourse around artificial intelligence (AI) and machine learning (ML) is inherently model-centric, focusing on the latest advancements in ML and deep learning. This model-first approach often comes with, at best, little regard for and, at worst, total disregard of the data being used to train said models. Fields like MLOps are exploding with ways to systematically train and utilize ML models with as little human interference as possible to "free up" the engineer's time.

Many prominent AI figures are urging data scientists to place more focus on a data-centric view of ML that focuses less on the model selection and hyperparameter-tuning process and more on techniques that enhance the data being ingested and used to train our models. Andrew Ng is on record saying that "machine learning is basically feature engineering" and that we need to be moving more toward a data-centric approach. Adopting a data-centric approach is especially useful when the following are true:

- Datasets have few observations (<10 K), so we can extract as much information as possible from fewer rows.
- Datasets have a large number of columns compared to the number of observations. This can lead to what is known as the *curse of dimensionality*, which describes an extremely sparse universe of data that ML models have difficulty learning from.
- Interpretability of the data and model is key.
- The domain of the data is inherently complex (e.g., accurate financial modeling is virtually impossible without clean and complete data).

We should be focusing on a part of the ML pipeline that requires arguably the most nuanced and careful deliberation: *feature engineering*.

In this book, we will dive into the different algorithms and statistical testing procedures used to identify the strongest features, create new ones, and measure ML model success as they relate to the strength of these features. For our purposes, we will define a *feature* as an attribute or column of data that is meaningful to an ML model. We will make these dives by way of several case studies, each of which belonging to different domains, including healthcare and finance, and will touch on several types of data, including tabular data, text data, image data, and time-series data.

1.1   *What is feature engineering, and why does it matter?*

The term *feature engineering* conjures different images for different data scientists. For some data scientists, feature engineering is how we narrow down the features needed for supervised models (e.g., trying to predict a response or outcome variable). For others, it is the methodology used to extract numerical representations from unstructured data for an unsupervised model (e.g., trying to extract structure from a previously unstructured dataset). Feature engineering is both of these and much more.

For the purposes of this book, feature engineering is the art of manipulating and transforming data into a format that optimally represents the underlying problem that an ML algorithm is trying to model and mitigates inherent complexities and biases within the data.

Data practitioners often rely on ML and deep learning algorithms to extract and learn patterns from data even when the data they are using are poorly formatted and non-optimal. Reasons for this range from the practitioner trusting their ML models too much to simply not knowing the best practices for dealing with messy and inconsistent data and hoping that the ML model will just "figure it out" for them. This approach never even gives the ML models a chance to learn from proper data and dooms the data scientist from the start.

It comes down to whether the data scientist is willing or able to use their data as much as possible by engineering the best possible features for their ML task. If we do not engineer proper features and rely on complex and slow ML models to figure it out for us, we will likely be left with poor ML models. If we instead take the time to understand our data and craft features for our ML models to learn from, we can end up with a smaller, faster models with on-par, or even superior, performance.

When it comes down to it, we want our ML models to perform as well as they possibly can, depending on whatever metric we choose to judge them on. To accomplish this, we can manipulate the data and the model (figure 1.1).

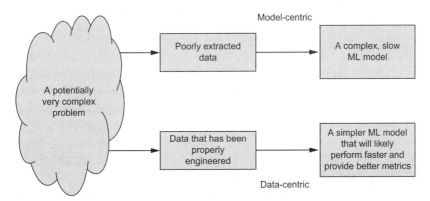

Figure 1.1 When taking a more data-centric approach to ML, we are not as concerned with improving the ML code, but instead, we are concerned with manipulating the impute data in such a way that the ML model has an easier time surfacing and using patterns in the data, leading to overall better performance in the pipeline.

This book focuses not on how to optimize ML models but, rather, on techniques for transforming and manipulating data to make it easier for ML models to process and learn from datasets. We will show that there is a whole world of feature engineering techniques that can help the overall ML pipeline that isn't just picking a better model with better hyperparameters.

1.1.1 Who needs feature engineering?

According to the 2020 State of Data Science survey by Anaconda (see https://www .anaconda.com/state-of-data-science-2020), data wrangling (which we can consider a stand-in term for feature engineering with the added step of data loading) takes up a disproportionate amount of time and, therefore, is on the mind of every data scientist. The survey shows how data management is still taking up a large portion of data scientists' time. Nearly half of the reported time was spent on data loading and "cleansing." The report claims that this was "disappointing" and that "data preparation and cleansing takes valuable time away from real data science work." One thing to note is that data "cleansing" is a pretty vague term and likely was used as a catchall for exploratory data analysis and all of feature engineering work. We believe that data preparation and feature engineering is a real, vital, and almost always unavoidable part of a data scientist's work and should be treated with as much respect as the portions of the pipeline that are focused on data modeling.

This book is dedicated to showcasing powerful feature engineering procedures, including model fairness evaluation (in our fairness case study chapter), deep learning–based representation learning (in both our NLP and image analysis case study chapters), hypothesis testing (in our healthcare case study), and more. These feature engineering techniques can affect model performance as much as the model selection and training process.

1.1.2 *What feature engineering cannot do*

It is important to mention that good feature engineering is not a silver bullet. Feature engineering cannot, for example, solve the problem of too little data for our ML models. While there is no magic threshold for how small is too small, in most cases, when working with datasets of under 1,000 rows, feature engineering can only do so much to squeeze as much information out of those observations as possible. Of course, there are exceptions to this. When we touch on transfer learning in our NLP and image case studies, we will see how pretrained ML models can learn from mere hundreds of observations, but this is only because they've been pretrained on hundreds of thousands of observations already.

Feature engineering also cannot create links between features and responses where there are not any. If the features we start with implicitly do not hold any predictive power to our response variable, then no amount of feature engineering will create that link. We could be able to achieve small bumps in performance, but we cannot expect either feature engineering or ML models to magically create relationships between features and responses for us.

1.1.3 *Great data, great models*

Great models cannot exist without great data. It is virtually impossible to guarantee an accurate and fair model without well-structured data that deeply represents the problem at hand.

I've spent the majority of my ML career working with natural language processing (NLP); specifically, I focus on building ML pipelines that can automatically derive and optimize conversational AI architecture from unstructured historical transcripts and knowledge bases. Early on, I spent most of my days focusing on deriving and implementing knowledge graphs and using state-of-the-art transfer learning and sequence-to-sequence models to develop conversational AI pipelines that could learn from raw human-to-human transcripts and be able to update on new topics as new conversations came in.

It was after my most recent AI startup was acquired that I met a conversational architecture designer and linguist named Lauren Senna, who taught me about the deep structure in conversations that she and her teams used to build bots that could outperform any of my auto-derived bots any day of the week. Lauren told me about the psychology of how people talk to and interact with bots and why it differed from how knowledge base articles are written. It was then that I finally realized I needed to spend more time focusing our ML efforts on preprocessing efforts to bring out these latent patterns and structures, so the predictive systems could grab hold of them and become more accurate than ever. She and I were responsible for, in some cases, up to 50% improvement in bot performance, and I would speak at various conferences about how data scientists could utilize similar techniques to unlock patterns in their own data.

Without understanding and respecting the data, I could have never brought out the greatness of the models trying their best to capture, learn from, and scale up the patterns locked within the data.

1.2 The feature engineering pipeline

Before we dive into the feature engineering pipeline, we need to back up a bit and talk about the overall ML pipeline. This is important because the feature engineering pipeline is itself a part of the greater ML pipeline, so this will give us the perspective we need to understand the feature engineering steps.

1.2.1 The machine learning pipeline

The ML pipeline generally consists of five steps (figure 1.2):

1 *Defining the problem domain*—What problem are we trying to solve with ML? This is the time to define any characteristics we want to prioritize, like the speed of model predictions or interpretability. These considerations will be crucial when it comes to model evaluation.

2 *Obtaining data that accurately represents the problem we are trying to solve*—Think about and implement methods of collecting data that are fair, safe, and respectful of the data providers' privacy. This is also a great time to perform an exploratory data analysis (EDA) to get a good sense of the data we are working with. I will assume you have done your fair share of EDA on data, and I will do my fair share in this book to help you understand our data as much as possible. If this is a supervised problem, are we going to deal with imbalanced classes? If this is an unsupervised problem, do we have a sample of data that will represent the population well enough to draw good enough insights?

3 *Feature engineering*—This is the main focus of this book and the pivotal point in our ML pipeline. This step involves all of the work of creating the optimal representation of data that can be fed into the ML models.

4 *Model selection and training*—This is a huge part of the data scientist's pipeline and should be done diligently and with care. At this stage, we are choosing

models that best fit our data and our considerations from step 1. If model interpretability was highlighted as a priority, perhaps, we will stay in the family of tree-based models over deep learning–driven models.

5   *Model deployment and evaluation*—At this stage, our data have been prepped, our models have been trained, and it's time to put our models into production. At this point, the data scientist can consider model versioning and prediction speeds as factors in the readiness of their models. For example, will we need some sort of user interface to obtain predictions synchronously, or can we perform predictions offline? Evaluation processes must be deployed to track out models' performance over time and look out for model decay.

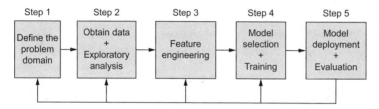

Figure 1.2   The ML pipeline. From left to right: we must understand the problem domain, obtain and understand data, engineer our features (which obviously is the main focus on this book), select and train our models, and then deploy models with the understanding that we may need to double back to any of the past steps if evaluations of the models show any kind of data or concept drift that would manifest as model decay—a drop in performance over time for our ML model.

TIP   Speaking of problem domain, it isn't required to be an expert in a particular domain to be a data scientist working on problems in said field. That being said, I would strongly encourage you to, at the very least, reach out to experts in a field and do some research to get yourself in a position where you can understand the potential pros and cons of architecting ML pipelines that may affect people.

In the last step of the ML pipeline, we also need to watch out for *concept drift* (when our interpretation of the data changes) and *data drift* (when the underlying distributions of our data change). These are references to how data may change *over time*. In this book, we will not need to worry about these concepts, but they are worth taking a moment to explore deeper.

Concept drift is the phenomenon that refers to the statistical properties of a feature or the response that has changed over time. If we train a model on a dataset at a point in time, we have, by definition, a snapshot of a function that relates our features to our response. As time progresses, the environment which that data represents may evolve, and how we perceive those features and responses may also change. This idea is most often applied to response variables but can also be considered for our features.

Imagine we are data scientists for a streaming media platform. We are tasked with building a model to predict when we should show a speed bump to the user and ask them whether they are still watching. We can build a basic model to predict this using metrics, such as *minutes since they pressed a button* or *average length of an episode of the show they are currently watching*, and our response would be a simple *True* or *False* to *should we show the speed bump or not?* At the time of model creation, our team sat down and, as domain experts, thought of all the ways we may want to show this speed bump. Maybe they fell asleep. Maybe they had to run out for an errand and left it on by accident. So we build a model and deploy it. Two months later, we start to receive requests to increase the time it takes to show the speed bump, and our team gets back together to read the requests. As it turns out, a large group of people (including this author) use streaming media apps to play soothing documentaries for their dogs and cats to help them with their separation anxiety when they leave for long stretches of time. This is a *concept* that our model was not trying to account for. We now have to add observations and features like *Is the show about animals?* to help account for this new concept.

Data drift refers to the phenomenon that our data's underlying distribution has shifted for some reason, but our interpretation of that feature remains unchanged. This is common when there are behavior changes that our models have not accounted for. Imagine we're back at the streaming media platform. We built a model in late 2019 to predict the number of hours someone would watch a show, given variables such as their past watching habits, types of shows they enjoy, and more, and it was going well. Suddenly, a global pandemic arises, and some of us (no judgment) start watching media online more often, maybe even while we are working to make it sound like people are still around us even while we are home alone. Our response variable's distribution (which is measured in hours of watch time) will dramatically shift to the right, and our model may not be able to keep up its past performance, given this distribution shift. This is data drift. The *concept* of hours watched hasn't changed, but it is our underlying distribution of that response that has changed.

This idea can be applied just as easily to a feature. If hours watched was a feature to a new response variable of *Will this person watch the next episode if we offer it to them?* the same principles apply, and that dramatic shift in the distribution is something our model hasn't seen before.

If we zoom in around the middle portion of the ML pipeline, we see feature engineering. Feature engineering, as it is a part of the larger ML pipeline, can be thought of as its own pipeline with its own steps. If we were to double-click and open up the feature engineering box in the ML pipeline, we would see the following steps:

1 *Feature understanding*—Recognizing the levels of data we are working with is crucial and will impact which types of feature engineering are available to us. It is at this stage that we will have to, for example, ascertain what level our data belong to. Don't worry; we will get into the levels of data in the next chapter.

2 *Feature structuring*—If any of our data are unstructured (e.g., text, image, video, etc.; see figure 1.3), we must convert them to a *structured format*, so our ML models can understand them. An example would be converting pieces of text into a vector representation or transforming images into a matrix form. We can use feature extraction or learning to accomplish this.

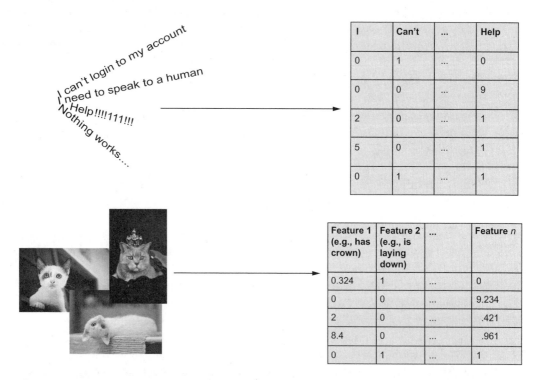

Figure 1.3   Raw data, such as text, audio, images, and videos, must be transformed into numerical vector representations to be processed by any ML algorithm. This process, which we will refer to as *feature structuring*, can be done through extraction techniques, such as applying a bag-of-words algorithm or using a nonparametric feature learning approach, like autoencoders (both bag-of-words and autoencoders are covered in our NLP case study). We will see both of these methods used in the fourth case study, on natural language processing.

3   *Feature optimization*—Once we have a structured representation for our data, we can apply optimizations, such as feature improvement, extraction, construction, and selection, to obtain the best data possible for our models. A majority of day-to-day feature engineering work is usually in this category. A majority of the code examples in this book will revolve around feature optimization. Every case study will have some instances of feature optimization, in which we will have to either create new features or take existing ones and make them more powerful for our ML model.

4   *Feature evaluation*—As we alter our feature engineering pipelines to try different scenarios, we will want to see just how effective the feature engineering techniques we've applied are going to be. We can achieve this by choosing a single learning algorithm and, perhaps, a few parameter options for quick tuning. We can then compare the applications of different feature engineering pipelines against a constant model to rank which steps of pipelines are performing, given a change in person with and without their appearance. If we are not seeing the performance where we need it to be, we will go back to previous optimization and structuring steps to attempt to get a better data representation (figure 1.4).

Feature engineering

1. Feature understanding
2. Feature structuring
3. Feature optimization
4. Feature evaluation

Figure 1.4   Zooming in on the feature engineering phase of our ML pipeline, we can see the steps it takes to develop proper and successful feature engineering pipelines.

1.3   *How this book is organized*

A book consisting of many case studies can be hard to organize. On one hand, we want to provide ample context and intuition behind the techniques we are going to use to engineer our features. On the other hand, we recognize the value of examples and code samples to help solidify the concepts.

To that end, we will put both hands together for a high five as we build a narrative around each case study to show end-to-end code that solves a domain-specific problem, while breaking up segments of the code with written sections to explain why we did what we just did and why we are about to do what we are. I hope this will offer up the best of both worlds, showing the reader both hands-on code and high-level thinking about the problem at hand.

1.3.1   *The five types of feature engineering*

The main focus of this book is on five main categories of feature engineering. We will touch on each of these five categories in the next chapter, and we will continually refer back to them throughout the entire book:

1 *Feature improvement*—Making existing features more usable through mathematical transformations

Example—Imputing (filling in) missing temperatures on a weather dataset by inferring them from the other columns

2 *Feature construction*—Augmenting the dataset by creating new interpretable features from existing interpretable features

Example—Dividing the *total price of home* feature by the *square foot of home* feature to create a *price per square foot* feature in a home-valuation dataset

3 *Feature selection*—Choosing the best subset of features from an existing set of features

Example—After creating the *price per square foot* feature, possibly removing the previous two features if they don't add any value to the ML model anymore

4 *Feature extraction*—Relying on algorithms to automatically create new, sometimes uninterpretable, features, usually based on making parametric assumptions about the data

Example—Relying on pretrained transfer learning models, like Google's BERT, to map unstructured text to a structured and generally uninterpretable vector space

5   *Feature learning*—Automatically generating a brand new set of features, usually by extracting structure and learning representations from raw unstructured data, such as text, images, and videos, often using deep learning

Example—Training generative adversarial networks (GANs) to deconstruct and reconstruct images for the purposes of learning the optimal representation for a given task

At this point, it is worth noting two things. First, it doesn't matter if we are working with an ML model that is supervised or unsupervised. This is because features, as we've defined them, are attributes that are meaningful to our ML model. So whether our goal is to cluster observations together or predict the price movement of a stock in a few hours, how we engineer our features will make all the difference. Secondly, oftentimes people will perform operations on data that are consistent with feature engineering without the intention of feeding the data into an ML model. For example, someone may want to vectorize text into a bag-of-words representation for the purpose of creating a word cloud visualization, or perhaps, a company needs to impute missing values on customer data to highlight churn statistics. This is, of course, valid, but it will not fit our relatively strict definition of feature engineering as it relates to ML.

If we were to look at the four steps of feature engineering and how our five types of feature engineering fit in, we would end up with a pipeline that shows an end-to-end pipeline for how to ingest and manipulate data for the purpose of engineering features that best help the ML model solve the task at hand. That pipeline would look something like figure 1.5.

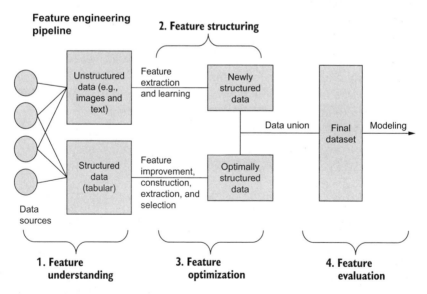

Figure 1.5   Our final zoom-in on the ML feature engineering pipeline. The feature engineering pipeline consists of four stages that include understanding our data, structuring and optimizing the data, and then evaluating that data using ML models. Note that the data union to combine the originally structured data and the newly structured data are optional and are at the discretion of the data scientist and the task at hand.

1.3.2   *A brief overview of this book's case studies*

The goal of this book is to showcase increasingly complex feature engineering procedures that build upon each other and to provide a basis for using these procedures through examples, code samples, and case studies. The first few case studies in this book focus on core feature engineering procedures that any data scientist should have a handle on and will apply to nearly every dataset out there. As we progress through the case studies presented in this book, the techniques will become more advanced and more specific to types of data.

These case studies are also presented in a way that, if you decide to come back (and we hope you do), you are free to jump right to any particular case study that uses a feature engineering technique you want to use and get started right away. This book has six case studies, each coming from distinct domains and using different data types. Each case study will build on top of previous ones by introducing more and more advanced feature engineering techniques.

Our first case study is the healthcare/COVID-19 diagnostics case study, wherein we will work with already structured data related to the global COVID-19 pandemic. In this case study, we will be attempting to make predictive diagnoses of COVID, using data structured in a tabular format. We will learn about the different levels of data: feature improvement, feature construction, and feature selection.

Our second case study is the fairness/predicting law school success dataset, wherein bias and ethics will take center stage. This case study focuses on looking beyond traditional ML metrics and what harm arises when we blindly follow algorithms' advice when real people's well-being is at stake. We will look at how to protect models from potential bias inherent in datasets by introducing different definitions of fairness and recognizing protected characteristics within data. Feature selection and feature construction will play a part as they relate to mitigating bias in data.

We will then look at our NLP/classifying tweet sentiment case study, wherein we will start to see more advanced feature engineering techniques like feature extraction and feature learning in action. The problem statement here is relatively simple: Is this tweet's author happy, neutral, or unhappy? We will look at how traditional parametric feature extraction methods, like principal component analysis, compare to more modern feature learning approaches, like transfer learning and autoencoders.

After working with text data, it's only fair that we dive into the *image/object recognition case study*. We will work with two different image datasets to try and teach a model how to recognize various objects. We will see yet another face-off between traditional parametric feature extraction methods, such as histograms of oriented gradients, and modern feature learning approaches, like generative adversarial networks, and how different feature engineering techniques have trade-offs between model performance and interpretability.

Moving on to the time series/day trading with deep learning case study, we will seek alpha (try to beat the market) and try to deploy deep learning to perform the most basic day trading question: in the next few hours, will this stock price significantly drop, rise, or stay about the same? It seems simple, but nothing is simple when it comes to the stock market. In this case study, time series techniques take center stage and feature selection, improvement, construction, and extraction all play a part.

Our last case study will take a detour down a beautiful and often overlooked backroad. The feature store/streaming data using Flask study will look at how we can deploy feature engineering techniques to a Flask service to make our feature engineering efforts more efficient and widely accessible to the greater engineer audience. We will be setting up a web service in Flask to create a *feature store* to store and serve real-time data from our previous day-trading case study.

In each case study, we will follow the same learning pattern:

1 We will introduce the dataset, often accompanied by a brief exploratory data analysis step to help us gain an understanding of the original dataset.
2 We will then set up the problem statement to help us understand what kinds of feature engineering techniques will be appropriate.
3 An implementation of the feature engineering process grouped by the type of feature engineering will follow.
4 Code blocks and visuals will help guide us along the pipeline and give us a clearer understanding of how the feature engineering techniques are affecting the ML models.
5 We will end with a recap and conclusion to summarize the main takeaways of each case study.

Summary

- Feature engineering as a part of the ML pipeline is the art of transforming data for the purpose of enhancing ML performance.
- Current discourse around ML is model-centric. More focus should be on a data-centric approach to ML.
- The four steps of feature engineering are feature understanding, feature structuring, feature optimization, and feature evaluation.
  - *Feature understanding*—To better interpret data
  - *Feature structuring*—To organize data for ML
  - *Feature optimization*—To extract as much signal from data as possible
  - *Feature evaluation*—To tune our feature engineering based on ML
- More than half of data scientists' time is spent cleaning and manipulating data; it's worth taking all of the time necessary to clean datasets to make all downstream tasks easier and more effective.
- Proper feature engineering can yield a more efficient dataset and allows us to use faster and smaller models, rather than relying on slow and complex models to just "figure out" messy data for us.
- This book has many case studies to help the reader see our feature engineering techniques in action.

The basics of
feature engineering

This chapter covers

- Understanding the differences between structured and unstructured data
- Discovering the four levels of data and how they describe the data's properties
- Looking at the five types of feature engineering and when we want to apply each one
- Differentiating between the ways to evaluate feature engineering pipelines

This chapter will provide an introduction to the basic concepts of feature engineering. We will explore the types of data we will encounter and the types of feature engineering techniques we will see throughout this book. Before jumping right into case studies, this chapter will set up the necessary underpinnings of feature engineering and data understanding. Before we can import a package in Python, we need to know what we are looking for and what the data want to convey to us.

Oftentimes, getting started with data can be difficult. Data can be messy, unorganized, large, or in an odd format. As we see various terms, definitions, and examples in this chapter, we will set ourselves up to hit the ground running with our first case study.

First, we will look at the two broad types of datasets: structured and unstructured. Then, we will zoom in on individual features and begin to assign each feature to one of four *levels* of data, which tells us a great deal about what we can or cannot do with the data while engineering features. Finally, once we have an understanding of the four levels of data and how to classify a feature as being one of the four levels, we will move on to the five types of feature engineering. All of this will provide us with a structured thought process when diving into our case studies. In general, we will begin by diagnosing our dataset as being either unstructured or structured. Then we will assign each feature to a level of data and, finally, use a technique in one or more of our five types of feature engineering, depending on the level of data each feature falls into. Let's get started.

2.1   Types of data

Along our feature engineering journey, we will encounter many different kinds of data we can broadly break down into two major categories: structured and unstructured. These terms are used to define entire datasets, rather than individual features. If someone is asking for analysis on a dataset, an appropriate question in response would be, are the data structured or unstructured?

2.1.1   Structured data

Structured data, or organized data, are data that fit a rigid data model or design. This is usually what people think of when they think of *data*. They are usually represented in a tabular (row/column) format, in which rows represent individual observations, and columns represent the characteristics or features.

Examples of structured data include the following:

- Relational databases and tables of data (e.g., SQL), in which each column has a specific data type and rules for what kind of value can exist
- An Excel document of data, in which each row is separate, and each column has a label that generally describes the kind of data in that column

2.1.2   Unstructured data

Unstructured data, on the other hand, have no predefined design and follow no particular data model. I know this is a bit vague, but the term *unstructured data* is a bit of a catch-all to define all nonstructured data. If the dataset you are working with doesn't really fit into a neat row-and-column structure, you are working with unstructured data.

Examples of unstructured data include the following:

- Transcripts of customer service conversations
- Videos from YouTube
- Audio from a podcast

Oftentimes, a dataset can have both a structured and an unstructured portion. For example, if we are dealing with a dataset of phone calls, we can consider the subset of data that includes the date the phone call was made and the name of the person who wrote it as being structured, whereas the raw audio of the call would be unstructured. Table 2.1 has some more examples of structured and unstructured portions of data.

Table 2.1 Examples of structured vs. unstructured portions of data

Example	Structured portion	Unstructured portion
Phone calls	Who called, who picked up, and what time the person called	The audio of the call
Insurance forms	The date filed, who filed it, who wrote it, and what kind of claim it is	The content of the open-ended questions
Podcasts	The date the podcast was released, the name of the host, and the category of the podcast	The audio of the podcast and the written transcript
Server logs	The datestamp of the log, the microservice it came from, and the level of the log (e.g., info, debug, etc.)	The content of the log

Analysts at Gartner (https://www.gartner.com/en/documents/3989657) estimate that 80% of enterprise data are unstructured, and the remaining 20% are structured. This may initially make it sound more urgent to deal with unstructured data, and that is a fair reaction, but it is worth noting that 80% of data are unstructured due to the fact that they take up much more space (it takes more megabytes to hold a raw, medium-length phone call than it would to hold thousands of Booleans), and most data-capturing systems capture everything we are doing—including emailing, texting, calling, and listening—and all of that data are unstructured. In this book, we will work with both structured and unstructured data. Our goal with any unstructured data is to transform them into a structured format because this is the format ML models are able to parse and learn from (table 2.2).

Table 2.2 Structured data, while comprising only about 20% of enterprise data, are generally easier to work with and cheaper to store, whereas unstructured data take up a much larger portion of enterprise data and are more difficult to work with. This book deals with both structured and unstructured data.

Structured data	Unstructured data
Tabular data can be represented in rows and columns and in a relational database.	Cannot be represented as tabular data. Generally thought of as a mass of data.
Generally easier to use as impute data for machine learning.	Harder to use as impute data, as they need to be structured first.
Require less storage capacity.	Require more storage capacity.
Estimated 20% of data in the enterprise.	Estimated 80% of data in the enterprise.
Examples include spreadsheets and CSV files.	Examples include text, video, and images.

2.2   *The four levels of data*

When working with structured datasets, individual columns or features can exist on one of four *levels of data*. Knowing what level your data belong to makes all the difference in deciding what kind of feature engineering technique is possible, let alone appropriate.

2.2.1   *Qualitative data vs. quantitative data*

Broadly speaking, a feature can be either *quantitative* (i.e., numerical in nature) or *qualitative* (i.e., categorical in nature). It is often obvious which data are quantitative and which are qualitative, and a lot of the time, it's enough to simply know which of the two broad categories your data fit in. For example, quantitative data can be anything from age, temperature, and price to white-blood-cell counts and GDP. Qualitative data are pretty much anything else that isn't numerical, like emails, tweets, blood types, and server logs.

Quantitative and qualitative data can be broken down further into four sublevels of data, and knowing on which level data live will give us insight into what operations are and are not allowed to be performed on them:

- The nominal level
- The ordinal level
- The interval level
- The ratio level

Data can exist on exactly one of these four levels, and knowing which level we are working with for each of our features will often dictate what kinds of operations are and aren't allowed to be used on them. Let's start by taking a look at our first level: the nominal level of data.

2.2.2   *The nominal level*

Our first level of data is the *nominal level.* Data at the nominal level are qualitative through and through. This includes categories, labels, descriptions, and classifications of things that involve no quantitative meaning whatsoever and have no discernable order.

Examples of data at the nominal level (figure 2.1) include the following:

- Blood types (e.g., A, AB, O, etc.)
- State of residence when filling out shipping information
- Phone brand owned (e.g., iPhone, Samsung, etc.)

There aren't many mathematical operations we can perform on data at the nominal level. We cannot take the "average" of blood types, nor can we find the median state of residence. We can, however, find the mode, or most frequent value, of nominal data. We can also visualize data at this level, using bar charts to get a count of the values of data at the nominal level.

Type of home	Neighborhood
Apartment	Soma
Single family	FiDi
Apartment	Russian Hill
Condo	Soma
Single family	Soma
Single family	FiDi
Apartment	Soma
Duplex	Russian Hill
Apartment	Soma
Apartment	FiDi
Condo	FiDi
Apartment	Russian Hill
Apartment	Soma
...	....

Count vs. neighborhood

Figure 2.1   At the nominal level, we can look at things like value distribution, but not much more. Nominal data are extremely common.

DEALING WITH DATA AT THE NOMINAL LEVEL

Simply put, we either need to transform data at the nominal level to be something that a machine can interpret, or we need to get rid of it. The most common way to transform nominal data is to *dummify* it—that is, create a brand-new binary feature (0 or 1) for each of the represented categories, and remove the original nominal feature (figure 2.2).

Neighborhood
Financial district
Outer Sunset
Inner Richmond
Financial district
Soma

Create *n* features, where *n* is the number of distinct categories. This way the machine learning pipeline has a numerical value to learn from.

Financial district	Outer Sunset	Inner Richmond	Soma
1	0	0	0
0	1	0	0
0	0	1	0
1	0	0	0
0	0	0	1

Figure 2.2   Creating dummy binary features from nominal features. We could also have chosen n × 1 features to dummify, as it is implied that if the rest of the values are 0, then the *n*th feature would be a 1.

Binary data are, yes, technically still at the nominal level because we don't have a way to meaningfully quantify *yes or no*, *true or false*, but machine learning algorithms can at least interpret 0s and 1s, as opposed to *Financial district* or *Soma*.

2.2.3   *The ordinal level*

Moving down the line, *ordinal data* depict qualitative data with some sense of order but stop short of having meaningful differences between values. One of the most common examples of data on the ordinal level is customer support satisfaction surveys. Your answer would live in the ordinal scale if I were to ask you, "How satisfied are you with this book so far?" with your choices being

- Very unhappy
- Unhappy
- Neutral
- Happy
- Very happy

It is still qualitative and still a category, but we have a sense of order. We have a scale of choices ranging from *very unhappy* (which I hope you aren't; I mean you've made it this far in the book) to *very happy* (I'll be honest, I hope you're here, but I'll settle for neutral or happy for now, until we get to the case studies).

Where these data stop short is expressing the difference between values. We don't have an easy way of defining the space between *happy* and *very happy*. The phrase *unhappy minus very unhappy* means nothing. We cannot subtract *unhappy* from *very unhappy*, nor can we add *happy* to *neutral*. Other examples of data at the ordinal level are

- *Ranks at a company*—intern, entry-level, director, VP, C-suite
- *Grades on an exam*—A, B, C, etc.

DEALING WITH DATA AT THE ORDINAL LEVEL

Dummifying data is an option at the ordinal level, but the more appropriate methodology would be to convert any ordinal data to a numerical scale, so the machine learning model can interpret them. Usually, this is as simple as assigning incrementing integers (e.g., 1, 2, 3, etc.) to the categories (figure 2.3).

Even though the proper way to deal with ordinal data is to convert to a numerical scale, we still cannot perform basic mathematical operations like addition, subtraction, multiplication, or division, as they hold no consistent meaning at this level. For example, $5 - 4$ is *not* the same thing as *very happy minus happy*, and the difference of $5 - 4 = 1$ doesn't mean that someone at a 5 is one unit happier than someone at a 4.

1. **Very unhappy**

2. **Unhappy**

3. **Neutral**

4. **Happy**

5. **Very happy**

Figure 2.3   Customer support surveys usually measure satisfaction on the ordinal level. We can convert the names of the categories *very unhappy* and *neutral* to numerical representations that preserve order. So *very unhappy* becomes 1, *unhappy* becomes 2, and so on.

2.2.4 *The interval level*

Here's where the fun really begins. Data at the *interval level* are similar to data at the ordinal level, except for the crucial fact that differences between values have a consistent meaning. This is our first level of quantitative data:

1 The quintessential example of data at the interval level is temperature. We clearly have a sense of order—68 degrees is hotter than 58 degrees. We also have the luxury of knowing that if we subtract one value from another, that difference has meaning: 68–58 degrees is a difference of 10 degrees. Likewise, if we subtracted 37 from 47 degrees, we also get a difference of 10 degrees.

2 We may also consider the survey from the ordinal level at the interval level *if* we choose to give meaning to differences between survey results. Most data scientists would agree that if we just showed people the words *unhappy, neutral, happy,* etc., then this would be at the ordinal scale. If we also showed them a number alongside the words and asked them to keep that number in mind when voting, then we could bring that data up to the interval level to allow us to perform arithmetic means.

I can hear some of you rolling your eyes at me, but this is actually groundbreaking and so crucial to understanding the data you are working with. When we have the ability to add and subtract numbers and can rely on those additions or subtractions being consistent, we can start to calculate things like *arithmetic means, medians,* and *standard deviations.* These formulas rely on the ability to add values together and to have those answers have meaning.

How could we ask for more than the interval level?! Well, one thing that data at the interval level do not have is the concept of a true zero. A *true zero* represents an absence of the thing you are trying to measure. Going back to our temperature example, the concept of 0 degrees does not indicate "an absence of temperature"; it is simply another measure of temperature.

Where data at the interval fall short is in our ability to define ratios between them. We know that 100 degrees is not twice as hot as 50 degrees, just as 20 degrees is not twice as cold as 40 degrees. We would never say those things because they don't really mean anything.

DEALING WITH DATA AT THE INTERVAL LEVEL

At the interval level, we have a lot we can do without data. If we have missing values, for example, we have the power to use the arithmetic mean or median to fill in any missing data. We can start to add and subtract features together if that is desired.

The arithmetic mean is useful when the data we are aggregating all have the same units (e.g., ft, ml, USD, etc.). The arithmetic mean, however, has the downside of being affected severely by outliers. For example, suppose we were taking the average of survey scores from 1–100, and our scores were 30, 54, 34, 54, 36, 44, 23, 93, 100, 99. Our arithmetic mean would be 56.7, but our median would be 49. Notice how our mean gets artificially pulled higher by our three outliers in the 90s and 100s, while our median stays more in the middle of the pack.

Note that we are taking survey data and considering it at the interval level, so we are implicitly giving meaning to differences. We are OK with saying that someone at a 95 is about 10 units happier than someone at an 85.

2.2.5 *The ratio level*

Our highest level of data is the *ratio level*. This is the scale of data most people think of when they think of qualitative data. Data at the ratio level are, as you've probably already guessed, identical to data at the interval level with a true zero existing.

Data at the ratio level are abundant and include

- *Money*—We can define a true zero as being the absence of money. We don't have any money if we have 0 dollars or 0 lira.
- *Age, height, and weight*—These would also count as being on the ratio level.

At the interval level, we can only add and subtract values together with meaning. At the ratio level, with the concept of a true zero, we can divide and multiply values together and have their results be meaningful. One hundred dollars is twice as much as $50, and $250 is half as much as $500. These sentences have meaning because we can visualize the concept of having no money (i.e., having $0; figure 2.4).

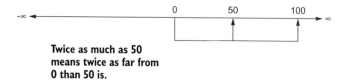

Twice as much as 50
means twice as far from
0 than 50 is.

Figure 2.4   When we say that numbers are "twice as much" or "a third as much," that intuitive meaning is derived from the fact that our brains are comparing each number to the concept of 0. To say that 100 is twice as much as 50 is to say that 100 is twice the distance from 0 than 50 is.

If you are trying to decide whether your quantitative data are at the interval or ratio level, try to divide two values, and ask yourself, "Does the answer have any generally accepted meaning?" If the answer is yes, you are probably dealing with data at the ratio level. If the answer is, "Ehh, I don't think so," you may be dealing with data at the interval level.

DEALING WITH DATA AT THE RATIO LEVEL

There isn't too much more you can do at the ratio level that you couldn't already do at the interval level. The main difference is that, now, we are allowed to multiply and divide values together. This gives us the ability to make sense of the geometric mean and the harmonic mean (figure 2.5). There are times we would want to use one of these three types of means, known collectively as the Pythagorean means.

We previously talked about the arithmetic mean when we were talking about data at the interval level. At the ratio level, we can still use the arithmetic mean for the same purposes, but in some cases, we should prefer to use the geometric or harmonic mean. The *geometric mean* is most useful when our data are either on different units (e.g., a mix of Celsius and Fahrenheit) or are on a mix of scales.

For example, let's say we want to compare two customer support departments to each other, and we measure each department using two metrics: the customer satisfaction (CSAT) score, which is on a scale from 1 to 5, and the net promoter score (NPS), which is on a scale from 0 to 10. Suppose our departments had the following scores (table 2.3).

Table 2.3 **CSAT and NPS scores for two departments**

Department	CSAT	NPS
A	3.5	8
B	4	6.5

We could, then, be tempted to use the arithmetic mean here and argue that

```
A = (3.5 + 8) / 2 = 5.75
B = (4.75 + 6.5) / 2 = 5.625
```

We would declare A the winner, but our numbers that we are averaging do not have the same unit, nor do they have the same scale. It is more proper to use the geometric mean here and say

```
A = sqrt(3.5 * 8) = 5.29
B = sqrt(5 * 6.5) = 5.56
```

And we would see that B actually had the better result after we normalized our CSAT and NPS scores.

The *harmonic mean* is the reciprocal of the arithmetic mean of the reciprocals of the data. That's a lot, but basically, the harmonic mean is best at finding the center of numbers at the ratio level that are a fraction of two values. You can see the obvious connection to the ratio level: this is the only level where we could even have ratios because we are allowing for division with our concept of zero.

For example, consider if we had a series of speed values (measured in mph) from point A to point B: 20 mph, 60 mph, 70 mph. If we wanted to know the average speed, we could try to use the arithmetic mean again, and we would get (60 + 70 + 20) / 3 = 50 mph, but if we stopped and thought about that for a minute, it would start to not make sense. The person who was going 70 mph spent less time traveling the same distance as the person who was going 20 mph. Our average speed should be taken into account. The harmonic mean of 20, 60, and 70 is 37.1 mph, which makes more sense because, put another way, the harmonic mean is telling us, "Of the total time these three people were traveling, the average speed was just above 37 mph." All of the different methods of calculating the mean of data are discussed in figure 2.5 and table 2.4.

Arithmetic mean   Geometric mean   Harmonic mean

$$\frac{1}{n} \cdot \sum_{i=1}^{n} a_i \qquad \left(\prod_{i=1}^{n} a_i \right)^{\frac{1}{n}} \qquad \left(\frac{1}{n} \cdot \sum_{i=1}^{n} a_i^{-1} \right)^{-1}$$

Figure 2.5   The various types of means are the following: arithmetic mean, which can be used at both the interval and ratio level; geometric mean, which is extremely powerful for data that live on varying units; and harmonic mean, which is used to calculate the F1 measure.

Table 2.4   Overview of the different types of means

Type of mean	Description	Level of data	When to use	When not to use
Arithmetic mean	Additive mean	Interval and ratio	▪ Data have consistent units. ▪ Data are additive in nature.	▪ When we don't want our mean to be skewed by outliers.
Geometric mean	Multiplicative mean	Ratio	▪ Data are multiplicative in nature. ▪ Data are on different scales or have differing units.	▪ If scales and units matter, the geometric mean will obscure them. ▪ Data have zeros or negative values.
Harmonic mean	The reciprocal of the arithmetic mean of the reciprocals of the data	Ratio	▪ Data values are ratios (fractions of other values).	▪ Difficult to interpret for those who are unfamiliar with the harmonic mean. ▪ Data have zeros or negative values.

With four levels of data (figure 2.6; table 2.5), it can be tricky to know which scale we are working on. In general, if we misdiagnose a feature as being in the ratio level when it should have been at the interval level, *usually* this is OK. We should not, however, mix up data that should be quantitative with data that was supposed to be qualitative, and vice versa.

Types of data

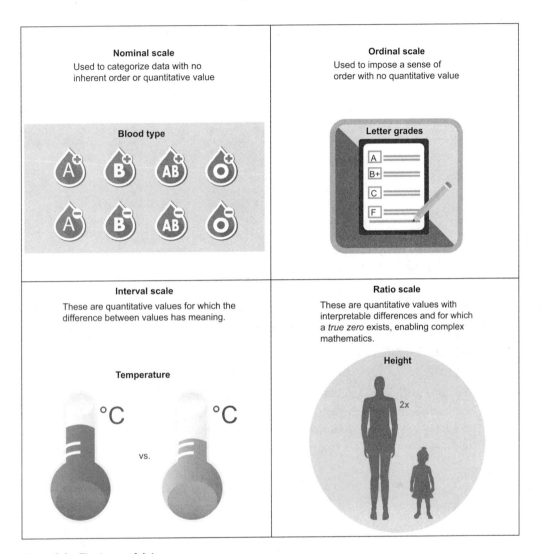

Figure 2.6 **The types of data**

WARNING I would not stop everything and memorize the four levels of data and how your own data fit into the levels. The different levels are a useful categorization system that can unlock certain ways of thinking. For example, if you are stuck trying to figure out if a number is useful for measuring engagement on a social media platform, it would be useful to stop and think if you want a number that is on the interval or ratio scale. If you end up with a metric not on the ratio scale, then you would have to think twice before marketing material goes out claiming "double your engagement score today to be twice as effective" because that is not necessarily what the metric means.

Table 2.5   A summary of the levels of data

Levels of data	Description	Examples	Types of operations allowed
Nominal	Qualitative variables with no order	▪ Blood types ▪ States of residence	▪ Mode ▪ Value count
Ordinal	Qualitative variables with a sense of order	▪ Grades ▪ Ranks at a company	▪ Mode ▪ Value count ▪ Median (to a certain extent)
Interval	Quantitative variables without a sense of zero	▪ Temperature	▪ Mean ▪ Standard deviation ▪ Arithmetic mean
Ratio	Quantitative variables with a true sense of zero	▪ Money ▪ Distance ▪ Height	▪ Mean ▪ Standard deviation ▪ Arithmetic mean ▪ Harmonic mean ▪ Geometric mean

2.3   *The types of feature engineering*

There are five types of feature engineering that we will refer to throughout the entire book. This group is the main structural unit of the case studies, and virtually every feature engineering step will fall under one of five categories.

2.3.1   *Feature improvement*

Feature improvement techniques deal with augmenting existing structured features through various transformations (figure 2.7). This generally takes the form of applying transformations to numerical features. Common improvement steps are imputing missing data values, standardization, and normalization. We will start to dive into these and other feature improvement techniques in the first case study.

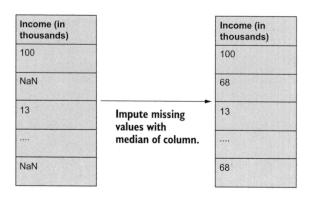

Figure 2.7   Feature improvement techniques rely on mathematical transformations to change the values and statistics of the data to make them better fit into our machine learning pipelines. This can take the form of applying z-score transformations, imputing missing values with the statistical median of the data, and much more. Feature improvement will play a big role in our early case studies.

Going back to our levels of data, the type of feature improvement we are allowed to perform depends on the level of data that the feature in question lives in. For example, let's say we are dealing with a feature that has missing values in the dataset. If we are dealing with data at the nominal or ordinal level, then we can *impute*—fill in—missing values by using the most common value (the mode) of that feature or by using the nearest neighbor algorithm to "predict" the missing value based on other features. If the feature lives in the interval or ratio level, then we can impute using one of our Pythagorean means or, perhaps, using the median. In general, if our data have a lot of outliers, we would rather use the median (or the geometric/harmonic mean, if appropriate), and we would use the arithmetic mean if our data didn't have as many outliers.

We want to perform feature improvement when

1   Features that we wish to use are unusable by an ML model (e.g., has missing values).
2   Features have outrageous outliers that may affect the performance of our ML model.

2.3.2   Feature construction

Feature construction is all about manually creating new features by directly transforming existing features or joining the original data with data from a new source (figure 2.8). For example, if we were working with a housing dataset, and we were trying to predict whether a given household would vote in a certain way on a bill, we may want to consider that household's total income. We may also want to find another source of data that has in it household head count and include that as one of our features. In this case, we are *constructing* a new feature by taking it from a new data source.

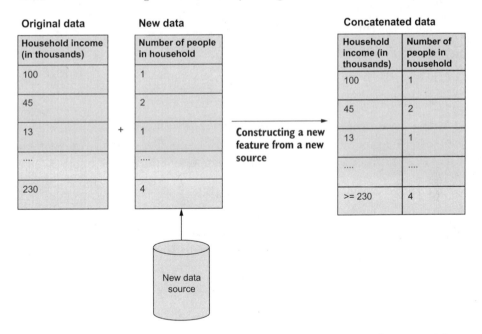

Figure 2.8   Feature construction often refers to concatenating new features from a new data source that is different from the source of the original dataset. The difficulty in this process often lies in merging the old and new data to make sure they align and make sense.

Examples of construction (figure 2.9) also include converting categorical features into numerical ones, or vice versa—converting numerical features into categorical ones via bucketing.

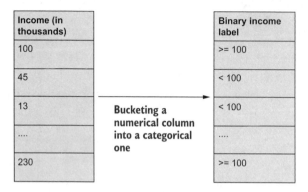

Figure 2.9   Feature construction also can look like feature improvement, wherein we apply some transformation to an existing feature. The difference here is that after applying the transformation, the interpretability of the feature drastically changes. In this case, we've changed the original numerical income feature to be a new categorical bucketed feature. The same information is generally there, but the machine learning algorithms must now process the feature in an entirely new way on an entirely new dimension.

We want to perform feature construction when one of the following is true:

- Our original dataset does not have enough signal in it to perform our ML task.
- A transformed version of one feature has more signal than its original counterpart (we will see an example of this in our healthcare case study).
- We need to map qualitative variables into quantitative features.

Feature construction is often laborious and time consuming, as it is the type of feature engineering that demands the most domain knowledge. It is virtually impossible to handcraft features without a deep understanding of the underlying problem domain.

2.3.3   *Feature selection*

Not all features are equally useful in an ML task. *Feature selection* involves picking and choosing the best features from an existing set of features to reduce both the total number of features the model needs to learn from as well as the chance that we encounter a case in which features are dependent on one another (figure 2.10). If the latter occurs, we are faced with possibly confounding features in our model, which often leads to poorer overall performance.

We want to perform feature selection when one of the following is true:

- We are face to face with the curse of dimensionality, and we have too many columns to properly represent the number of observations in our dataset.
- Features exhibit dependence among each other. If features are dependent on one another, then we are violating a common assumption in ML that our features are independent.
- The speed of our ML model is important. Reducing the number of features our ML model has to look at generally reduces complexity and increases the speed of the overall pipeline.

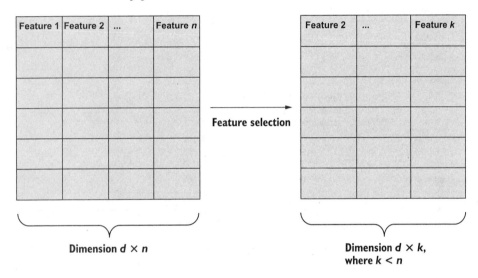

Figure 2.10 Feature selection is simply the process of selecting the best subset of existing features to reduce feature dependence (which can confuse machine learning models) and maximize data efficiency (less data usually means smaller and faster models).

We will be performing feature selection in nearly every one of our case studies, using multiple selection criteria, including hypothesis testing and information gain from tree-based models.

2.3.4 Feature extraction

Feature extraction automatically creates new features, based on making assumptions about the underlying shape of the data. Examples of this include applying linear algebra techniques to perform principal component analysis (PCA) and singular value decomposition (SVD). We will cover these concepts in our NLP case study. The key here is that any algorithm that fits under feature extraction is making an assumption about the data that, if untrue, may render the resulting dataset less useful than its original form.

A common feature extraction technique involves learning a vocabulary of words and transforming raw text into a vector of word counts, in which each feature represents a *token* (usually a word or phrase), and the values represent how often that token appears in the text. This multi-hot encoding of text is often referred to as a *bag-of-words model* and has many advantages, including ease of implementation and yielding interpretable features (figure 2.11). We will be comparing this classic NLP technique to its more modern deep learning–based feature learning model—cousins, in our NLP case study.

Text		What	A	...	Godzilla
What a great success!		1	1	...	0
Godzilla is here.		0	0	...	1
What is Godzilla?	Applying a bag-of-words model to convert text to vectors	1	0	...	1
What is up? Godzilla is what is up.		2	0	...	1
Kong could beat Godzilla in a fight.		0	1	...	1

Figure 2.11   Bag-of-words models convert raw text to multi-hot encodings of word counts.

We want to perform feature extraction when one of the following is true:

- We can make certain assumptions about our data and rely on fast mathematical transformations to discover new features (we will dive into these assumptions in future case studies).
- We are working with unstructured data, such as text, images, and videos.
- Like in feature selection, when we are dealing with too many features to be useful, feature extraction can help us reduce our overall dimensionality.

2.3.5   *Feature learning*

Feature learning—sometimes referred to as representation learning—is similar to feature extraction in that we are attempting to automatically generate a set of features from raw, unstructured data, such as text, images, and videos. Feature learning is different, however, in that it is performed by applying a *nonparametric* (i.e., making no assumption about the shape of the original underlying data) deep learning model with the intention of automatically discovering a latent *representation* of the original data. Feature learning is an advanced type of feature engineering, and we will see examples of this in the NLP and image case studies (figure 2.12).

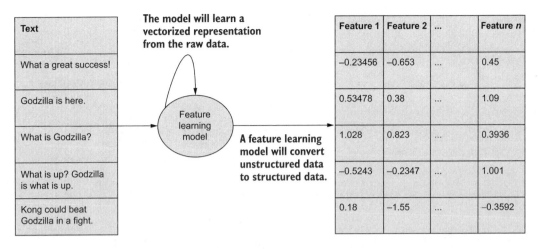

Figure 2.12   Often considered the most difficult feature engineering technique, feature learning is the process of learning an entirely new set of features, usually by way of some nonparametric feature learning model, like an autoencoder (which we will use in our NLP case study) or generative adversarial networks (which we will see in our Image case study).

Feature learning is often considered the alternative to manual feature engineering, as it promises to discover features for us instead of us having to do so. Of course, there are downsides to this approach:

- We need to set up a preliminary learning task to learn our representations, which could require a lot more data.
- The representation that is automatically learned may not be as good as the human-driven features.
- Features that are learned are often uninterpretable, as they are created by the machine with no regard for interpretability.

Overall, we want to perform feature learning when one of the following is true:

- We cannot make certain assumptions about our data, like in feature extraction, and we are working with unstructured data, such as text, images, and videos.
- Also, like in feature selection, feature learning can help us reduce our overall dimensionality and expand our dimensionality, if necessary.

Table 2.6 provides descriptions and previews examples of feature engineering techniques that will be presented later in the book.

Table 2.6   A summary of the types of feature engineering

Feature engineering technique	Description	Examples we will see and use throughout this book
Feature improvement	Using mathematical formulas to augment the predictiveness of a particular feature	- Imputing - Scaling/normalization

Table 2.6   A summary of the types of feature engineering *(continued)*

Feature engineering technique	Description	Examples we will see and use throughout this book
Feature construction	Creating new features from existing features or a new data source	▪ Multiplying/dividing features together ▪ Joining with a new dataset
Feature selection	Eliminating a subset of existing features to isolate the most useful subset of features	▪ Hypothesis testing ▪ Recursive feature elimination
Feature extraction	Applying parametric mathematical transformations to a subset of features to create a new set of features	▪ Principal component analysis ▪ Singular value decomposition
Feature learning	Using nonparametric methods to create a set of structured features, usually from an unstructured source	▪ Generative adversarial networks ▪ Autoencoders ▪ Restricted Boltzmann machines

2.4   *How to evaluate feature engineering efforts*

It bears repeating: great models cannot exist without great data. Garbage in, garbage out. When we have bad data, models are prone to harmful bias, and performance is difficult to improve. Throughout this book, we will define *great* in many ways.

2.4.1   *Evaluation metric 1: Machine learning metrics*

Compared to baseline, *machine learning metrics* is likely the most straightforward method; this entails looking at model performance before and after applying feature engineering methods to the data. The steps are as follows:

1 Get a baseline performance of the machine learning model we are planning to use before applying any feature engineering.

2 Perform feature engineering on the data.

3 Get a new performance metric value from the machine learning model, and compare it to the value obtained in the first step. If performance improves and passes some threshold defined by the data scientist, then our feature engineering endeavor was a success. Note that we should take into account both the delta in model performance and ease of feature engineering. For example, whether or not paying a third-party data platform to augment our data for a gain of 0.5% accuracy on our validation set is worth it is entirely up to the model stakeholders.

NOTE   Supervised metrics, such as precision and recall (which we will cover in the first case study), are just a few of the many metrics that we can use to gauge how well the model is doing. We can also rely on unsupervised metrics, like the Davies-Bouldin index, for clustering, but this will not be the focus of any of our case studies in this book.

2.4.2 *Evaluation metric 2: Interpretability*

Data scientists and other model stakeholders should care deeply about pipeline interpretability, as it can impact both business and engineering decisions. Interpretability can be defined as how well we can ask our model "why" it made the decision it did and tie that decision back to individual features or groups of features that were most relevant in making the model's decision.

Imagine we are data scientists building an ML model that predicts a user's probability of being a spamming bot. We can build a model using a feature like the speed of clicks. When our model is in production, we run the risk of seeing some false positives and kicking people off of our site when our model thinks they are bots. To be transparent with people, we would want our model to have a level of interpretability, so we could diagnose which features the model thinks are the most important in making this prediction and redesign the model if necessary. The choice of feature engineering procedure can greatly increase or severely hinder our ability to explain how or why the model is performing the way it is. Feature improvement, construction, and selection will often help us gain insight into model performance, while feature learning and feature extraction techniques will often lessen the transparency of the machine learning pipeline.

2.4.3 *Evaluation metric 3: Fairness and bias*

Models must be evaluated against fairness criteria to make sure they are not generating predictions based on biases inherent in the data. This is especially true in domains of high impact to individuals, such as financial loan-granting systems, recognition algorithms, fraud detection, and academic performance prediction. In the same 2020 data science survey, over half of respondents said they had implemented or are planning to implement a solution to make models more explainable (interpretable), while only 38% of respondents said the same about fairness and bias mitigation. AI and machine learning models are prone to exploiting biases found in data and scaling them up to a degree that can become harmful to those the data is biased against. Proper feature engineering can expose certain biases and help reduce them at model training time.

2.4.4 *Evaluation metric 4: ML complexity and speed*

Often an afterthought, machine learning pipeline complexity, size, and speed can sometimes make or break a deployment. As mentioned before, sometimes data scientists will turn to large learning algorithms, like neural networks or ensemble models, in lieu of proper feature engineering in the hopes that the model will *figure it out* for itself. These models have the downside of being large in memory and being slow to train and sometimes slow to predict. Most data scientists have at least one story about how after weeks of data wrangling, model training, and intense evaluation it was revealed that the model wasn't able to generate predictions fast enough or was taking up too much memory to be considered *production ready*. Techniques, such as dimension reduction (a school of feature engineering under feature extraction and feature learning), can play a big part here. By reducing the size of the data, we can expect a reduction in the size of our models and an improvement in model speed.

HOW WE WILL APPROACH THE FEATURE ENGINEERING PROCESS

Throughout this book, we will follow a set of guidelines set forth by what we've learned in this chapter (figure 2.13). In general:

1 We will deal with unstructured data and transform it to be structured through feature extraction or feature learning.
2 We will assign features a level of data and, from that level, use all four feature engineering types to further enhance our structured data.
3 We will use these data to evaluate our ML model.
4 We will iterate as needed, until we reach a performance threshold we are satisfied with.

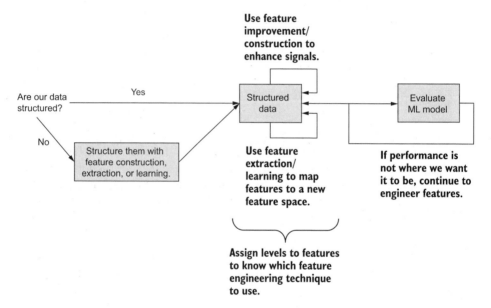

Figure 2.13   A high-level pipeline of how we will approach feature engineering in this book

We may deviate from this general set of rules for individual case studies, but this is how we will approach our feature engineering process.

Summary

- Every feature lives on exactly one of the four levels of data (nominal, ordinal, interval, and ratio), and knowing which level of data we are working in lets us know what kinds of transformations are allowed.

- There are generally five types of feature engineering techniques (feature improvement, construction, selection, extraction, and learning), and each one has pros and cons, and they work in specific situations.
- We can evaluate our feature engineering pipelines by looking at ML metrics, interpretability, fairness and bias, and ML complexity and speed.
- There is a general feature engineering procedure we will follow throughout this book to help guide us on what steps we should be taking next.

Healthcare: Diagnosing COVID-19

In our first case study, we will focus on the more classic feature engineering techniques that can be applied to virtually any tabular data (data in a classic row and column structure), such as value imputation, categorical data dummification, and feature selection via hypothesis testing. Tabular datasets (figure 3.1) are common, and no doubt, any data scientist will have to deal with tabular data at some point in their careers. There are many benefits to working with tabular data:

- It is an interpretable format. Rows are observations, and columns are features.
- Tabular data are easy to understand by most professionals, not just data scientists. It is easy to distribute a spreadsheet of rows and columns that can be understood by a breadth of people.

	Feature 1	Feature 2	Feature 3	Feature 4
Observation 1	Value 1, 1	Value 1, 2	Value 1, 3	Value 1, 4
Observation 2	Value 2, 1	Value 2, 2	Value 2, 3	Value 2, 4

Figure 3.1 Tabular data consist of rows (also known as observations or samples) and columns (which we will often refer to as features).

There are also downsides to working with tabular data. The main downside is that there are virtually unlimited feature engineering techniques that apply to tabular data. No book can reasonably cover every single feature engineering technique that can be feasibly applied to tabular data. Our goal in this chapter is to showcase a handful of common and useful techniques, including end-of-tail imputations, Box-Cox transformations, and feature selection, and provide enough intuition and code samples to have the reader be able to understand and apply techniques as they see fit.

We will begin the chapter by performing an exploratory data analysis on our dataset. We will be looking to understand each one of our features and assign them to one of our four levels of data. We will also do some visualizations to get a better sense of what we are working with. Once we have a good idea of our data, we will move on to improving the features in our dataset, so they are more useful in our ML pipeline. Once we've improved our features, we will turn to constructing new ones that add even more signal for our ML pipeline. Finally, we will take a step back and look at some feature selection procedures to see if we can remove any extraneous features that are not helping in the hopes of speeding up our ML pipeline and improving performance. Finally, we will summarize our findings and land on a feature engineering pipeline that works best for our task.

By following this procedure, I hope that you will be able to see and follow an end-to-end workflow for dealing with tabular data in Python. I hope this will provide a framework for thinking about other tabular data that the reader may encounter. Let's get started by looking at our first dataset.

3.1   The COVID flu diagnostic dataset

The dataset for this case study consists of observations that represent patients who came into a doctor presenting with an illness. Features represent information about the patient as well as symptoms they are presenting. The data are sourced from various publications from well-known sources, including the *New England Journal of Medicine.*

As for our response variable, we have two classes to choose from. We can diagnose either:

- *COVID-19*—A disease caused by SARS-CoV-2
- *H1N1*—A subtype of influenza

Of course, this dataset is not a perfect diagnostic dataset, but for our purposes this is OK. Our assumption about this data is that a patient has come in presenting symptoms of an illness, and our model should be able to provide a recommendation.

Our plan for our projects will generally follow these steps:

1 First we will download/ingest our data and do initial preparations, such as renaming any columns, etc.
2 Perform some exploratory data analysis to understand what data columns we have and assign data levels to each column.
3 Split our data into train and test sets, so we can train our models on the training set and get a less biased set of metrics by evaluating our model on the test set.
4 Set up an ML pipeline with our feature engineering algorithms along with a learning algorithm, such as logistic regression, random forest, etc.
5 Perform cross-validation on our training set to find the best set of parameters for our pipeline.
6 Fit our best model on the entire training set, evaluate it on our testing set, and print our ML pipeline's performance metrics.
7 Repeat steps 4–6 using different feature engineering techniques to see how well our feature engineering efforts are paying off.

> **NOTE**   It should be noted explicitly that this case study is not presuming to be a diagnostic tool for COVID-19. Our goal is to showcase feature engineering tools and how they can be used on a binary classification task where the features are healthcare oriented.

3.1.1   The problem statement and defining success

With all of our datasets, it is crucial that we define what it is we are trying to accomplish. If we blindly dive into the data and start applying transformations with no eye for what we consider success, we run the risk of altering our data and worsening our situation.

In our case of using ML to diagnose illnesses, we only have two options to choose from: COVID-19 or H1N1. We have a binary classification problem on our hands.

We could simply define our problem as doing whatever we need to do to raise our ML model's accuracy in diagnosis. This seems innocuous enough until we eventually learn (as we will see in our exploratory data analysis phase) that nearly 3/4 of our dataset consists of samples with an H1N1 diagnosis. Accuracy as an aggregated metric of success is unreliable for imbalanced datasets and will weigh accuracy on H1N1 samples higher than accuracy on COVID-19 cases, as it will correspond to an overall higher accuracy of our dataset, but we will need to be a bit more granular than that. For example, we'd want to understand our ML model's performance broken down by our two categories to understand how well our model is doing at predicting each class individually instead of just looking at the aggregated accuracy metric.

To that end, let's write a function that takes in training and test data (listing 3.1), along with a feature engineering pipeline that we will assume will be a the scikit-learn `Pipeline` object that will do a few things:

1 Instantiate an `ExtraTreesClassifier` model and a `GridSearchCV` instance.
2 Fit our feature engineering pipeline to our training data.
3 Transform our test data using the now-fit data pipeline.
4 Do a quick hyperparameter search to find the set of parameters that gives us the best accuracy on our test set.
5 Calculate a classification report on the testing data to see granular performance.
6 Return the best model.

Listing 3.1 Base grid search code

```
def simple_grid_search(
    x_train, y_train, x_test, y_test, feature_engineering_pipeline):
    '''
    simple helper function to grid search an
    ExtraTreesClassifier model and print out a classification report
    for the best model where best here is defined as having
    the best cross-validated accuracy on the training set
    '''

    params = {  # some simple parameters to grid search
        'max_depth': [10, None],
        'n_estimators': [10, 50, 100, 500],
        'criterion': ['gini', 'entropy']
    }

    base_model = ExtraTreesClassifier()

    model_grid_search = GridSearchCV(base_model, param_grid=params, cv=3)
    start_time = time.time()  # capture the start time
    # fit FE pipeline to training data and use it to transform test data
    if feature_engineering_pipeline:
        parsed_x_train = feature_engineering_pipeline.fit_transform(
            x_train, y_train)
        parsed_x_test = feature_engineering_pipeline.transform(x_test)
    else:
```

```
        parsed_x_train = x_train
        parsed_x_test = x_test

    parse_time = time.time()
    print(f"Parsing took {(parse_time - start_time):.2f} seconds")

    model_grid_search.fit(parsed_x_train, y_train)
    fit_time = time.time()
    print(f"Training took {(fit_time - start_time):.2f} seconds")

    best_model = model_grid_search.best_estimator_

    print(classification_report(
        y_true=y_test, y_pred=best_model.predict(parsed_x_test)))
    end_time = time.time()
    print(f"Overall took {(end_time - start_time):.2f} seconds")

    return best_model
```

With this function defined, we have an easy-to-use helper function, where we can pass in training and test data along with a feature engineering pipeline and quickly get a sense of how well that pipeline is working for us. More importantly, it will help drive the point that our goal is not to perform long and tedious hyperparameter searches on models but, rather, to see the effects of manipulating data on our machine learning performance.

We are almost ready to start digging into our first case study! First, we need to talk about how we will be defining success. For every chapter, we will take some time to talk about how we want to define success in our work. Just like a statistical test, it is crucial that we define success before we look at any data, so we can prevent biasing ourselves. For the most part, success will come in the form of measuring a certain metric and, in some cases, an aggregation of several metrics.

As is the case with most health diagnostic models, we will want to look beyond simple measures, like accuracy, to truly understand our ML model's performance. For our purposes, we will focus on each class's *precision*—the percentage of correctly labeled diagnoses in the class/attempted diagnoses of the class—and our *recall*—the percentage of correctly labeled diagnoses in the class/all observations in the class.

PRECISION AND RECALL

It's worth taking a quick refresher on precision and recall. In a binary classification task, the precision (i.e., the *positive predictive value*), as defined for a specific class, is defined as being

```
True Positives / Predicted Positives
```

Our precision will tell us how confident we should be of our model; if the COVID-19 model has a precision of 91%, then in our test set, of all the times the model predicted COVID-19, it was correct 91% of the time, and the other 9% we misdiagnosed H1N1 as COVID-19.

Recall (i.e., *sensitivity*) is also defined for individual classes, and its formula is

```
True Positives / All Positive Cases
```

Our recall tells us how many cases of COVID-19 our model was able to catch. If the COVID-19 model has a recall of 85%, that means that in our test, of the true instances of actual COVID-19, our model correctly classified 85% of them as COVID-19 and the other 15% incorrectly as H1N1.

3.2 Exploratory data analysis

Before we dive into our feature engineering techniques, let's ingest our data, using the popular data manipulation tool pandas, and perform a bit of exploratory data analysis (EDA) to get a sense of what our data look like (figure 3.2). For all of our case studies, we will rely on the power and ease of pandas to wrangle our data. If you are unfamiliar with pandas,

```
import pandas as pd
covid_flu = pd.read_csv('../data/covid_flu.csv')
covid_flu.head()  # take a look at the first 5 rows
```

Diagnosis	InitialPCRDiagnosis	Age	Sex	NumberOfFamilyMembersInfected	neutrophil	serumLevelsOfWhiteBloodCell	lymphocytes	Plateletes
H1N1	NaN	67.0	F		NaN	NaN	NaN	NaN	NaN
H1N1	NaN	29.0	M		NaN	NaN	NaN	NaN	NaN
H1N1	NaN	22.0	F		NaN	NaN	NaN	NaN	NaN
H1N1	NaN	20.0	F		NaN	NaN	NaN	NaN	NaN
H1N1	NaN	21.0	M		NaN	NaN	NaN	NaN	NaN

Figure 3.2 A look at the first five rows of our `covid_flu` dataset

Something that stands out immediately is the number of NaN (not a number) values in our data, which indicate values that are missing. That will be the first thing we deal with. Let's see what percent of values are missing for each feature:

```
covid_flu.isnull().mean()  # percent of missing data in each column
```

```
Diagnosis                       0.000000
InitialPCRDiagnosis             0.929825
Age                             0.018893
Sex                             0.051282
neutrophil                      0.930499
serumLevelsOfWhiteBloodCell     0.898111
lymphocytes                     0.894737
CReactiveProteinLevels          0.907557
DurationOfIllness               0.941296
CTscanResults                   0.892713
RiskFactors                     0.858974
GroundGlassOpacity              0.937247
Diarrhea                        0.696356
```

```
Fever                        0.377193
Coughing                     0.420378
ShortnessOfBreath            0.949393
SoreThroat                   0.547908
NauseaVomiting               0.715924
Temperature                  0.576248
Fatigue                      0.641700
```

We can see that we have our work cut out for us. Every single feature in our model has some missing data, with some features missing over 90% of their values! Most ML models are unable to deal with missing values. Our first section of feature improvement will begin to deal immediately with these missing values by talking about ways to fill in these missing values to make them usable for our ML model.

The only column that doesn't have any missing data is the `Diagnosis` column because this is our response variable. Let's see a percent breakdown of our categories:

```
covid_flu['Diagnosis'].value_counts(normalize=True)  # percent breakdown of
➡ response variable

H1N1       0.723347
COVID19    0.276653
```

Our most common category is H1N1, with just over 72% of our response variable belonging to that category. Our *null accuracy* is 72%—the accuracy of a classification model that just guesses the most common category over and over again. Our absolute baseline for our machine learning pipeline will have to be beating the null accuracy. If our model just guessed H1N1 for every person coming in, *technically*, that model would be accurate 72% of the time, even though it isn't really doing anything. But hey, even a guessing ML model is right 72% of the time.

> **NOTE** If our classification ML model cannot beat the null accuracy, our model is no better than just guessing the most common response value.

Last, and certainly not least, we will want to get a sense of which columns are quantitative and which are qualitative. We will want to do this for virtually every tabular dataset we investigate for ML because this will help us better understand which feature engineering techniques we can and should apply to which columns, as shown in the following listing.

Listing 3.2   Checking data types of our dataset

```
covid_flu.info()

RangeIndex: 1482 entries, 0 to 1481
Data columns (total 20 columns):
 #   Column                   Non-Null Count   Dtype
---  ------                   --------------   -----
 0   Diagnosis                1482 non-null    object
```

```
1   InitialPCRDiagnosis          104 non-null      object
2   Age                          1454 non-null     float64
3   Sex                          1406 non-null     object
4   neutrophil                   103 non-null      float64
5   serumLevelsOfWhiteBloodCell  151 non-null      float64
6   lymphocytes                  156 non-null      float64
7   CReactiveProteinLevels       137 non-null      object
8   DurationOfIllness            87 non-null       float64
9   CTscanResults                159 non-null      object
10  RiskFactors                  209 non-null      object
11  GroundGlassOpacity           93 non-null       object
12  Diarrhea                     450 non-null      object
13  Fever                        923 non-null      object
14  Coughing                     859 non-null      object
15  ShortnessOfBreath            75 non-null       object
16  SoreThroat                   670 non-null      object
17  NauseaVomitting              421 non-null      object
18  Temperature                  628 non-null      float64
19  Fatigue                      531 non-null      object
dtypes: float64(6), object(14)
memory usage: 231.7+ KB
```

The `info` method reveals a breakdown of which columns have been cast as an `object`, pandas' recognition of a qualitative column and which are `float64` types, which are quantitative. Now that we have more of a sense of our data, let's move into our feature engineering efforts.

> **NOTE**   Pandas will make assumptions about data based on the values it finds within the dataset. It's possible that pandas could ingest a column that has been cast as quantitative but, in fact, may be qualitative, based solely on its values (e.g., phone numbers or ZIP codes).

3.3   Feature improvement

As we saw previously, we have a lot of missing values in our feature columns. In fact, every single feature has missing data that we will need to fill in to use a vast majority of ML models. We will see two forms of feature improvement in this case study:

- *Imputing data*—This is the most common way to improve features. We will look at a few ways to impute data, or fill in missing values, for both qualitative and quantitative data.
- *Value normalizing*—This involves mapping values from a perceived value to a hard value. For our dataset, we will see that the binary features are conveying values through strings like `Yes` and `No`. We will want to map those to being `True` and `False` values, so our ML model can use them.

3.3.1   Imputing missing quantitative data

As we saw in our EDA, we have a lot of missing data to account for. We have two options for dealing with missing values:

- We can remove observations and rows that have missing data in them, but this can be a great way to throw out a lot of useful data.
- We can impute the values that are missing, so we don't have to throw away the entire observation or row.

Let's now learn how to impute the missing values using scikit-learn, and we will start with the quantitative data. Let's grab the numerical columns and put them in a list:

```
numeric_types = ['float16', 'float32', 'float64', 'int16', 'int32', 'int64']
➡ # the numeric types in Pandas
numerical_columns =
➡ covid_flu.select_dtypes(include=numeric_types).columns.tolist()
```

Now, we should have a list with the following elements in it:

```
['Age',
 'neutrophil',
 'serumLevelsOfWhiteBloodCell',
 'lymphocytes',
 'DurationOfIllness',
 'Temperature']
```

We can make use of the `SimpleImputer` class in scikit-learn to fill in most of the missing values we have. Let's take a look at a few ways we could handle this.

MEAN/MEDIAN IMPUTATION

Our first option for *numerical data imputation* is to fill in all missing values with the mean or the median of the feature. To see this using scikit-learn, we can use the `SimpleImputer`:

```
from sklearn.impute import SimpleImputer    ⟵⎯⎯  Sklearn class to impute missing data
num_impute = SimpleImputer(strategy='mean') ⟵⎯  Could be mean or median for numerical values
print(covid_flu['lymphocytes'].head())      ⟵⎯⎮
print(f"\n\nMean of Lymphocytes column is      │ Shows the first five values before imputing
    {covid_flu['lymphocytes'].mean()}\n\n")
print(num_impute.fit_transform(covid_flu[['lymphocytes']])[:5])   ⟵⎯⎮
0    NaN
1    NaN                                            Transforming turns the
2    NaN                                           column into a NumPy array.
3    NaN
4    NaN
Name: lymphocytes, dtype: float64

Mean of Lymphocytes column is 1.8501538461538463

[[1.85015385]
 [1.85015385]
 [1.85015385]
 [1.85015385]
 [1.85015385]]
```

So we can see that our missing values have been replaced with the mean of the column.

ARBITRARY VALUE IMPUTATION

Arbitrary value imputation consists of replacing missing values with a constant value that indicates that this value is not missing at random. Generally, for numerical features we can use values like −1, 0, 99, 999. These values are not technically arbitrary, but they appear arbitrary to the ML model and indicate that this value may not be missing by accident; there may be a reason why it is missing. When choosing an arbitrary value, the only real rule is *pick a value that cannot reasonably be among the non-missing values*. For example, if the temperature values range from 90–110, then the value 99 isn't quite arbitrary. A better choice for this would be 999.

The goal of arbitrary imputation is to highlight the missing values by making them look like they don't belong to the non-missing values. When performing arbitrary value imputation, best practice tells us not to impute values that may seem like they belong in the distribution.

Arbitrary value imputations for both numerical and categorical variables are useful in that they help give meaning to missing values by giving meaning to the concept of, "Why is this value missing?" It also has the benefit of being very easy to implement in scikit-learn through our `SimpleImputer`:

```
arbitrary_imputer = SimpleImputer(strategy='constant', fill_value=999)
arbitrary_imputer.fit_transform(covid_flu[numerical_features])
```

END-OF-TAIL IMPUTATION

End-of-tail imputation is a special type of arbitrary imputation in which the constant value we use to fill in missing values is based on the distribution of the feature. The value is at the *end* of the distribution. This method still has the benefit of calling out missing values as being different from the rest of the values (which is what imputing with the mean/median does) but also has the added benefit of making the values that we pick more automatically generated and easier to impute (figure 3.3):

- If our variable is normally distributed, our arbitrary value is the mean + 3 × the standard deviation. Using 3 as a multiplier is common but also can be changed at the data scientist's discretion.
- If our data are skewed, then we can use the IQR (interquartile range) rule to place values at either end of the distribution by adding 1.5 times the IQR (which is the 75th percentile minus the 25th percentile) to the 75th or subtracting 1.5 times the IQR from the 25th percentile.

To implement this, we will use a third-party package called `feature-engine`, which has an implementation of end-of-tail imputation that fits into our scikit-learn pipeline well. Let's begin by taking a look at the original histogram of the `lymphocytes` feature (figure 3.4):

```
covid_flu['lymphocytes'].plot(
    title='Lymphocytes', kind='hist', xlabel='cells/µL'
)
```

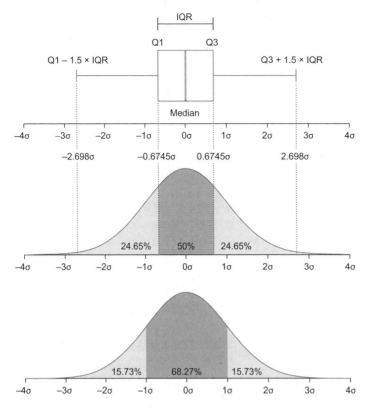

Figure 3.3   The IQR visualized. For skewed data, we want to place missing values at either Q1 − 1.5 × IQR or Q3 + 1.5 × IQR.

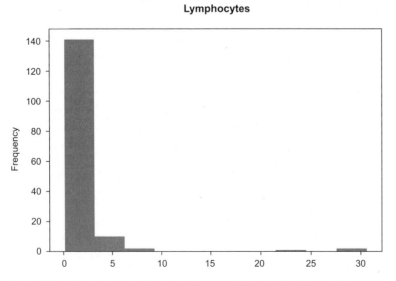

Figure 3.4   The lymphocytes feature before applying end-of-tail imputation

The original data show a right-skewed distribution with a bump on the left side of the distribution and a tail on the right-hand side. Let's import the `EndOfTailImputer` (figure 3.5) class now and impute values into the feature, using the default Gaussian method, which is computed by the following formula:

Apply the end-of-tail imputer to the lymphocytes feature, and plot the histogram.

For more info, see https://feature-engine .readthedocs.io.

```
arithmetic mean + 3 * standard deviation
```

Import our end-of-tail imputer.

```
from feature_engine.imputation import EndOfTailImputer

EndOfTailImputer().fit_transform(covid_flu[['lymphocytes']]).plot(
    title='Lymphocytes (Imputed)', kind='hist', xlabel='cells/µL'
)
```

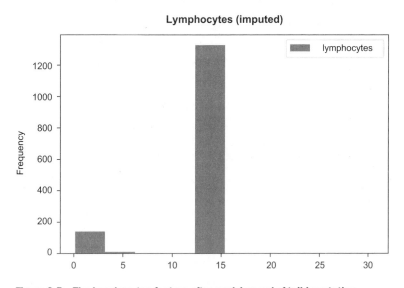

Figure 3.5   The lymphocytes feature after applying end-of-tail imputation

Our imputer has filled in values, and we now can see a large bar at around the value of 14. These are our imputed values. If we wanted to calculate how this happens, our arithmetic mean of the feature is 1.850154, and our standard deviation is 3.956668. So our imputer is imputing the following value:

```
1.850154 + (3 * 3.956668) = 13.720158
```

This lines up with the bump we see in our histogram.

EXERCISE 3.1 If our arithmetic mean was 8.34 and our standard deviation was 2.35, what would the `EndOfTailImputer` fill in missing values with?

We have many options when filling in quantitative data, but we also need to talk about how to impute values for qualitative data. This is because the techniques to do so, while familiar, are different.

3.3.2 Imputing missing qualitative data

Let's turn our focus on our qualitative data, so we can start building our feature engineering pipelines. Let's begin by grabbing our categorical columns and putting them in a list, as shown in the following listing.

Listing 3.3 Counting values of qualitative features

```
categorical_types = ['O']  # The "object" type in pandas
categorical_columns = covid_flu.select_dtypes(
    include=categorical_types).columns.tolist()
categorical_columns.remove('Diagnosis')              ◁
for categorical_column in categorical_columns:
    print('=======')
    print(categorical_column)
    print('=======')
    print(covid_flu[categorical_column].value_counts(dropna=False))
```

> **We want to remove our response variable from this list because it is not a feature in our ML model.**

```
=======
InitialPCRDiagnosis
=======
NaN    1378
Yes     100
No        4
Name: InitialPCRDiagnosis, dtype: int64
=======
Sex
=======
M       748
F       658
NaN      76
Name: Sex, dtype: int64
...
=======
RiskFactors
=======
NaN                         1273
asthma                        36
pneumonia                     21
immuno                        21
diabetes                      16
                             ...
HepB                           1
pneumonia                      1
Hypertension and COPD          1
asthma, chronic, diabetes      1
Pre-eclampsia                  1
Name: RiskFactors, Length: 64, dtype: int64
```

It looks like all of our categorical columns are binary except for `RiskFactors`, which looks to be a pretty dirty, comma-separated list of factors. Before we attempt to deal with `RiskFactors`, let's clean up our binary features.

Let's start by turning the `Sex` column into a true/false binary column and then mapping all instances of `Yes` to `True` and `No` to `False` in our DataFrame. This will allow these values to be machine readable, as Booleans are treated as 0s and 1s in Python. The following code snippet performs both of these functions for us. The code will

1 Create a new column called `Female`, which will be `True` if the `Sex` column indicated `Female` and `False`, otherwise.

2 Use the replace feature in pandas to replace `Yes` with `True` and `No` with `False` everywhere in our dataset.

```
covid_flu['Female'] = covid_flu['Sex'] == 'F'      ◄─── Turn our Sex column
del covid_flu['Sex']                                     into a binary column.

covid_flu = covid_flu.replace({'Yes': True, 'No': False})   ◄── Replace Yes and No
                                                                with True and False.
```

MOST-FREQUENT CATEGORY IMPUTATION

As with numerical data, there are many ways we can impute missing categorical data. One such method is called the most-frequent category imputation or *mode imputation*. As the name suggests, we simply replace missing values with the most common non-missing value:

```
cat_impute = SimpleImputer(strategy='most_frequent')   ◄── Could be most_frequent
                                                            or constant (arbitrary)
print(covid_flu['Coughing'].head())                         for categorical values

print(cat_impute.fit_transform(
    covid_flu[['Coughing']])[:5])       ◄── Transforming turns the column
0    Yes                                    into a NumPy array.
1    NaN
2    NaN
3    Yes
4    NaN
Name: Coughing, dtype: object
[['Yes']
 ['Yes']
 ['Yes']
 ['Yes']
 ['Yes']]
```

With our data, I believe we can make an assumption that allows us to use another kind of imputation.

ARBITRARY CATEGORY IMPUTATION

Similar to arbitrary value imputation for numerical values, we can apply this to categorical values by either creating a new category, called `Missing` or `Unknown`, that the machine learning algorithm will have to learn about or by making an assumption about the missing values and filling in the values based on that assumption.

For our purposes, let's make an assumption about missing categorical data and say that if a categorical value (which, in our data, represents a symptom) is missing, the doctor in charge of writing this down did not think they were presenting this symptom, so it is more likely than not that they did not have this symptom. Basically, we will replace all missing categorical values with `False`.

This is done pretty simply with our `SimpleImputer`:

```
fill_with_false = SimpleImputer(strategy='constant', fill_value=False)
fill_with_false.fit_transform(covid_flu[binary_features])
```

That's it!

3.4   Feature construction

Just like we talked about in the last chapter, feature construction is the manual creation of new features by directly transforming existing features, and we are going to do just that. In this section, we are going to take a look at our features and make transformations to them based on their data level (e.g., ordinal, nominal, etc).

3.4.1   Numerical feature transformations

In this section, we are going to go over some ways of creating new features from the ones we started with. Our goal is to create new, more useful features than the ones we started with. Let's begin by applying some mathematical transformations to our features.

LOG TRANSFORMS

Log transforms are probably the most common feature transformation technique that replaces each value in a column x with the value $\log(1 + x)$. Why $1 + x$ and not just x? One reason is that we want to be able to handle 0 values, and $\log(0)$ is undefined. In fact, the log transform only works on strictly positive data.

The log transform's overall purpose is to make the data look more normal. This is preferred in many cases, mostly because data being normal is one of the most overlooked assumptions in data science. Many underlying tests and algorithms assume that data are normally distributed, including chi-squared tests and logistic regressions. Another reason we would prefer to transform our skewed data into normally distributed data is that the transformation tends to leave behind fewer outliers, and machine learning algorithms don't tend to work well with outliers.

Luckily, in NumPy, we have an easy way to do the log transformation (figures 3.6 and 3.7 show the before and after of a log transformation):

```
covid_flu['lymphocytes'].plot(
    title='Lymphocytes', kind='hist', xlabel='cells/µL'
)                                                 ⊲————————— Before log transform
covid_flu['lymphocytes'].map(np.log1p).plot(
    title='Lymphocytes (Log Transformed)', kind='hist', xlabel='cells/µL'
)                            ⊲——————
                                   | Log transform of lymphocytes
```

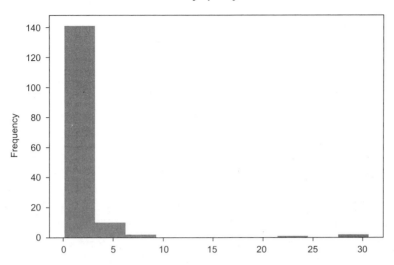

Figure 3.6 Histogram of the lymphocytes columns before applying a log transform

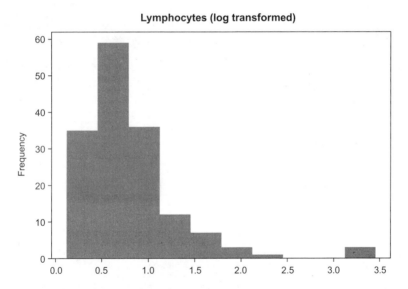

Figure 3.7 Histogram of the lymphocytes columns after applying a log transform. The data are much more normal.

Our data look much more normal after applying the log transform (figure 3.7). However, we do have a way of taking this transformation even further, using another kind of feature transformation.

BOX-COX TRANSFORMS

A less common, but oftentimes more useful transformation, is the *Box-Cox transformation*. The Box-Cox transformation is a transformation parameterized by a parameter lambda that will shift the shape of our data to be more normal.

The formula for Box-Cox is as follows:

$$x_i^{(\lambda)} = \begin{cases} \dfrac{x_i^\lambda - 1}{\lambda} & \text{if } \lambda \neq 0, \\[2ex] \ln(x_i) & \text{if } \lambda = 0, \end{cases}$$

Lambda is a parameter here that is chosen to make the data look the most normal. It's also worth noting that the Box-Cox transform only works on strictly positive data.

It is not crucial to fully internalize the formula for Box-Cox, but it is worth seeing it for reference. For our purposes, we can use the `PowerTransformer` class in scikit-learn to perform the Box-Cox transformation (figures 3.8 and 3.9 show the before and after of a Box-Cox transformation).

First, let's deal with the fact that our `Age` column has some zeros in it, making it not strictly positive:

```
covid_flu[covid_flu['Age']==0].head(3)      It looks like Age may have some zeros
                                             in it, which won't work with Box-Cox.

covid_flu['Age'] = covid_flu['Age'] + 0.01      To make Age strictly positive
pd.DataFrame(covid_flu[numerical_columns]).hist(figsize=(10, 10))
```

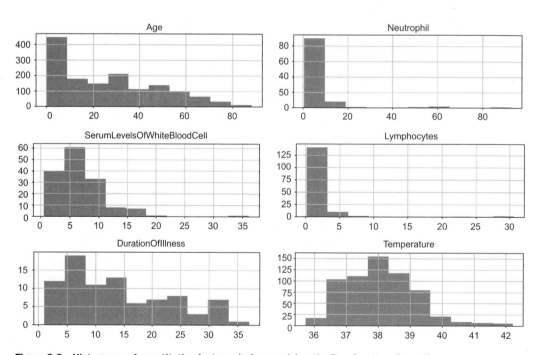

Figure 3.8 Histograms of quantitative features before applying the Box-Cox transformation

Now, we can apply our transformation:

```
from sklearn.preprocessing import PowerTransformer

boxcox_transformer = PowerTransformer(method='Box-Cox', standardize=False)
pd.DataFrame(
    boxcox_transformer.fit_transform(covid_flu[numerical_columns]),
    columns=numerical_columns
).hist(figsize=(10, 10))
```

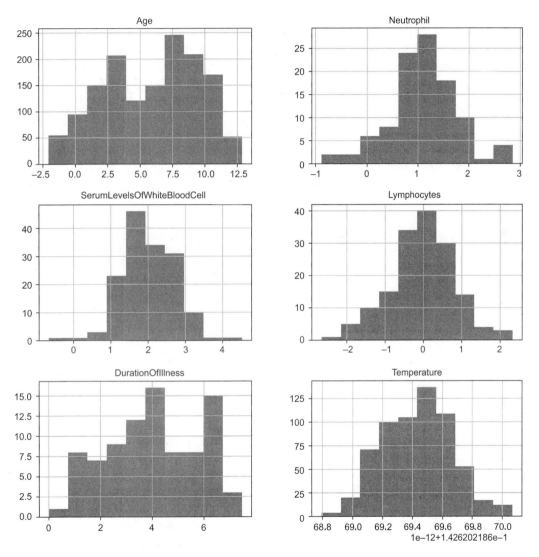

Figure 3.9 Histograms of quantitative features after applying Box-Cox look much more *normal* than the original features.

We can even take a look at the lambdas that were chosen to make our data more normal (figure 3.9). A lambda value of 1 would not change the shape of our distribution, so if we see a value very close to 1, our data were already close to normally distributed:

```
boxcox_transformer.lambdas_

array([ 0.41035252, -0.22261792,  0.12473207,
       -0.24415703,  0.36376996, -7.01162857])
```

> **NORMALIZING NEGATIVE DATA**   The `PowerTransformer` class also supports the Yeo-Johnson transformation, which also attempts to distort distributions to be more normal but has a modification in it that allows it to be utilized on negative data. Our data do not have any negatives in them, so we did not need to use it.

Feature transformations seem like they are a great catchall for forcing our data to be normal, but there are disadvantages to using the log and Box-Cox transformations:

- We are distorting the original variable distribution, which may lead to decreased performance.
- We are also changing various statistical measures, including the covariance between variables. This may become an issue when relying on techniques that use the covariance, like PCA.
- Transformations run the risk of hiding outliers in our data, which may sound good at first but means that we lose control over dealing with outliers manually if we rely entirely on these transformations.

We will be applying the Box-Cox transformation later in this chapter in our feature engineering. In general, if the goal is to enforce normally distributed data, I recommend using the Box-Cox transformation, as the log transform is a special case of the Box-Cox transformation.

FEATURE SCALING

In most datasets with numerical features, we run into the issue that the scales of the data are vastly different from one another, and some scales are just too big to be efficient. This can be an issue for algorithms where the distance between points is important, like in k-nearest neighbors (k-NN), k-means, or algorithms that rely on a gradient descent, like neural networks and SVMs.

Moving forward, we will talk about two kinds of standardization: min-max standardization and z-score standardization. *Min-max standardization* scales values in a feature to be between 0 and 1, while *z-score standardization* scales values to have a mean of 0 and a variance of 1, allowing for negative values. While min-max standardization ensures that each feature is on the same scale (from 0 to 1), z-score standardization ensures that outliers are handled more properly but will not guarantee that the data will end up on the exact same scale.

Both transformations do not affect the distribution of the feature like the log and Box-Cox transformations, and they both help deal with the effects of outliers on our models. Min-max standardization has a harder time dealing with outliers, so if our data have many outliers, it is generally better to stick with *z*-score standardization. Let's see this in action by first looking at our data before applying any transformations (figure 3.10):

```
covid_flu[numerical_columns].describe()
```
⟵ **Before any transformations, scales are all over the place, as are means and standard deviations.**

	Age	Neutrophil	SerumLevelsOfWhiteBloodCell	Lymphocytes	DurationOfIllness	Temperature
count	1454.000000	103.000000	151.000000	156.000000	87.000000	628.000000
mean	26.481040	6.854078	6.885159	1.850154	13.988506	38.068312
std	21.487982	12.690131	4.346668	3.956668	9.043171	1.094468
min	0.010000	0.446000	0.500000	0.130000	1.000000	35.722222
25%	7.010000	2.160000	3.995000	0.637500	7.000000	37.222222
50%	24.010000	3.310000	5.690000	0.905500	12.000000	38.000000
75%	42.010000	6.645000	9.155000	1.605000	20.000000	38.722222
max	88.010000	93.000000	36.070000	30.600000	37.000000	42.222222

Figure 3.10   Descriptive statistics of our quantitative features

We can see that our scales, mins, maxes, standard deviations, and means are all over the place (figure 3.11)!

	Age	Neutrophil	SerumLevelsOfWhiteBloodCell	Lymphocytes	DurationOfIllness	Temperature
count	1.454000e+03	103.000000	1.510000e+02	1.560000e+02	8.700000e+01	6.280000e+02
mean	1.368308e-16	0.000000	-1.411674e-16	-1.708035e-17	-5.614921e-17	1.708471e-15
std	1.000344e+00	1.004890	1.003328e+00	1.003221e+00	1.005797e+00	1.000797e+00
min	-1.232324e+00	-0.507435	-1.473866e+00	-4.361482e-01	-1.444604e+00	-2.145299e+00
25%	-9.064480e-01	-0.371709	-6.671264e-01	-3.074706e-01	-7.772737e-01	-7.736770e-01
50%	-1.150359e-01	-0.280644	-2.758748e-01	-2.395187e-01	-2.211651e-01	-6.246559e-02
75%	7.229298e-01	-0.016556	5.239403e-01	-6.215921e-02	6.686088e-01	5.979450e-01
max	2.864398e+00	6.821614	6.736646e+00	7.289577e+00	2.559378e+00	3.798396e+00

Figure 3.11   Descriptive statistics of our quantitative features after applying *z*-score standardization

Let's start by applying the `StandardScalar` class from scikit-learn to standardize our data:

```
from sklearn.preprocessing import StandardScaler, MinMaxScaler

pd.DataFrame(  # mean of 0 and std of 1 but ranges are different (see min and max)
    StandardScaler().fit_transform(covid_flu[numerical_columns]),
    columns=numerical_columns
).describe()
```

We can see that all features now have a mean of 0 and a standard deviation (and there-fore variance) of 1, but the ranges are different if we look at the min and max of the features (figure 3.12). Let's see this now for min-max standardization:

```
pd.DataFrame(  # mean and std are different but min and max are 0s and 1s
    MinMaxScaler().fit_transform(covid_flu[numerical_columns]),
    columns=numerical_columns
).describe()
```

	Age	Neutrophil	SerumLevelsOfWhiteBloodCell	Lymphocytes	DurationOfIllness	Temperature
count	1454.000000	103.000000	151.000000	156.000000	87.000000	628.000000
mean	0.300807	0.069236	0.179510	0.056454	0.360792	0.360937
std	0.244182	0.137111	0.122200	0.129855	0.251199	0.168380
min	0.000000	0.000000	0.000000	0.000000	0.000000	0.000000
25%	0.079545	0.018519	0.098257	0.016656	0.166667	0.230769
50%	0.272727	0.030944	0.145909	0.025451	0.305556	0.350427
75%	0.477273	0.066977	0.243323	0.048408	0.527778	0.461538
max	1.000000	1.000000	1.000000	1.000000	1.000000	1.000000

Figure 3.12   Descriptive statistics of our quantitative features after applying min-max standardization

Now, our scales are spot on with all features having a min of 0 and a max of 1, but our standard deviations and means are no longer identical.

3.4.2   *Constructing categorical data*

Constructing quantitative features generally involves transforming original features, using methods like Box-Cox and log transforms. When constructing qualitative data, however, we only have a few options to extract as much signal as possible from our features. Of those methods, *binning* transforms quantitative data into qualitative data.

BINNING

Binning refers to the act of creating a new categorical (usually ordinal) feature from a numerical or categorical feature. The most common way to bin data is to group numerical data into bins based on threshold cutoffs, similar to how a histogram is created.

The main goal of binning is to decrease our model's chance of overfitting the data. Usually, this will come at the cost of performance, as we are losing granularity in the feature that we are binning.

In scikit-learn, we have access to the KBinsDiscretizer class, which can bin data for us using three methods:

- Uniform bins are of equal width (figure 3.13):

```
from sklearn.preprocessing import KBinsDiscretizer
```
We will use this module for binning our data.

```
binner = KBinsDiscretizer(n_bins=3, encode='ordinal', strategy='uniform')
binned_data = binner.fit_transform(covid_flu[['Age']].dropna())
pd.Series(binned_data.reshape(-1,)).plot(
    title='Age (Uniform Binning)', kind='hist', xlabel='Age'
)
```
The uniform strategy will create bins of equal width.

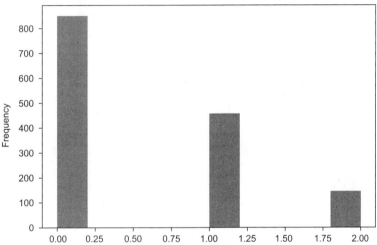

Figure 3.13   Uniform binning yields bins of equal width.

- Quantile bins are of equal height (figure 3.14):

```
binner = KBinsDiscretizer(n_bins=3, encode='ordinal', strategy='quantile')
binned_data = binner.fit_transform(covid_flu[['Age']].dropna())
pd.Series(binned_data.reshape(-1,)).hist()
```
Quantile will create bins of roughly equal height.

- K-means bins are chosen by assigning them to the nearest cluster on a one-dimensional k-means algorithm outcome (figure 3.15):

```
binner = KBinsDiscretizer(n_bins=3, encode='ordinal', strategy='kmeans')
binned_data = binner.fit_transform(covid_flu[['Age']].dropna())
pd.Series(binned_data.reshape(-1,)).plot(
    title='Age (KMeans Binning)', kind='hist', xlabel='Age'
)
```
KMeans will run a k-means cluster on each feature independently.

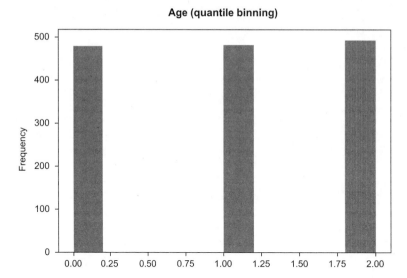

Figure 3.14   Quantile binning yields bins of equal height.

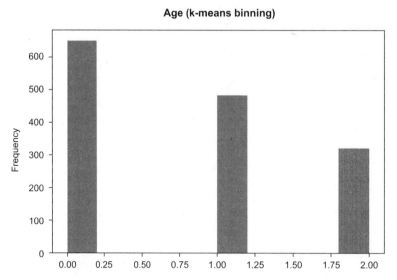

Figure 3.15   K-means binning yields bins based on a k-means run, with *k* set to the number of desired bins.

ONE-HOT ENCODINGS

The RiskFactors feature is a bit of a mess and will require us to get our hands dirty and create a custom feature transformer that will work in our machine learning pipeline. Our goal is to transform a feature on the nominal level and create a *one-hot encoding* matrix, where each feature represents a distinct category, and the value is either 1 or 0, representing the presence of that value in the original observation (figure 3.16).

Color
Red
Red
Yellow
Green
Yellow

Red	Yellow	Green
1	0	0
1	0	0
0	1	0
0	0	1

Figure 3.16   One-hot encoding a categorical variable, turning it into a matrix of binary values

We will need to create a custom scikit-learn transformer that will split the RiskFactors columns' values by comma and then dummify them into a matrix, where each column represents a risk factor, and the value is either 0 (for the patient either not presenting the symptom or the value being null) or 1 (where the patient is presenting that risk factor). This is shown in the following listing.

Listing 3.4   Custom transformer for `RiskFactors`

```
from sklearn.base import BaseEstimator, TransformerMixin      A custom data
from sklearn.preprocessing import MultiLabelBinarizer          transformer to deal
                                                               with our messy
class DummifyRiskFactor(BaseEstimator,TransformerMixin):   ◁── RiskFactors column
    def __init__(self):
        self.label_binarizer = None

    def parse_risk_factors(self, comma_sep_factors):
        ''' asthma,heart disease -> ['asthma', 'heart disease'] '''
        try:
            return [s.strip().lower() for s in comma_sep_factors.split(',')]
        except:
            return []
                                                          Class to help
                                                          make dummy
    def fit(self, X, y=None):                             variables
        self.label_binarizer = MultiLabelBinarizer()   ◁──
        self.label_binarizer.fit(X.apply(self.parse_risk_factors))   ◁───
        return self
                                                    Creates a dummy variable
    def transform(self, X, y=None):                 for each risk factor
        return
      self.label_binarizer.transform(X.apply(self.parse_risk_factors))
```

Our DummifyRiskFactor transformer works by first applying the fit method to data. The fit method will

1 Normalize the RiskFactors text by setting it in lowercase
2 Separate the now lowercase string by comma
3 Apply the MultiLabelBinarizer class from scikit-learn to create dummy variables for each risk factor

We can then use the `transform` method in our custom transformer to map a list of messy risk factor strings to a neat matrix of risk factors! Let's use our transformer just like any other scikit-learn transformer, as shown in the following listing.

Listing 3.5   Dummifying risk factors

```
drf = DummifyRiskFactor()
risks = drf.fit_transform(covid_flu['RiskFactors'])
print(risks.shape)
pd.DataFrame(risks, columns=drf.label_binarizer.classes_)
```

We can see the resulting DataFrame in figure 3.17.

	Asthma	Athero	Atopic dermatitis and repetitive respiratory infections	Begin tumor (removed)	Chronic	Chronic endocrine disorder	Chronic liver disease	Chronic liver disorder	Chronic neurological disorders	Chronic obstructive pulmonary disease		Lung disease	Myxoma of abdominal cavity	Obesity
0	0	0	0	0	0	0	0	0	0	0	...	0	0	0
1	0	0	0	0	0	0	0	0	0	0	...	0	0	0
2	0	0	0	0	0	0	0	0	0	0	...	0	0	0
3	0	0	0	0	0	0	0	0	0	0	...	0	0	0
4	0	0	0	0	0	0	0	0	0	0	...	0	0	0
...	...	...	...	...	...	...	...	...	...	...	...	...	...	...
1477	0	0	0	0	0	0	0	0	0	0	...	0	0	0
1478	0	0	0	0	0	0	0	0	0	0	...	0	0	0
1479	0	0	0	0	0	0	0	0	0	0	...	0	0	0
1480	0	0	0	0	0	0	0	0	0	0	...	0	0	0
1481	0	0	0	0	0	0	0	0	0	0	...	0	0	0

1482 rows × 41 columns

Figure 3.17   One-hot encoded risk factors with one row for every row in our original dataset and 41 columns representing the 41 risk factors we have parsed out

We can see that our transformer turns our single `RiskFactors` column into a brand-new matrix with 41 columns. We can also pretty quickly notice that this matrix will be pretty sparse. When we get to our feature selection portion of this chapter, we will attempt to remove unnecessary features to try and reduce sparsity.

It is important to note that when we fit our custom transformer to data, it will *learn* the risk factors in the training set and only apply those factors to the test set. This means that if a risk factor appears in our test set that was not in the training set, then our transformer will throw away that risk factor and forget it ever even existed.

DOMAIN-SPECIFIC FEATURE CONSTRUCTION

In different domains, data scientists have the option of applying domain-specific knowledge to create new features that they believe will be relevant. We will attempt to do this at least once per case study. In this study, let's create a new column called

FluSymptoms, which will be another Boolean feature that will be True if the patient is presenting with at least two symptoms and False otherwise:

```
covid_flu['FluSymptoms'] = covid_flu[
    ['Diarrhea', 'Fever', 'Coughing', 'SoreThroat',
     'NauseaVomitting', 'Fatigue']].sum(axis=1) >= 2  ◁
```

Construct a new categorical column that is an amalgamation of several flu symptoms.

```
print(covid_flu['FluSymptoms'].value_counts())
False    753
True     729
```

```
print(covid_flu['FluSymptoms'].isnull().sum())   ◁—— No missing values
0
```

```
binary_features = [            ◁———— Aggregate all binary columns in a list.
    'Female', 'GroundGlassOpacity', 'CTscanResults',
    'Diarrhea', 'Fever', 'FluSymptoms',
    'Coughing', 'SoreThroat', 'NauseaVomitting',
    'Fatigue', 'InitialPCRDiagnosis'
]
```

> **EXERCISE 3.2**   If we instead decided to define the FLuSymptoms feature as having at least one of the symptoms in that list, what would the distribution be between Trues and Falses?

We highly encourage all data scientists to think about constructing new domain-specific features, as they tend to lead to more interpretable and useful features. Some other features we could have created include

- Number of risk factors (count of risk factors noted in the dataset)
- Bucketing numerical values, using research-driven thresholds, rather than relying on k-means or a uniform distribution

For now, let's move into building our feature engineering pipeline in scikit-learn, so we can start to see these techniques in action.

3.5 Building our feature engineering pipeline

Now that we've seen a few examples of feature engineering, let's put them to the test. Let's set up our dataset for machine learning by splitting our data into training and testing sets.

3.5.1 Train/test splits

To effectively train an ML pipeline that can generalize well to unseen data is to follow the train/test split paradigm (figure 3.18). The steps we will take are

1. Split our entire dataset into a training set (80% of the data) and a testing set (20% of the data).
2. Use the training dataset to train our ML pipeline and perform a cross-validated grid search to choose from a small set of potential parameter values.

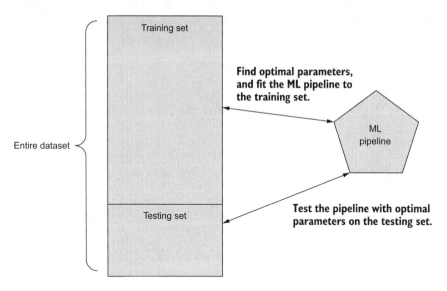

Figure 3.18 **By splitting up our entire dataset into training and testing sets, we can use the training data to find optimal parameter values for our pipeline and use the testing set to output a classification report to give us a sense of how well our pipeline predicts data it hasn't seen yet.**

   3 Take the best set of parameters and use that to train the ML pipeline on the entire training set.

   4 Output a classification report using scikit-learn by testing our ML pipeline on the testing set, which, as of now, we haven't touched.

This procedure will give us a good sense of how well our pipeline does at predicting data that it did not see during the training phase and, therefore, how our pipeline generalizes to the problem we are trying to model. We will take this approach in virtually all of our case studies in this book to make sure that our feature engineering techniques are leading to generalizable ML pipelines.

```
from sklearn.model_selection import train_test_split
X, y = covid_flu.drop(['Diagnosis'], axis=1), covid_flu['Diagnosis']
x_train, x_test, y_train, y_test = train_test_split(
    X, y, stratify=y, random_state=0, test_size=.2
)
```

We can rely on scikit-learn's `train_test_split` to perform this split for us.

   Note that we want to stratify our train/test splits, so our training and test sets resemble the response split of the original dataset as closely as possible. We will rely heavily on scikit-learn's `FeatureUnion` and `Pipeline` classes to create flexible chains of feature engineering techniques that we can pass into our grid search function, as shown in the following listing.

Listing 3.6 Creating feature engineering pipelines

```
from sklearn.preprocessing import FunctionTransformer
from sklearn.pipeline import Pipeline, FeatureUnion


risk_factor_pipeline = Pipeline(          ◁──── Deal with risk factors.
    [
        ('select_and_parse_risk_factor', FunctionTransformer(lambda df:
df['RiskFactors'])),
        ('dummify', DummifyRiskFactor())  ◁──┐  Using our custom risk factor
    ]                                         │  transformer to parse risk factors
)

# deal with binary columns

binary_pipeline = Pipeline(
    [
        ('select_categorical_features', FunctionTransformer(lambda df:
df[binary_features])),
        ('fillna', SimpleImputer(strategy='constant', fill_value=False))  ◁──┐
    ]                                                    Assume missing values
)                                                          are not present.

# deal with numerical columns

numerical_pipeline = Pipeline(
    [
        ('select_numerical_features', FunctionTransformer(lambda df:
df[numerical_columns])),
        ('impute', SimpleImputer(strategy='median')),
    ]
)
```

We have three very simple feature engineering pipelines to give ourselves a baseline metric:

- The `risk_factor_pipeline` selects the `RiskFactors` column and then applies our custom transformer to it (figure 3.20).
- The `binary_pipeline` selects the binary columns and then imputes missing values in each column with `False` (making the assumption that if the dataset didn't explicitly say the patient was presenting this symptom, they don't have it; figure 3.21).
- The `numerical_pipeline` selects the numerical columns and then imputes missing values with the median of each feature (figure 3.19).

Let's see how each pipeline alone does by passing them into our helper function:

**Only using numerical values has a good
precision on the COVID class but awful recall.**

```
  simple_grid_search(x_train, y_train, x_test, y_test,
└▷ numerical_pipeline)
  simple_grid_search(x_train, y_train, x_test, y_test,
```

```
    risk_factor_pipeline)
    simple_grid_search(x_train, y_train, x_test, y_test,
    binary_pipeline)
```

Only using binary columns is
also not performing well.

Only using risk factors
has a horrible recall and
accuracy is barely higher
than the null accuracy.

```
Parsing took 0.01 seconds
Training took 8.93 seconds
              precision    recall  f1-score   support

    COVID19        0.76      0.70      0.73        82
       H1N1        0.89      0.92      0.90       215

   accuracy                            0.86       297
  macro avg        0.82      0.81      0.81       297
weighted avg       0.85      0.86      0.85       297

Overall took 8.96 seconds
```

**Figure 3.19   Results after
using only our numerical
feature engineering pipeline**

```
Training took 8.66 seconds
              precision    recall  f1-score   support

    COVID19        0.73      0.10      0.17        82
       H1N1        0.74      0.99      0.85       215

   accuracy                            0.74       297
  macro avg        0.73      0.54      0.51       297
weighted avg       0.74      0.74      0.66       297

Overall took 8.67 seconds
```

**Figure 3.20   Results after
using only our risk factor
feature engineering
pipeline. Barely beats the
null accuracy with 74%.**

```
Parsing took 0.01 seconds
Training took 8.75 seconds
              precision    recall  f1-score   support

    COVID19        0.83      0.59      0.69        82
       H1N1        0.86      0.95      0.90       215

   accuracy                            0.85       297
  macro avg        0.84      0.77      0.79       297
weighted avg       0.85      0.85      0.84       297

Overall took 8.76 seconds
```

**Figure 3.21   Results
after using only our
binary features**

Let's now get our first real baseline metric by concatenating all three of these pipelines
together into one dataset and passing that into our helper function (figure 3.22).

```
simple_fe = FeatureUnion([                    ◁──── Put all of our features together.
    ('risk_factors', risk_factor_pipeline),
    ('binary_pipeline', binary_pipeline),
    ('numerical_pipeline', numerical_pipeline)
```

```
])

simple_fe.fit_transform(x_train, y_train).shape
best_model = simple_grid_search(x_train, y_train, x_test, y_test, simple_fe)
```

```
Training took 9.75 seconds
              precision    recall  f1-score   support

     COVID19       0.86      0.87      0.86        82
        H1N1       0.95      0.94      0.95       215

    accuracy                          0.92◄────────297
   macro avg       0.90      0.91      0.90       297
weighted avg       0.92      0.92      0.92       297

Overall took 9.77 seconds
```

Figure 3.22   The results after concatenating our three feature engineering pipelines show that we've already boosted our performance up to 92% accuracy. We can see the benefit of joining together our feature engineering efforts.

That's a big increase in performance! Accuracy has shot up to 92%, and our precision and recall for COVID-19 is looking much better. But let's see if we can't make it even better. Let's try altering our numerical pipeline to impute the mean as well as scale the data (figure 3.23):

```
numerical_pipeline = Pipeline(
    [
        ('select_numerical_features', FunctionTransformer(lambda df:
df[numerical_columns])),
        ('impute', SimpleImputer(strategy='mean')),◄──┐  Try mean instead of median.
        ('scale', StandardScaler())  # scale our numerical features
    ]
)

simple_fe = FeatureUnion([
    ('risk_factors', risk_factor_pipeline),
    ('binary_pipeline', binary_pipeline),
    ('numerical_pipeline', numerical_pipeline)
])

best_model = simple_grid_search(x_train, y_train, x_test, y_test, simple_fe)
```

```
Training took 10.46 seconds
              precision    recall  f1-score   support

     COVID19       0.85      0.84      0.85        82
        H1N1       0.94      0.94      0.94       215

    accuracy                          0.92       297
   macro avg       0.90      0.89      0.89       297
weighted avg       0.92      0.92      0.92       297

Overall took 10.54 seconds
```

Figure 3.23   Performance is worse all around after attempting to impute values with the mean.

Our model got slower, and performance is not as good. Looks like this isn't the way to go here. How about imputing our missing values with an arbitrary 999 (figure 3.24) and then applying a scaling to reduce the impact of the outliers we are introducing?

```
numerical_pipeline = Pipeline(
    [
        ('select_numerical_features', FunctionTransformer(lambda df:
df[numerical_columns])),
        ('impute', SimpleImputer(strategy='constant', fill_value=999)),   ⟵
        ('scale', StandardScaler())
    ]                                                              Try a constant 999.
)

simple_fe = FeatureUnion([
    ('risk_factors', risk_factor_pipeline),
    ('binary_pipeline', binary_ipeline),
    ('numerical_pipeline', numerical_pipeline)
])         ⟵
                   Gained some precision for the COVID class
best_model = simple_grid_search(x_train, y_train, x_test, y_test, simple_fe)
```

```
Training took 9.90 seconds
               precision   recall  f1-score   support

   COVID19 ──────▶ 0.88     0.88◀──── 0.88        82
      H1N1         0.95     0.95      0.95        215

  accuracy                           0.93        297
 macro avg         0.92     0.92      0.92        297
weighted avg       0.93     0.93      0.93        297

Overall took 9.96 seconds
```

Figure 3.24   Results after applying arbitrary imputation, showing a boost in precision/recall for COVID-19

We are getting somewhere! Looks like arbitrary imputation is helpful. Let's go a step further and try end-of-tail imputation (figure 3.25), which we know is a type of arbitrary imputation. Let's apply the Box-Cox transformation on our numerical features to make them normal and then apply a Gaussian end-of-tail imputation, which will replace missing values with the mean of the data (which, after scaling, would be 0) + 3 times the standard deviation (the standard deviation is 1 after scaling, so that would be 3).

```
numerical_pipeline = Pipeline(
    [
        ('select_numerical_features', FunctionTransformer(lambda df:
           ⇨ df[numerical_columns])),
        ('Box-Cox', PowerTransformer(
        ⇨  method='Box-Cox', standardize=True)),
        ('turn_into_df', FunctionTransformer(lambda matrix:
           ⇨ pd.DataFrame(matrix))),   # turn back into dataframe
        ('end_of_tail', EndOfTailImputer(imputation_method='gaussian'))

    ]
```

Apply Box-Cox transformation after scaling data and impute using Gaussian end of tail.

```
)

simple_fe = FeatureUnion([
    ('risk_factors', risk_factor_pipeline),
    ('binary_pipeline', binary_pipeline),
    ('numerical_pipeline', numerical_pipeline)
])

best_model = simple_grid_search(x_train, y_train, x_test, y_test, simple_fe)
```

```
Training took 9.86 seconds
                    precision    recall   f1-score   support

        COVID19 ──────▶ 0.87       0.88      0.87        82
           H1N1        0.95       0.95      0.95       215

       accuracy                 ────────▶ 0.93       297
      macro avg        0.91       0.91      0.91       297
   weighted avg        0.93       0.93      0.93       297

Overall took 9.88 seconds
```

Figure 3.25   Results after using the end-of-tail imputer show a slightly better overall accuracy but a slightly worse precision for COVID-19.

Just about as good as imputing with a simple 999, but let's keep the pipeline with the end-of-tail imputation. Let's apply binning to our pipeline to see its effect on performance:

```
numerical_pipeline = Pipeline(    ◀─── Bin data after scaling and imputing.
    [
        ('select_numerical_features', FunctionTransformer(lambda df:
           ⮕ df[numerical_columns])),
        ('Box-Cox', PowerTransformer(method='Box-Cox', standardize=True)),
        ('turn_into_df', FunctionTransformer(lambda matrix:
           ⮕ pd.DataFrame(matrix))),
        ('end_of_tail', EndOfTailImputer(imputation_method='gaussian')),
        ('ordinal_bins', KBinsDiscretizer(n_bins=10, encode='ordinal',
         strategy='kmeans'))
    ]
)
```

Turn back into DataFrame.

```
simple_fe = FeatureUnion([
    ('risk_factors', risk_factor_pipeline),
    ('binary_pipeline', binary_pipeline),
    ('numerical_pipeline', numerical_pipeline)
])

best_model = simple_grid_search(x_train, y_train, x_test, y_test, simple_fe) ◀─┘
```

So far, this is one of our best sets of results!

This is actually one of our best results so far (figure 3.26)! Binning seems to have helped our model's precision at the cost of a bit of recall. We've had success creating and transforming features, but let's move into how we might improve our pipeline with some feature selection.

```
Parsing took 0.06 seconds
Training took 8.74 seconds
              precision    recall   f1-score    support

    COVID19        0.92      0.85       0.89         82
       H1N1        0.95      0.97       0.96        215

   accuracy                     ────▶   0.94        297
  macro avg        0.93      0.91       0.92        297
weighted avg       0.94      0.94       0.94        297

Overall took 8.80 seconds
```

Figure 3.26 Results after binning our quantitative features show one of our best results overall.

3.6 *Feature selection*

Over the last few sections, we have made it a point to add features and improve them to make our model more effective. However, we ended up with dozens of features, many of which likely do not hold a lot of predictive power. Let's apply a few feature selection techniques to reduce our dataset's dimension.

3.6.1 *Mutual information*

Mutual information is a measure between two variables that measure the reduction in uncertainty of the first variable given that you know the second variable. Put another way, it measures dependence between two variables. When we apply this to feature engineering, we want to keep the features that have the highest mutual information with our response, meaning that the uncertainty in knowing the response is minimized given that we know the useful feature. We then throw out the bottom features that aren't in the top n features.

Let's apply this concept to our risk factor pipeline because it is by far the biggest subset of features (figure 3.27):

```
from sklearn.feature_selection import SelectKBest
from sklearn.feature_selection import mutual_info_classif
risk_factor_pipeline = Pipeline(          ◁────     Add feature selection.
    [
        ('select_risk_factor', FunctionTransformer(
                        lambda df: df['RiskFactors'])),
        ('dummify', DummifyRiskFactor()),
        ('mutual_info', SelectKBest(mutual_info_classif, k=20)),   ◁────
    ]                                         Feature selection based on
)                                                  mutual information


simple_fe = FeatureUnion([
    ('risk_factors', risk_factor_pipeline),
    ('binary_pipeline', binary_pipeline),
    ('numerical_pipeline', numerical_pipeline)
])

best_model = simple_grid_search(x_train, y_train, x_test, y_test, simple_fe)
```

```
Parsing took 0.20 seconds
Training took 9.34 seconds
                 precision    recall   f1-score    support

       COVID19        0.91      0.83       0.87         82
          H1N1        0.94      0.97       0.95        215

      accuracy                   ──────▶   0.93        297
     macro avg        0.92      0.90       0.91        297
  weighted avg        0.93      0.93       0.93        297

Overall took 9.41 seconds
```

Figure 3.27   Feature selection via mutual information did not show a boost in performance.

We lost a bit of performance here, so we could increase the number of features to select or try our next technique.

3.6.2   *Hypothesis testing*

Another method for feature selection is to utilize the chi-squared test, which is a statistical test that works only on categorical data and is used to test for independence between two variables. In ML, we can use the chi-squared test to select features that the test deems the most dependent on the response, implying that it is useful in predicting the response variable. Let's apply the chi-squared test to the risk factors (figure 3.28):

```
from sklearn.feature_selection import chi2

risk_factor_pipeline = Pipeline(      ◁─── Add feature selection.
    [
        ('select_risk_factor', FunctionTransformer(
                        lambda df: df['RiskFactors'])),
        ('dummify', DummifyRiskFactor()),
        ('chi2', SelectKBest(chi2, k=20))    ◁─── Use chi2 to select features.
    ]
)


simple_fe = FeatureUnion([
    ('risk_factors', risk_factor_pipeline),
    ('binary_pipeline', binary_pipeline),
    ('numerical_pipeline', numerical_pipeline)
])

best_model = simple_grid_search(x_train, y_train, x_test, y_test, simple_fe)
```

Performance is pretty much the same as our mutual information run.

```
Training took 9.43 seconds
             precision    recall   f1-score    support

   COVID19       0.92       0.85       0.89          82
      H1N1       0.95       0.97       0.96         215

  accuracy                             0.94         297
 macro avg       0.93       0.91       0.92         297
weighted avg     0.94       0.94       0.94         297

Overall took 9.50 seconds
```

Figure 3.28 Results after feature selection via chi-squared are showing results on par with previous results but using fewer features.

3.6.3 *Using machine learning*

The last two feature selection methods had something in common that may have been holding us back. They operate independently on each feature. This means that they don't take into account any interdependence between the features themselves. One method we can use to take feature correlation into account is to use a secondary ML model that has either the `feature_importances` or the `coef` attribute and uses those values to select features (figure 3.29).

```
from sklearn.feature_selection import SelectFromModel
from sklearn.tree import DecisionTreeClassifier

risk_factor_pipeline = Pipeline(
    [
        ('select_risk_factor', FunctionTransformer(
                        lambda df: df['RiskFactors'])),
        ('dummify', DummifyRiskFactor()),
        ('tree_selector', SelectFromModel(
              max_features=20, estimator=DecisionTreeClassifier()))
    ]
)

simple_fe = FeatureUnion([
    ('risk_factors', risk_factor_pipeline),
    ('binary_pipeline', binary_pipeline),
    ('numerical_pipeline', numerical_pipeline)
])

best_model = simple_grid_search(x_train, y_train, x_test, y_test, simple_fe)
```

Use a decision tree classifier to select features.

Let's stop here for now.

```
Parsing took 0.07 seconds
Training took 8.98 seconds
             precision    recall   f1-score    support

   COVID19       0.92       0.85       0.89          82
      H1N1       0.95       0.97       0.96         215

  accuracy                             0.94         297
 macro avg       0.93       0.91       0.92         297
weighted avg     0.94       0.94       0.94         297

Overall took 9.05 seconds
```

Figure 3.29 Results after using a decision tree's important feature attribute to select features

It looks like we may be bumping up against the peak performance of our chosen model (figure 3.26). Let's stop here and assess our findings.

As a final step, let's take a look at our feature engineering pipeline as it stands:

```
simple_fe.transformer_list
[('risk_factors',
  Pipeline(steps=[('select_risk_factor',
                   FunctionTransformer(func=<function <lambda>)),
                  ('dummify', DummifyRiskFactor()),
                  ('tree_selector',
                   SelectFromModel(estimator=DecisionTreeClassifier(),
                                   max_features=20))])),
 ('binary_pipeline',
  Pipeline(steps=[('select_categorical_features',
                   FunctionTransformer(func=<function <lambda>)),
                  ('fillna',
                   SimpleImputer(fill_value=False, strategy='constant'))])),
 ('numerical_pipeline',
  Pipeline(steps=[('select_numerical_features',
                   FunctionTransformer(func=<function <lambda>)),
                  ('Box-Cox', PowerTransformer(method='Box-Cox')),
                  ('turn_into_df',
                   FunctionTransformer(func=<function <lambda>)),
                  ('end_of_tail', EndOfTailImputer(variables=[0, 1, 2, 3, 4,
                  ➡ 5])),
                  ('ordinal_bins',
                   KBinsDiscretizer(encode='ordinal', n_bins=10,
                                    strategy='kmeans'))])]]
```

If we were to visualize this, it would look like figure 3.30.

When working with tabular data, there is a universe of feature engineering techniques to choose from. This case study only scratches the surface of our options and, hopefully, provides a framework for how to work with tabular data end to end. Our overall goal is to

1 Ingest the data.
2 Explore the data to get a sense of what features we have.
3 Assign features to a level of data to maximize understanding them.
4 Apply feature improvements to fix columns we wish to use.
5 Apply feature construction and selection to fine-tune our data.
6 Apply an ML model to the engineered features to test how well our feature engineering efforts are working.

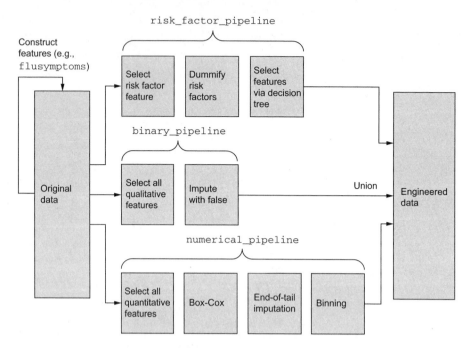

Figure 3.30   Our final feature engineering pipeline

3.7   *Answers to exercises*

EXERCISE 3.1

If our arithmetic mean was 8.34 and our standard deviation was 2.35, what would the `EndOfTailImputer` fill in missing values with?

ANSWER:

The following code will calculate the value:

```
8.34 + (3 * 2.35) = 15.39
```

EXERCISE 3.2

If we, instead, decided to define the `FluSymptoms` feature as having at least one of the symptoms in that list, what would the distribution be between `Trues` and `Falses`?

ANSWER:

```
covid_flu['FluSymptoms'] = covid_flu[['Diarrhea', 'Fever', 'Coughing',
    'SoreThroat', 'NauseaVomitting', 'Fatigue']].sum(axis=1) >= 1

print(covid_flu['FluSymptoms'].value_counts())

True      930
False     552
```

Summary

- By looking at qualitative and quantitative features separately and applying appropriate feature engineering techniques to each type, we were able to see improvements in our model up until we were in the low- to mid-90s for precision/accuracy.
- Quantitative features were imputed, transformed, and binned to achieve our peak performance.
- Engineering our qualitative features, such as dummifying our risk factors, helps keep up recall.
- Feature selection did not provide a boost in performance for us, most likely due to the fact that the classifier we chose (the extra trees classifier) was doing its own version of feature selection by applying low importance scores to features.

Bias and fairness: Modeling recidivism

4

This chapter covers

- Recognizing and mitigating bias in our data and ML models
- Quantifying fairness through various metrics
- Applying feature engineering techniques to remove bias from our model without sacrificing model performance

In our last chapter, we focused on building a feature engineering pipeline that would maximize our model's performance on our dataset. This is generally the stated goal of an ML problem. Our goal in this chapter will be to not only monitor and measure model performance but also to keep track of how our model treats different groups of data because sometimes *data are people*.

In our case study today, data are people whose lives are on the line. Data are people who simply want to have the best life they can possibly have. As we navigate the waters around bias and discrimination, around systemic privilege and racial discrepancies, *we urge you to keep in mind that when we are talking about rows of data, we are talking about people, and when we are talking about features, we are talking about aggregating years—if not decades—of life experiences into a single number, class, or Boolean.* We must be respectful of our data and of the people our data represents. Let's get started.

4.1   *The COMPAS dataset*

The dataset for this case study is the Correctional Offender Management Profiling for Alternative Sanctions (COMPAS) dataset, which is a collection of criminal offenders screened in Broward County, Florida, in the years of 2013–2014. In particular, we are looking at a subset of this data that corresponds to a binary classification problem of predicting recidivism (whether or not a person will reoffend), given certain characteristics about an individual. A link to the dataset can be found here: https://www.kaggle .com/danofer/compass.

  On its face, the problem is pretty simple—binary classification, no missing data— let's go! The problem arises when our ML models have very real downstream effects on people's lives and well being. As ML engineers and data scientists, much of this burden is on us to create models that are not only performing well but are also generating predictions that can be considered fair.

  As we go through this chapter, we will define and quantify *fair* in many ways, and ultimately, a decision must be rendered on what fairness criteria is best for a particular problem domain. It will be our goal in this chapter to introduce various definitions of fairness and give examples throughout on how each one is meant to be interpreted. Let's jump in and start by ingesting our data and taking a look around in listing 4.1 (figure 4.1).

> **NOTE**   This case study does not represent a statistical study, nor should it be used to make any generalizations about America's criminal justice system. Our goal is to highlight instances of bias in data and promote tools to maximize fairness in our ML systems.

Listing 4.1   Ingesting the data

```
import pandas as pd          Import packages.
import numpy as np
compas_df = pd.read_csv('../data/compas-scores-two-years.csv')   Show the first
compas_df.head()                                                 five rows.
```

In the original ProPublica study from 2016 that looked into the fairness of the COMPAS algorithm, software, and underlying data, they focused on the *decile score* given to each person. A decile score is a score from 1–10 that scales data into buckets of 10%. If this word looks somewhat familiar, it's because it is closely related to the idea of a percentile. The idea is that a person can be given a score between 1–10, where each score represents a bucket of a population in which a certain percentage of people above and below rank higher in a metric. For example, if we give someone a decile score of 3, that means 70% of people should have a higher risk of recidivism (people with scores of 4, 5, 6, 7, 8, 9,

	sex	age	race	juv_fel_count	juv_misd_count	juv_other_count	priors_count	c_charge_degree	is_violent_recid	two_year_recid
0	Male	69	Other	0	0	0	0	F	0	0
1	Male	34	African American	0	0	0	0	F	1	1
2	Male	24	African American	0	0	1	4	F	0	1
3	Male	23	African American	0	1	0	1	F	0	0
4	Male	43	Other	0	0	0	2	F	0	0

Figure 4.1 The first five rows of our COMPAS dataset, which shows some sensitive information about people who have been incarcerated in Broward County, Florida. Our response label here is `two_year_recid`, which represents an answer to the binary question, "Did this person return to incarceration within 2 years of being released?"

and 10), and 20% of people have a lower risk of recidivism (people with scores of 1 and 2). Likewise, a score of 7 means 30% of people have a higher rate of recidivism (people with scores of 8, 9, and 10), where 60% of people have a lower rate of recidivism (people with scores of 1, 2, 3, 4, 5, and 6).

The study went further to show the disparities between how decile scores are used and how they don't always look fair. For example, if we look at how scores are distributed, we can see that scores are given out differently by race. The following snippet will plot a histogram of decile scores by race (figure 4.2) and highlight a few things:

- African American decile scores are spread out relatively evenly, with about 10% of the population residing in each decile score. By definition of a decile score, this on its face is appropriate. In theory, 10% of the population should live in each decile score.
- The Asian, Caucasian, Hispanic, and other categories seem to have a right skew on decile scores with a larger-than-expected portion of the category having a decile score of 1 or 2.

```
compas_df.groupby('race')['decile_score'].value_counts(
    normalize=True
).unstack().plot(
    kind='bar', figsize=(20, 7),
    title='Decile Score Histogram by Race', ylabel='% with Decile Score'
)
```

We can see this more clearly by inspecting some basic statistics around decile scores by race, as shown in figure 4.3.

```
compas_df.groupby('race')['decile_score'].describe()
```

We could go on looking at how the ProPublica study interpreted this data, but rather than attempting to recreate these results, our approach to this dataset will be focused on building a binary classifier with the data, ignoring the decile score already given to people.

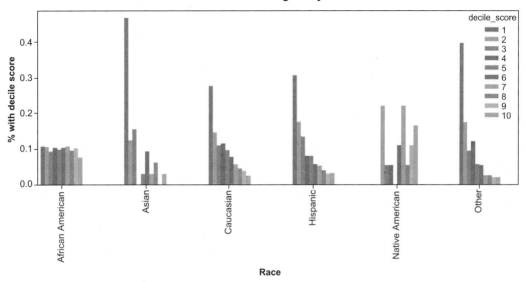

Figure 4.2   We can see clear differences in how decile scores are distributed when broken down by race.

	count	mean	std	min	25%	50%	75%	max
race								
African American	3696.0	5.368777	2.831122	1.0	3.00	5.0	8.00	10.0
Asian	32.0	2.937500	2.601953	1.0	1.00	2.0	3.50	10.0
Caucasian	2454.0	3.735126	2.597926	1.0	1.00	3.0	5.00	10.0
Hispanic	637.0	3.463108	2.599100	1.0	1.00	3.0	5.00	10.0
Native American	18.0	6.166667	2.975389	2.0	3.25	7.0	8.75	10.0
Other	377.0	2.949602	2.350895	1.0	1.00	2.0	4.00	10.0

Figure 4.3   Taking a look at the means and medians of decile scores by race, we can see, for example, that the median decile score for African Americans is 5 (which is expected), but for Caucasians and Hispanics it is 3.

4.1.1   The problem statement and defining success

As mentioned in the previous section, the ML problem here is one of binary classification. The goal of our model can be summarized by this question: "Given certain aspects about a person, can we predict recidivism both accurately *and fairly*?"

The term *accurately* should be easy enough. We have plenty of metrics to measure model performance, including accuracy, precision, and AUC. When it comes to the term *fairly*, however, we will need to learn a few new terms and metrics. Before we get into how to quantify bias and fairness, let's first do some EDA knowing the problem at hand.

4.2   *Exploratory data analysis*

Our goal is to directly model our response label two_year_recid, based on features about people in this dataset. Specifically, we have the following features:

- sex—Qualitative (binary Male or Female)
- age—Quantitative ratio (in years)
- race—Qualitative nominal
- juv_fel_count—Quantitative (the number of prior juvenile felonies this person has)
- juv_misd_count—Quantitative (the number of prior juvenile misdemeanors this person has)
- juv_other_count—Quantitative (the number of juvenile convictions that are neither a felony nor a misdemeanor)
- priors_count—Quantitative (the number of prior crimes committed)
- c_charge_degree—Qualitative, binary (F for felony and M for misdemeanor)

And our response label is

- two_year_recid—Qualitative, binary (did this person recidivate, commit another crime, within 2 years)

Note that we have three separate columns to count juvenile offenses. We should note that for our models, we may want to combine these into a single column that simply counts the number of juvenile offenses this person had.

Given our problem statement of creating an accurate and fair model, let's look at the breakdown of recidivism by race (figure 4.4). When we group our dataset by race and look at the rate of recidivism, it becomes clear that there are differences in the base rates of recidivism. Without breaking down further (e.g., by age, criminal history, etc.) there are pretty big differences in recidivism rates between different race categories.

```
compas_df.groupby('race')['two_year_recid'].describe()
```

race	count	mean	std	min	25%	50%	75%	max
African American	3696.0	0.514340	0.499862	0.0	0.0	1.0	1.0	1.0
Asian	32.0	0.281250	0.456803	0.0	0.0	0.0	1.0	1.0
Caucasian	2454.0	0.393643	0.488657	0.0	0.0	0.0	1.0	1.0
Hispanic	637.0	0.364207	0.481585	0.0	0.0	0.0	1.0	1.0
Native American	18.0	0.555556	0.511310	0.0	0.0	1.0	1.0	1.0
Other	377.0	0.352785	0.478472	0.0	0.0	0.0	1.0	1.0

Figure 4.4   Descriptive statistics of recidivism by race. We can see clear difference in recidivism rates between our different racial groups.

We should also note that we have two race categories (Asian and Native American) with extremely small representation in our data. This is an example of a *sample bias*, where the population may not be represented appropriately. These data are taken from Broward County, Florida, where, according to the US census, those identifying as Asian, for example, make up about 4% of the population, whereas in this dataset, they make up about .44% of the data.

For our purposes in this book, we will relabel data points with race as either Asian or Native American as Other to avoid any misconceptions in our metrics in relation to having two categories of race being so underrepresented. Our main reason for doing this relabeling is to make the resulting classes more balanced. In our last figure, it's clear that the counts of people in the Asian and Native American classes are vastly underrepresented, and therefore, it would be inappropriate to try and use this dataset to make meaningful predictions about them. Once we relabel these data points, let's then plot the actual 2-year recidivism rates for our, now, four considered race categories, as shown in the following listing and the resulting figure 4.5.

Listing 4.2   Relabeling underrepresented races

```
compas_df.loc[compas_df['race'].isin(['Native American', 'Asian']), 'race'] =
➡ 'Other'                                                          ◄─── Relabel rows with
                                                                        Asian/Native American
                                                                        races as Other.
compas_df.groupby('race')['two_year_recid'].value_counts(
    normalize=True
).unstack().plot(
    kind='bar', figsize=(10, 5), title='Actual Recidivism Rates by Race'
)   ◄───────────  Plot recidivism rates for the four races we are considering.
```

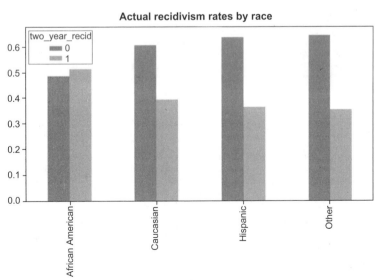

Figure 4.5   Bar chart showing recidivism rates by group

Again, we can see that our data are showing that African American people recidivate at a higher rate than Caucasian, Hispanic, or other. This is true due to numerous systemic reasons that we cannot begin to touch on in this book. For now, let's note that, even though recidivism rates are different between groups, the difference between a near 50/50 split for African Americans and the 60/40 split for Caucasians is not radically different rates.

> **NOTE**   We also could have chosen to look at bias in sex, as there are definitely disparities between those identified as males and females in this dataset. For the purposes of this case study, we chose to focus on the racial biases present in the data.

Let's continue on by looking at our other features a bit more. We have a binary charge degree feature that we will have to encode as a Boolean but otherwise looks usable in its current form (figure 4.6):

```
compas_df['c_charge_degree'].value_counts(normalize=True).plot(
    kind='bar', title='% of Charge Degree', ylabel='%', xlabel='Charge Degree'
)
```

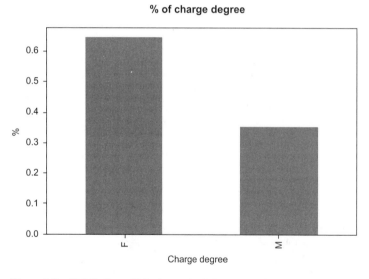

Figure 4.6   Distribution of felonies and misdemeanors in our dataset by degree. We have about 65% of our charges as *F* for felonies, and the rest are *M* for misdemeanors.

Let's wrap up our EDA by looking at a histogram of our remaining quantitative features: age and priors_count. Both of these variables are showing a pretty clear right skew and would benefit from some standardization to reel in those outliers a bit, as shown in the following listing with resulting graphs in figure 4.7.

Listing 4.3 Plotting histograms of our quantitative variables

```
compas_df['age'].plot(
    title='Histogram of Age', kind='hist', xlabel='Age', figsize=(10, 5)
)                    ◁──────  Right skew on Age
compas_df['priors_count'].plot(
    title='Histogram of Priors Count', kind='hist', xlabel='Priors',
    ⮕ figsize=(10, 5)
)                    ◁────────  Right skew on Priors, as well
```

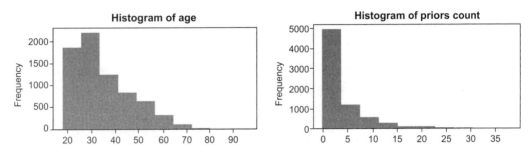

Figure 4.7 Age and Priors Count are showing a right skew in the data. It's showing that most of the people in our dataset are on the young side, but we do have some outliers pulling the average to the right. This will come up again when we investigate model fairness.

With our EDA giving us some initial insight, let's move on to discussing and measuring the bias and fairness of our models.

4.3 Measuring bias and fairness

When tasked with making model predictions fair and as unbiased as possible, we need to look at a few different ways of formulating and quantifying fairness. Doing so will help us quantify how well our ML models are doing.

4.3.1 Disparate treatment vs. disparate impact

In general, a model—or really, any predictive or decision-making process—can suffer from two forms of bias: disparate treatment and disparate impact. A model is considered to suffer from *disparate treatment* if predictions are in some way based on a sensitive attribute (e.g., sex or race). A model could also have a *disparate impact* if the predictions or downstream outcomes of the predictions disproportionately hurt or benefit people with specific sensitive features, which can look like predicting higher rates of recidivism for one race over another.

4.3.2 Definitions of fairness

There are at least dozens of ways of defining fairness in a model, but let's focus on three for now. When we are building our baseline model, we will see these again and more.

UNAWARENESS

Unawareness is likely the easiest definition of fairness. It states that a model should not include sensitive attributes as a feature in the training data. This way our model will not have access to the sensitive values when training. This definition aligns well with the idea of disparate treatment in that we are literally not allowing the model to see the sensitive values of our data.

The surface-level pro of using unawareness as a definition is that it is very easy to explain to someone that we simply did not use a feature in our model; therefore, how could it have obtained any bias? The counterargument to this statement and the major flaw of relying on unawareness to define fairness is that, more often than not, the model will be able to reconstruct sensitive values by relying on other features that are highly correlated to the original sensitive feature we were trying to be unaware of.

For example, if a recruiter is deciding whether or not to hire a candidate and we wish for them to be sensitive to the sex of the candidate, we could simply blind the recruiter to the candidate's sex; however, if the recruiter also notices that the candidate listed *fraternities* as a prior volunteer or leadership experience, the recruiter may reasonably put together that the candidate is likely a male.

STATISTICAL PARITY

Statistical parity, also known as demographic parity or disparate impact, is a very common definition for fairness. Simply put, it states that our model's prediction of being in a certain class (whether they will recidivate or not) is independent of the sensitive feature. Put as a formula

$$P(\text{recidivism} \mid \text{race} = \text{African American}) = P(\text{recidivism} \mid \text{race} = \text{Caucasian}) = P(\text{recidivism} \mid \text{race} = \text{Hispanic}) = P(\text{recidivism} \mid \text{race} = \text{Other})$$

Put yet another way, to achieve good statistical parity, our model should predict equal rates of recidivism for every racial category. The above formula is pretty strict, and to relax this we can lean on the *four-fifths rule,* which states that if the selection rate (the rate at which we predict recidivism) of a certain group is either less than 80% or greater than 125% of the selection rate of another group, then we are possibly looking at disparate impact. As a formula, this looks like the following:

$$0.8 < P(\text{recidivism} \mid \text{race} = \text{disadvantaged}) \ / \ P(\text{recidivism} \mid \text{race} = \text{advantaged}) < 1 \ / \ .8 \ (1.25)$$

The pros of using statistical parity as a definition of fairness is that it is relatively easy to explain the metric, and there is evidence that using statistical parity as a definition can lead to both short-term and long-term benefits for the disadvantaged groups (see Hu and Chen, https://arxiv.org/pdf/1712.00064.pdf).

One caveat of relying on statistical parity is that it ignores any possible relationship between our label and our sensitive attribute. In our case, this is actually a good thing because we want to ignore any correlation between our response (will this person recidivate) and our sensitive attribute in question (race), as that correlation is driven by much bigger factors than our case study can deal with. For any use case you may consider in the future, this may not be desired, so please take this into consideration!

Another caveat of relying solely on statistical parity is that our ML model, in theory, could just be *lazy* and select random people from each group, and we would still technically achieve statistical parity. Obviously, our ML metrics should prevent our models from doing this, but it's always something to look out for.

EQUALIZED ODDS

Also known as positive rate parity, the *equalized odds* definition of fairness states that our model's prediction of our response should be independent of our sensitive feature, conditional on our response value. In the context of our example, equalized odds would mean the following two conditions are met:

- P(recidivism | race = Hispanic, actually recidivated = True) = P(recidivism | race = Caucasian, actually recidivated = True) = P(recidivism | race = African American, actually recidivated = True) = P(recidivism | race = Other, actually recidivated = True)
- P(recidivism | race = Hispanic, actually recidivated = False) = P(recidivism | race = Caucasian, actually recidivated = False) = P(recidivism | race = African American, actually recidivated = False) = P(recidivism | race = Other, actually recidivated = False)

Another way to view this would be to say our model has equalized odds if

- Independent of race, our model predicted recidivism rates equally for people who did actually recidivate.
- Independent of race, our model predicted recidivism rates equally for people who did not actually recidivate.

The pros of using equalized odds for our definition are that it penalizes the same *laziness* we talked about with statistical parity; and it encourages the model to become more accurate in all groups, rather than allowing the model to simply randomly predict recidivism to achieve similar rates of prediction between groups.

The biggest flaw is those equalized odds are sensitive to different underlying base rates of the response. In our data, we saw that African Americans recidivated at a higher rate than the other three racial categories. If this was a scenario wherein we believed there were some natural differences between racial groups and recidivism rates, then equalized odds would not be a good metric for us. In our case, this will not be an issue, as we reject the idea that these base rates relating to race and recidivism reflect natural recidivism rates.

> **NOTE**   There are dozens of established metrics for measuring fairness and bias. Our case study will touch on a few of them, but we recommend looking at other texts that focus exclusively on bias and fairness for a comprehensive treatment.

4.4   Building a baseline model

It's time to build our baseline ML model. For our first pass at our model, we will apply a bit of feature engineering to ensure our model interprets all of our data correctly and spend time analyzing the fairness/performance results of our model.

4.4.1   Feature construction

As we saw in our EDA, we have three features that each count the number of juvenile offenses of the person in question. Let's take another look at our three juvenile features (figure 4.8).

```
compas_df[["juv_fel_count", "juv_misd_count", "juv_other_count"]].describe()
```

	juv_fel_count	juv_misd_count	juv_other_count
count	7214.000000	7214.000000	7214.000000
mean	0.067230	0.090934	0.109371
std	0.473972	0.485239	0.501586
min	0.000000	0.000000	0.000000
25%	0.000000	0.000000	0.000000
50%	0.000000	0.000000	0.000000
75%	0.000000	0.000000	0.000000
max	20.000000	13.000000	17.000000

Figure 4.8   We have three different features that each count a subset of prior juvenile offenses. Our goal will be to combine them together into one feature.

Let's combine these features into one by adding them all up into a new column called juv_count that should be a bit easier to interpret, as shown in the following listing.

Listing 4.4   Constructing a new juvenile offense count feature

```
compas_df['juv_count'] = compas_df[["juv_fel_count", "juv_misd_count",
➡ "juv_other_count"]].sum(axis=1)                                      ◁──── Construct our
compas_df = compas_df.drop(["juv_fel_count", "juv_misd_count",                new total juvenile
➡ "juv_other_count"], axis=1) ◁──┐                                            offense count.
                                  └── Remove the original
                                      juvenile features.
```

EXERCISE 4.1   Plot the distribution of the new juv_count feature. What is the arithmetic mean and standard deviation?

We now have one new feature, and we have removed three features as a result. Figure 4.9 shows the current state of our training data.

	sex	age	race	priors_count	c_charge_degree	two_year_recid	juv_count
0	Male	69	Other	0	F	0	0
1	Male	34	African American	0	F	1	0
2	Male	24	African American	4	F	1	1
3	Male	23	African American	1	F	0	1
4	Male	43	Other	2	F	0	0

Figure 4.9 The current state of our training data with our combined juvenile offense count

4.4.2 Building our baseline pipeline

Let's start putting our pipeline together to create our baseline ML model. Let's begin by splitting up our data into training and testing sets, and let's also instantiate a static random forest classifier. We have chosen a random forest model here because random forest models have the useful feature of calculating feature importances. This will end up being very useful for us. We could have chosen a decision tree or even a logistic regression, as they both also have representations of feature importances, but for now, we will go with a random forest. Remember that our goal is to manipulate our features and not our model, so we will use the same model with the same parameters for all of our iterations. In addition to splitting up our x and our y, we will also split the race column, so we have an easy way to split our test set by race.

Listing 4.5 Splitting up our data into training and testing sets

```
from sklearn.model_selection import train_test_split
from sklearn.ensemble import RandomForestClassifier

X_train, X_test, y_train, y_test, race_train, race_test = train_test_split(
    compas_df.drop('two_year_recid', axis=1),        ◁──┐ Split up our data.

compas_df['two_year_recid'],

                                                     compas_df['race'],

stratify=compas_df['two_year_recid'],

                                                     test_size=0.3,
                                                     random_state=0)

classifier = RandomForestClassifier(
    max_depth=10, n_estimators=20, random_state=0)   ◁──── Our static classifier
```

Now that we have our data split up and our classifier ready to go, let's start creating our feature pipelines just like we did in our last chapter. First up is our categorical data. Let's create a pipeline that will one-hot encode our categorical columns and only drop the second dummy column if the categorical feature is binary, as shown in the following listing.

Listing 4.6   Creating our qualitative pipeline

```
from sklearn.compose import ColumnTransformer
from sklearn.pipeline import Pipeline, FeatureUnion
from sklearn.preprocessing import OneHotEncoder, StandardScaler

categorical_features = ['race', 'sex', 'c_charge_degree']
categorical_transformer = Pipeline(steps=[
    ('onehot', OneHotEncoder(drop='if_binary'))
])
```

And for our numerical data, we will scale our data to bring down those outliers that we saw in our EDA.

Listing 4.7   Creating our quantitative pipeline

```
numerical_features = ["age", "priors_count"]
numerical_transformer = Pipeline(steps=[
    ('scale', StandardScaler())
])
```

Let's introduce the `ColumnTransformer` object from scikit-learn that will help us quickly apply our two pipelines to our specific columns with minimal code, as shown in the following listing.

Listing 4.8   Putting our pipelines together to create our feature preprocessor

```
preprocessor = ColumnTransformer(transformers=[
        ('cat', categorical_transformer, categorical_features),
        ('num', numerical_transformer, numerical_features)
])

clf_tree = Pipeline(steps=[
    ('preprocessor', preprocessor),
    ('classifier', classifier)
])
```

With our pipeline set up, we can train it on our training set and run it on our test set.

Listing 4.9   Running our bias-unaware model on our test set

```
clf_tree.fit(X_train, y_train)
unaware_y_preds = clf_tree.predict(X_test)
```

Unaware_y_preds will be an array of 0s and 1s, where 0 represents our model predicting that this person will not recidivate, and a 1 represents our model, predicting that this person will recidivate. Now that we have our predictions of our model predicting on our test set, it's time to start investigating how fair our ML model truly is.

4.4.3 Measuring bias in our baseline model

To help us dive into our fairness metrics, we are going to be using a module called *Dalex*. Dalex has some excellent features that help visualize different kinds of bias and fairness metrics. Our base object is the `Explainer` object, and with our explainer object we can obtain some basic model performance, as shown in the following listing with results in figure 4.10.

Listing 4.10 Using Dalex to explain our model

```
import dalex as dx

exp_tree = dx.Explainer(
    clf_tree, X_test, y_test,
    label='Random Forest Bias Unaware', verbose=True)
exp_tree.model_performance()
```

	recall	precision	f1	accuracy	auc
Random forest bias unaware	0.560451	0.628736	0.592633	0.652656	0.693935

Figure 4.10 Baseline model performance with our bias-unaware model

Our metrics are not amazing, but we are concerned with both performance and fairness, so let's dig into fairness a bit. Our first question is, "How much did our model rely on race as a way to predict recidivism?" This question goes hand in hand with our model's disparate treatment. Dalex has a very handy plot that can be used with tree-based models and linear models to help visualize the features our model is learning the most from (figure 4.11).

```
exp_tree.model_parts().plot()
```

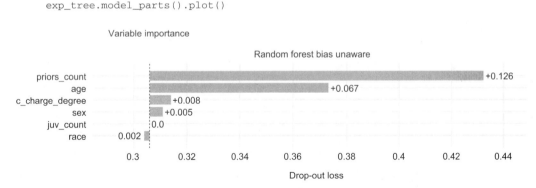

Figure 4.11 Feature importance of our bias-unaware model as reported by Dalex. This visualization is taking feature importances directly from the random forest's feature importance attribute and is showing that `priors_count` and `age` are our most important features.

Dalex is reporting importance in terms of *drop-out loss*, or how much the overall *fit* of our model would decrease if the feature in question were entirely removed. According to this chart, our model would lose a lot of information if we lost `priors_count`, but in theory, it would have been better if we dropped `race`. It would seem that our model isn't even learning from the race at all! This speaks to the model's unawareness of sensitive features.

Before we begin our no-bias-here dance, we should look at a few more metrics. Dalex also has a `model_fairness` object we can look at that will calculate several metrics for each of our racial categories, as shown in the following listing with results in figure 4.12.

Listing 4.11   Outputting model fairness

```
mf_tree = exp_tree.model_fairness(
    protected=race_test, privileged = "Caucasian")
mf_tree.metric_scores
```

	TPR	TNR	PPV	NPV	FNR	FPR	FDR	FOR	ACC	STP
African American	0.665	0.658	0.674	0.650	0.335	0.342	0.326	0.350	0.662	0.508
Caucasian	0.407	0.799	0.581	0.662	0.593	0.201	0.419	0.338	0.639	0.285
Hispanic	0.356	0.785	0.447	0.714	0.644	0.215	0.553	0.286	0.644	0.261
Other	0.562	0.714	0.509	0.756	0.438	0.286	0.491	0.244	0.662	0.381

Figure 4.12   A breakdown of 10 fairness metrics for our bias-unaware model

This package gives us 10 metrics here by default; let's break down how to calculate each one in terms of true positives (TP), false positives (FP), false negatives (FN), actual positives (AP), actual negatives (AN), predicted positives (PP), and predicted negatives (PN). Keep in mind that we can calculate each of these metrics by race:

1 $TPR(r) = TP / AP$ (aka sensitivity)
2 $TNR(r) = TN / AN$ (aka specificity)
3 $PPV(r) = TP / (PP)$ (aka precision)
4 $NPV(r) = TN / (PN)$
5 $FNR(r) = FN / AP$ *or* $1 - TPR$
6 $FPR(r) = FP / AN$ *or* $1 - TNR$
7 $FDR(r) = FP / (PP)$ *or* $1 - PPV$
8 $FOR(r) = FN / (PN)$ *or* $1 - NPV$
9 $ACC(r) = TP + TN / (TP + TN + FP + FN)$ (overall accuracy by race)
10 $STP(r) = TP + FP / (TP + FP + FP + FN)$ (aka $P[\text{recidivism predicted} \mid \text{Race} = r]$)

These numbers on their own will not be very helpful, so let's perform a fairness check by comparing our values to the privileged group of people: Caucasians. Why are we choosing Caucasians as our privileged group? Well, among a lot of other reasons, if we look at how often our baseline model predicted recidivism between our groups, we will notice that the model is vastly underpredicting Caucasian recidivism compared to actual rates in our test set (listing 4.12 and figure 4.13).

For our purposes, we will focus on TPR, ACC, PPV, FPR, and STP as our main metrics. The reason we are choosing these metrics is that

- TPR relates to how well our model captures actual recidivism. Of all the times people recidivate, did our model predict them as positive? We want this to be higher.
- ACC is our overall accuracy. It is a fairly well-rounded way to judge our model but will not be taken into consideration in a vacuum. We want this to be higher.
- PPV is our precision. It measures how much we can trust our model's positive predictions. Of the times our model predicts recidivism, how often was the model correct in that positive prediction? We want this to be higher.
- FPR relates to our model's rate of predicting recidivism when someone will not actually recidivate. We want this to be lower.
- STP is statistical parity per group. We want this to be roughly equal to each other by race, meaning our model should be able to reliably predict recidivism based on nondemographic information.

Listing 4.12 Highlighting Caucasian privilege

```
y_test.groupby(race_test).mean()     ◁─┤  Recidivism by race
                                         │  in our test set
pd.Series(unaware_y_preds, index=y_test.index).groupby(
    race_test).mean()                                    ◁──
```

Predicted recidivism by race in our bias-unaware model

```
race                                    race
African American    0.514652           African American    0.508242
Caucasian           0.407162           Caucasian           0.285146
Hispanic            0.327778           Hispanic            0.255556
Other               0.345324           Other               0.381295
Name: two_year_recid, dtype: float64   dtype: float64
```

Figure 4.13 On the left we have actual recidivism rates by group in our test set, and the right has the rates of recidivism predicted by our baseline bias-unaware model. Our model is vastly underpredicting Caucasian recidivism. Nearly 41% of Caucasian folk recidivated; meanwhile, our model only thought 28% of them would. That means that our model underpredicted recidivism for Caucasians by over 30%.

The rates of recidivism predicted among African American people are very similar, while Caucasians seem to only get a recidivism prediction less than 29% of the time, even though the actual rate is almost 41%. The fact that our model is underpredicting the Caucasian group is an indicator that Caucasians are privileged by our model. Part of the reason this is happening is that the data are representative of an unfair justice system. Thinking back to the fact that African Americans have a higher priors count and that the priors count was the most important feature in our model, and it is still unable to accurately predict Caucasian recidivism, our model is clearly unable to reliably predict recidivism based on the raw data.

Let's run that fairness check now to see how our bias-unaware model is doing across our five bias metrics:

```
mf_tree = exp_tree.model_fairness(protected=race_test, privileged =
➥ "Caucasian")
mf_tree.fairness_check()
```

Our output is outlined in the following table, and at first glance, it is a lot! We've high-lighted the main areas to focus on. We want each of the values to be between 0.8 and 1.25, and the boldface values are those that are outside of that range and, therefore, being called out as being evidence of bias.

```
Bias detected in 4 metrics: TPR, PPV, FPR, STP
Conclusion: your model is not fair because 2 or more criteria exceeded
acceptable limits set by epsilon.
Ratios of metrics, based on 'Caucasian'. Parameter 'epsilon' was set to 0.8
and, therefore, metrics should be within (0.8, 1.25)
                       TPR        ACC        PPV        FPR        STP
African American    1.633907   1.035994   1.160069   1.701493   1.782456
Hispanic            0.874693   1.007825   0.769363   1.069652   0.915789
Other               1.380835   1.035994   0.876076   1.422886   1.336842
```

Each value in the table above is the value from the metric_scores table divided by the Caucasian value (our privileged group). For example, the African American TPR value of 1.633907 is equal to the TPR(African American) / TPR(Caucasian), which is calculated as 0.665 / 0.407.

These ratios are then checked against a four-fifth range of (0.8, 1.25), and if our metric falls outside of that range, we consider that ratio unfair. The ideal value is 1, which indicates that the specified metric for that race is equal to the value of that metric for our privileged group. If we count up the number of ratios outside of that range, we come up with 7 (they are in boldface). We can plot the numbers in the previous table using Dalex as well (figure 4.14):

```
mf_tree.plot()   # Same numbers from the fairness_check in a plot
```

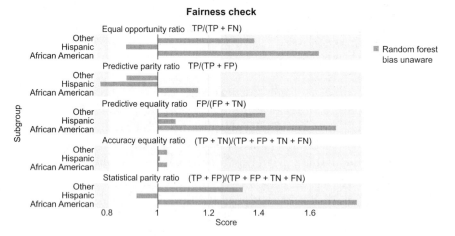

Figure 4.14   Dalex offers a visual breakdown of the five main ratios we will focus on, broken down by subgroup. The lighter areas of the bars are meant to convey acceptable ranges for fairness. Any bar in the darker regions are out of range of (.8, 1.25) and are considered unfair. We can see that we have some work to do!

To make things a bit simpler, let's focus on the parity loss of each of the five metrics from our fairness check. *Parity loss* represents a total score across our disadvantaged groups. Dalex calculates parity loss for a metric as being the sum of the absolute value of the log of the metric ratios in our fairness checks.

$$metric_{parity\_loss} = \sum_{i \in \{a, b, \ldots z\}} \left| log \left(\frac{metric_i}{metric_{privileged}} \right) \right|$$

For example, if we look at the statistical parities of our groups (STP), we have the following:

$$STP(\text{African American}) = 0.508$$
$$STP(\text{Hispanic}) = 0.261$$
$$STP(\text{Other}) = 0.381$$
$$STP(\text{Caucasian}) = 0.285$$

We can calculate our parity loss for STP for our bias-unaware model should be 0.956. Luckily, Dalex gives us an easier way to calculate parity loss for all five metrics and stack them together in a chart. Figure 4.15 is the one we will use to compare across our models, and the five stacks represent the values for each of our five bias metrics. They are stacked up together to represent the overall bias of the model. We want to see the overall stacked length to *decrease* as we become more bias aware. We will be pairing this stacked parity loss graph with classic ML metrics, like accuracy, precision, and recall as seen in figure 4.15.

EXERCISE 4.2 Write Python code to calculate the STP parity loss.

```
mf_tree.plot(type = 'stacked')
```
◁────── **Plot of parity loss of each metric**

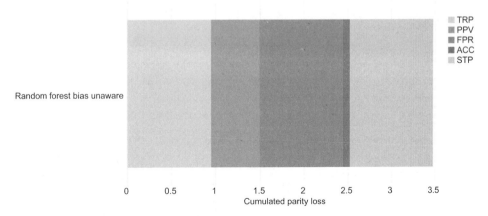

Figure 4.15 Cumulative parity loss. In this case, smaller is better, meaning less bias. For example, the far-right section represents the 0.956 we previously calculated by hand. Overall, our bias-unaware model is scoring around 3.5, which is our number to beat on the bias front.

We now have both a baseline for model performance (from our model performance summary) and a baseline for fairness given by our stacked parity loss chart. Let's move on now to how we can actively use feature engineering to mitigate bias in our data.

4.5   *Mitigating bias*

When it comes to mitigating bias and promoting fairness in our models, we have three main opportunities to do so:

1   *Preprocessing*—Bias mitigation, as applied to the training data (i.e., before the model has had a chance to train on the training data)
2   *In-processing*—Bias mitigation applied to a model during the training phase
3   *Postprocessing*—Bias mitigation applied to the predicted labels after the model has been fit to the training data

Each phase of bias mitigation has pros and cons, and preprocessing directly refers to feature engineering techniques and, therefore, will be the main focus of this chapter.

4.5.1   *Preprocessing*

Preprocessing bias mitigation takes place in the training data before modeling takes place. Preprocessing is useful when we don't have access to the model itself or the downstream predictions, but we do have access to the initial training data.

Two examples of preprocessing bias mitigation techniques that we will implement in this chapter are

- *Disparate impact removal*—Editing feature values to improve group fairness
- *Learning fair representations*—Extracting a new feature set by obfuscating the original information regarding protected attributes

By implementing these two techniques, we will be hoping to reduce the overall bias that our model is exhibiting, while also trying to enhance our ML pipeline's performance.

4.5.2   *In-processing*

In-processing techniques are applied during training time. They usually come in the form of some regularization term or an alternative objective function. In-processing techniques are only possible when we have access to the actual learning algorithm. Otherwise, we'd have to rely on pre- or postprocessing.

Some examples of in-processing bias mitigation techniques include

- *Meta fair classifier*—Uses fairness as an input to optimize a classifier for fairness
- *Prejudice remover*—Implementing a privilege-aware regularization term to our learning objective

4.5.3   *Postprocessing*

Postprocessing techniques, as the name implies, are applied after training time and are most useful when we need to treat the ML model as a black box, and we don't have access to the original training data. Some examples of postprocessing bias mitigation techniques include

- *Equalized odds*—Modifying predicted labels, using a separate optimization objective to make the predictions fairer
- *Calibrated equalized odds*—Modifying the classifier's scores to make for fairer results

4.6   Building a bias-aware model

Let's begin to construct a more bias-aware model, using two feature engineering techniques. We will begin by applying a familiar transformation to construct a new less-biased column and then move on to new feature extraction methods. Our goal is to minimize the bias of our model without sacrificing a great deal of model performance.

4.6.1   Feature construction: Using the Yeo-Johnson transformer to treat the disparate impact

In the last chapter, we used the Box-Cox transformation to transform some of our features to make them appear more normal. We will want to do something similar here. We have to investigate why our model is underpredicting recidivism for non–African American people. One approach would be to remove race entirely from our dataset and expect the ML model to remove all bias. This rarely is the answer.

Unprivileged and privileged groups of people experience different opportunities, and this likely presents itself in the data through correlated features. The most likely cause for our model's bias is that at least one of our features is highly correlated with race, and our model is able to reconstruct someone's racial identity through this feature. To find this feature, let's start by finding the correlation coefficient of our numerical features and being African American:

```
compas_df.corrwith(compas_df['race'] == 'African-American').sort_values()
age            -0.179095
juv_count       0.111835
priors_count    0.202897
```

Both `age` and `priors_count` are highly correlated with our Boolean label of simply being African American, so let's take a closer look at each of those. Let's start by looking at age. We can plot a histogram and print out some basic statistics (figure 4.16), and we will see that across our four racial categories, age seems to be relatively similar with a similar mean, standard deviation, and median. This signals to us that even though age is negatively correlated to being African American, this relationship is likely not a huge contributing factor to our model's bias.

```
compas_df.groupby('race')['age'].plot(
    figsize=(20,5),
    kind='hist', xlabel='Age', title='Histogram of Age'    ⬅──┐ Age is not
)                                                              └─ very skewed.
compas_df.groupby('race')['age'].describe()
```

	count	mean	std	min	25%	50%	75%	max
race								
African American	3696.0	32.740801	10.858391	18.0	25.0	30.0	38.00	77.0
Caucasian	2454.0	37.726569	12.761373	18.0	27.0	35.0	47.75	83.0
Hispanic	637.0	35.455259	11.877783	19.0	26.0	33.0	43.00	96.0
Other	427.0	35.131148	11.634159	19.0	25.0	33.0	43.00	76.0

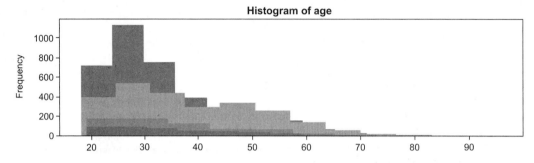

Histogram of age

Figure 4.16 **Distribution of age by group. The table on top implies that age distribution is not drastically different across groups, thereby implying less impact to disparate treatment and impact. It is worth noting that the average and the median age of African Americans is about 10%–15% younger than those identified in the other categories, which is probably why we are seeing a strong correlation between our age column and our African American identifying column.**

Let's turn our attention to `priors_count` and do the same printout. When we do, we will see some stark contrasts from age, as seen in figure 4.17.

```
compas_df.groupby('race')['priors_count'].plot(
    figsize=(20,5),
    kind='hist', xlabel='Count of Priors',
title='Histogram of Priors'
)
compas_df.groupby('race')['priors_count'].describe()
```

> **Priors is extremely skewed by looking at the differences in mean/median/std across the racial categories.**

There are two things to note:

- African American priors are hugely right skewed, as evidenced by the mean being over twice the median.
- African American priors are nearly twice as high as the other racial groups combined, due to a long history of systemic criminal justice issues.

The facts that `priors_count` is so correlated to race, and it is skewed differently for the different racial categories, are huge problems mainly because the ML model can likely pick up on these and bias itself against certain races, simply by looking at the `priors_count` column.

race	count	mean	std	min	25%	50%	75%	max
African American	3696.0	4.438853	5.579835	0.0	1.0	2.0	6.0	38.0
Caucasian	2454.0	2.586797	3.798803	0.0	0.0	1.0	3.0	36.0
Hispanic	637.0	2.252747	3.647673	0.0	0.0	1.0	2.0	26.0
Other	427.0	2.016393	3.695856	0.0	0.0	1.0	2.5	31.0

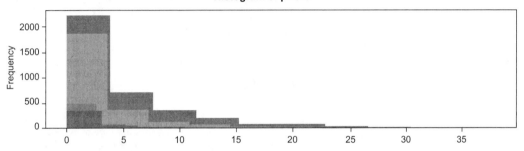

Figure 4.17 At first glance, it may seem like the patterns of priors for all races are similar. Distributions of priors count show a similar right skew between racial groups. However, for reasons out of many people's control, the median and mean priors counts for African Americans are nearly twice that of the other groups.

To remedy this, we will create a custom transformer that will modify a column in place by applying the Yeo-Johnson transformation—as discussed in our previous chapter— to each racial category's subset of values. This will help to remove the disparate impact that this column would have on our group fairness.

As pseudocode, it would look like this:

```
For each group label:
    Get the subset of priors_count values for that group
    Apply the yeo-johnson transformation to the subset
    Modify the column in place for that group label with the new values
```

By applying the transformation on each subset of values, rather than on the column as a whole, we are forcing each group's set of values to be normal with a mean of 0 and a standard deviation of 1, making it harder for the model to reconstruct a particular group label from a given priors_count value. Let's construct a custom scikit-learn transformer to perform this operation, as shown in the following listing.

Listing 4.13   Disparate treatment mitigation through Yeo-Johnson

Imports from scikit-learn for our yeo-johnson transformation and base transformer classes

```
from sklearn.preprocessing import PowerTransformer
from sklearn.base import BaseEstimator, TransformerMixin

class NormalizeColumnByLabel(BaseEstimator, TransformerMixin):
    def __init__(self, col, label):
        self.col = col
        self.label = label
        self.transformers = {}

    def fit(self, X, y=None):
        for group in X[self.label].unique():
            self.transformers[group] = PowerTransformer(
                method='yeo-johnson', standardize=True
            )
            self.transformers[group].fit(
                X.loc[X[self.label]==group][self.col].values.reshape(-1, 1)
            )
        return self

    def transform(self, X, y=None):
        C = X.copy()
        for group in X[self.label].unique():
            C.loc[
                X[self.label]==group, self.col
            ] = self.transformers[group].transform(
                X.loc[X[self.label]==group][self.col].values.reshape(-1, 1)
            )
        return C
```

Fit a PowerTransformer for each group label.

When transforming a new DataFrame, we use the transform method of our already fit transformers and modify the DataFrame in place.

Let's apply our new transformer to our training data to see our priors counts modified (figure 4.18), so each group label has a mean priors count of 0 and a standard deviation of 1:

```
n = NormalizeColumnByLabel(col='priors_count', label='race')

X_train_normalized = n.fit_transform(X_train, y_train)

X_train_normalized.groupby('race')['priors_count'].hist(figsize=(20,5))
X_train_normalized.groupby('race')['priors_count'].describe()
```

	count	mean	std	min	25%	50%	75%	max
race								
African American	2604.0	1.119176e-17	1.000192	-1.394037	-0.549932	-0.092417	0.784661	2.276224
Caucasian	1700.0	-2.388286e-16	1.000294	-1.190914	-1.190914	-0.104396	0.733866	2.293665
Hispanic	457.0	-5.538968e-17	1.001096	-1.124116	-1.124116	0.098333	0.620238	2.060623
Other	288.0	1.780983e-16	1.001741	-0.921525	-0.921525	-0.921525	0.878567	1.871600

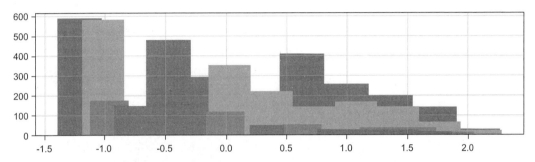

Figure 4.18 After applying the Yeo-Johnson transformation on each subgroup's subset of priors counts, the distributions begin to look much less skewed and different from one another. This will make it difficult for the ML model to reconstruct race from this feature.

Listing 4.14 Our first bias-aware model

```
clf_tree_aware = Pipeline(steps=[
    ('normalize_priors', NormalizeColumnByLabel(
                         col='priors_count', label='race')),        ⟵
    ('preprocessor', preprocessor),
    ('classifier', classifier)
])

clf_tree_aware.fit(X_train, y_train)
aware_y_preds = clf_tree_aware.predict(X_test)

exp_tree_aware = dx.Explainer(
    clf_tree_aware, X_test, y_test,
    label='Random Forest DIR', verbose=False)        ⟵
mf_tree_aware = exp_tree_aware.model_fairness(
    protected=race_test, privileged = "Caucasian")

# performance is virtually unchanged overall
pd.concat(
    [exp.model_performance().result for exp in [exp_tree, exp_tree_aware]])

# We can see a small drop in parity loss
mf_tree.plot(objects=[mf_tree_aware], type='stacked')        ⟵
```

Add in our new transformer before our preprocessor to fix the priors_count before doing anything else.

Check out our model performance.

Investigate the change in parity loss.

Our new bias-aware model (listing 4.14) with disparate impact removal is working quite well! We can actually see a small boost in model performance and a small decrease in cumulative parity loss (figure 4.19).

	recall	precision	f1	accuracy	auc
Random forest bias unaware	0.560451	0.628736	0.592633	0.652656	0.693935
Random forest DIR	0.560451	0.633835	0.594889	0.655889	0.694213

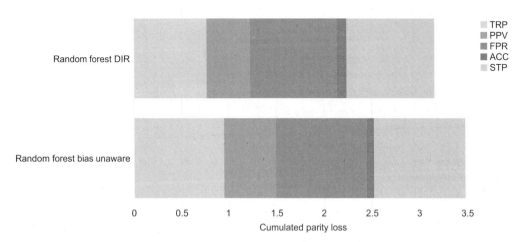

Figure 4.19   The top bar represents the sum of our bias metrics for our bias-aware model, which is seeing a minor boost in model performance (noted in the metric table) in all metrics, except recall, where it is unchanged. The bottom bar shows the original bias-unaware stacked plot we saw earlier. Overall, our new bias-unaware model is performing better in some ML metrics and is showing a decrease in bias based on our parity loss bar chart. We are on the right track!

4.6.2   *Feature extraction: Learning fair representation implementation using AIF360*

Up until now, we haven't done anything to address our model's unawareness of sensitive features. Rather than remove race completely, we are going to use AI Fairness 360 (AIF360), which is an open source toolkit developed by IBM to help data scientists get access to preprocessing, in-processing, and postprocessing bias mitigation techniques, to apply our first feature extraction technique, called *learning fair representation (LFR)*. The idea of LFR is to map our data *x* onto a new set of features that represent a more fair representation with respect to sensitive variables, including gender and race.

For our use case, we are going to attempt to map our categorical variables (4 / 6 of them representing race) into a new *fairer* vector space that preserves statistical parity and retains as much information as possible from our original *x*.

AIF360 can be a bit tricky to use, as it forces you to use its own version of a Data-Frame called the `BinaryLabelDataset`. Listing 4.15 is a custom scikit-learn transformer that will

1 Take in *x*, a DataFrame of binary values, which are created from our categorical preprocessor
2 Convert the DataFrame into a `BinaryLabelDataset`
3 Fit the LFR module from the AIF360 package
4 Transform any new dataset, using the now-fit LFR to map it onto our new fair representation

Listing 4.15 Custom LFR transformer

```
from aif360.algorithms.preprocessing.lfr import LFR
from aif360.datasets import BinaryLabelDataset

class LFRCustom(BaseEstimator, TransformerMixin):
    def __init__(
        self, col, protected_col,
        unprivileged_groups, privileged_groups
    ):
        self.col = col
        self.protected_col = protected_col
        self.TR = None
        self.unprivileged_groups = unprivileged_groups
        self.privileged_groups = privileged_groups

    def fit(self, X, y=None):
        d = pd.DataFrame(X, columns=self.col)
        d['response'] = list(y)

        binary_df = BinaryLabelDataset(         ◁─── Conversion to and from the AIF360
            df=d,                                    BinaryLabelDataset object
            protected_attribute_names=self.protected_col,
            label_names=['response']
        )

        self.TR = LFR(unprivileged_groups=self.unprivileged_groups,
                privileged_groups=self.privileged_groups, seed=0,
                k=2, Ax=0.5, Ay=0.2, Az=0.2,        ◁───
                verbose=1
                )
        self.TR.fit(binary_df, maxiter=5000, maxfun=5000)
        return self

    def transform(self, X, y=None):
        d = pd.DataFrame(X, columns=self.col)
        if y:
            d['response'] = list(y)
        else:
            d['response'] = False
```

These parameters can be found on the AIF360 website and were discovered through offline grid searching.

```
        binary_df = BinaryLabelDataset(
            df=d,
            protected_attribute_names=self.protected_col,
            label_names=['response']
        )
        return self.TR.transform(
            binary_df).convert_to_dataframe()[0].drop(
                ['response'], axis=1)   #B
```

To use our new transformer, we will need to modify our pipeline slightly and make use of the `FeatureUnion` object, as shown in the following listing.

Listing 4.16 Model with disparate impact removal and LFR

Tell AIF360 that rows with a Caucasian label of 1 are privileged, and rows with a Caucasian label of 0 are unprivileged. Right now, the AIF360 package can only support one privileged and one unprivileged group.

```
categorical_preprocessor = ColumnTransformer(transformers=[
    ('cat', categorical_transformer, categorical_features)
])

#
privileged_groups = [{'Caucasian': 1}]
unprivileged_groups = [{'Caucasian': 0}]

lfr = LFRCustom(
    col=['African-American', 'Caucasian', 'Hispanic', 'Other', 'Male', 'M'],
    protected_col=sorted(X_train['race'].unique()) ,
    privileged_groups=privileged_groups,
    unprivileged_groups=unprivileged_groups
)

categorical_pipeline = Pipeline([
    ('transform', categorical_preprocessor),
    ('LFR', lfr),
])

numerical_features = ["age", "priors_count"]
numerical_transformer = Pipeline(steps=[
    ('scale', StandardScaler())
])

numerical_preprocessor = ColumnTransformer(transformers=[
        ('num', numerical_transformer, numerical_features)
])

preprocessor = FeatureUnion([
    ('numerical_preprocessor', numerical_preprocessor),
    ('categorical_pipeline', categorical_pipeline)
])

clf_tree_more_aware = Pipeline(
```

Isolate the numerical and categorical preprocessor, so we can fit the LFR to the categorical data separately.

Use FeatureUnion to combine our categorical data and our numerical data.

```
        steps=[
            ('normalize_priors', NormalizeColumnByLabel(
                col='priors_count', label='race')),
            ('preprocessor', preprocessor),
            ('classifier', classifier)
    ])
```

Our new pipeline will remove
disparate impact/treatment
via Yeo-Johnson and will apply
LFR to our categorical data to
address model unawareness.

```
clf_tree_more_aware.fit(X_train, y_train)

more_aware_y_preds = clf_tree_more_aware.predict(X_test)
```

That was a lot of code to simply apply an LFR module to our DataFrame. Truly, the only reason it was so much was the need to transform our pandas DataFrame into AIF360's custom data object and back. Now that we have fit our model, let's take a final look at our model's fairness:

```
exp_tree_more_aware = dx.Explainer(
    clf_tree_more_aware, X_test, y_test,
    label='Random Forest DIR + LFR', verbose=False)

mf_tree_more_aware = exp_tree_more_aware.model_fairness(
    protected=race_test, privileged="Caucasian")

pd.concat(
    [exp.model_performance().result for exp in [exp_tree,
        exp_tree_aware, exp_tree_more_aware]
])
```

We can see that our final model with disparate impact removal and LFR applied has arguably better model performance than our original baseline model (figure 4.20).

	recall	precision	f1	accuracy	auc
Random forest bias unaware	0.560451	0.628736	0.592633	0.652656	0.693935
Random forest DIR	0.560451	0.633835	0.594889	0.655889	0.694213
Random forest DIR + LFR	0.558402	0.639671	0.596280	0.659122	0.693426

Figure 4.20   Our final bias-aware model has improved accuracy, f1, and precision and is seeing only a minor drop in recall and AUC. This is wonderful because it shows that by reducing bias, we have gotten our ML model to perform better in more *classical* metrics, like accuracy, at the same time. Win-win!

We also want to check in on our cumulative parity loss to make sure we are heading in the right direction:

```
Mf_tree.plot(objects=[mf_tree_aware, mf_tree_more_aware], type='stacked')
```

When we check our plot, we can see that our fairness metrics are decreasing as well! This is all-around great news. Our model is not suffering performance-wise from our baseline model, and our model is also acting much more fairly (figure 4.21).

Stacked parity loss metrics

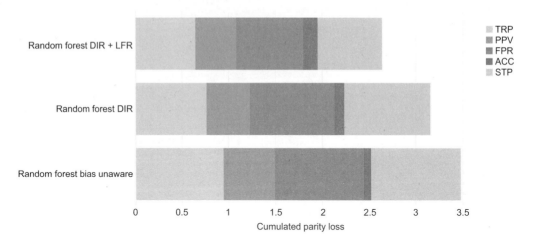

Figure 4.21   Our final, bias-aware model that has disparate impact removal and LFR is the fairest model yet. Again, keep in mind that smaller means less bias, which is generally better for us. We are definitely making some right moves here to see such a drop in bias and an increase in model performance after doing some pretty simple transformations to our data!

Let's take a look at our Dalex model fairness check one last time. Recall that for our unaware model, we had seven numbers outside of our range of (0.8, 1.25), and we had bias detected in four of five metrics.

```
mf_tree_more_aware.fairness_check()      ⊲──── 3 / 15 numbers out of the range of (08, 1.25)
Bias detected in 3 metrics: TPR, FPR, STP

Conclusion: your model is not fair because 2 or more criteria exceeded
    acceptable limits set by epsilon.

Ratios of metrics, based on 'Caucasian'. Parameter 'epsilon' was set to 0.8
➥ and therefore metrics should be within (0.8, 1.25)
                       TPR         ACC         PPV         FPR         STP
African-American  1.626829    1.058268    1.198953    1.538095    1.712329
Hispanic          1.075610    1.102362    0.965096    0.828571    0.893836
Other             0.914634    0.996850    0.806283    1.100000    0.962329
```

We now only have three metrics out of our range, as opposed to the seven previously, and bias is now only being detected in three metrics, rather than four. All in all, our work has seemed to improve our model performance slightly and reduced our cumulative parity loss at the same time.

We've done a lot of work on this data, but would we be comfortable submitting this model as is to be considered an accurate and fair recidivism predictor? *Absolutely not!* Our work in this chapter barely scratched the surface of bias and fairness awareness and only focused on a few preprocessing techniques, not even beginning to discuss, in depth, the other forms of bias mitigation available to us.

4.7 Answers to exercises

EXERCISE 4.1

Plot the distribution of the new `juv_count` feature. What is the arithmetic mean and standard deviation?

ANSWER:

```
compas_df['juv_count'].plot(
    title='Count of Juvenile Infractions', kind='hist', xlabel='Count'
)
```

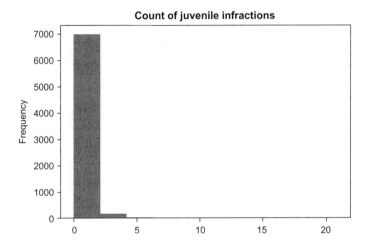

To calculate the mean and standard deviation, we could run the following code:

```
compas_df['juv_count'].mean(), compas_df['juv_count'].std()
```

The mean is 0.2675, and the standard deviation is 0.9527.

EXERCISE 4.2

Write Python code to calculate the STP parity loss.

ANSWER:

```
unpriv_stp = [0.508, 0.261, 0.381]    ◁——— STP metrics for unprivileged groups

caucasian_stp = 0.285    ◁——— STP metrics for privileged group

sum([abs(np.log(u / caucasian_stp)) for u in unpriv_stp])    ◁——— 0.956
```

Summary

- Model fairness is as important as, if not more important than, model performance alone.
- There are multiple ways of defining fairness in our model, each with its pros and cons:

- – Relying on the unawareness of a model is almost always not enough because of correlating factors in our data.
  - – Statistical parity and equalized odds are two common definitions of fairness but can sometimes contradict one another.
- We can mitigate bias before, during, and after training a model.
- Disparate impact removal and learning of fair representation helped our model become more fair and also led to a small bump in model performance.
- Preprocessing alone is *not enough* to mitigate bias. We would also have to work on in-processing and postprocessing methods to further minimize our bias.

Natural language processing: Classifying social media sentiment

This chapter covers
- Preparing text vectorization for quantitative features
- Practicing cleaning and tokenizing raw text into features
- Extracting and learning features with deep learning
- Taking advantage of transfer learning with BERT

Our last two case studies focused on completely different domains but had a major component in common: we were working with structured tabular data. In the next two case studies, we are going to look at special cases where we need to deploy specific feature engineering techniques to make machine learning possible. In this case study, we will be looking at techniques from the world of *natural language processing (NLP)*, which is a branch of ML focused on working with raw text data.

As discussed in previous chapters, unstructured data are widely prevalent, and data scientists often need to perform machine learning tasks on unstructured data like text and images. A common NLP task is performing *text classification* or *text regression*, which consists of performing classification or regression given only raw text.

Figure 5.1 consists of three different examples of text classification. Example 1—"I love this restaurant!"—is a common sentiment analysis, in which the goal is to predict whether or not a piece of text is positive or negative. The second example—LIMITED OFFER, BIG WINNER, OPEN NOW!!!11!!—is a spam classification task that would likely run on email subject lines. The last example is how a home automation system decides what task was asked of it given a voice command is converted to text.

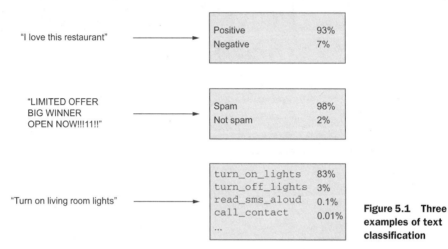

Figure 5.1   Three examples of text classification

Before we dive into the intricacies of natural language processing and the feature engineering techniques in this domain, we should lay out some basic terminology. Throughout this chapter, I will refer to a *document* as a piece of text of variable length. A document could be a movie review, a tweet, a research paper—really, anything! Documents are the main input to our NLP models. When we have a collection of documents, we call this collection a *corpus* (figure 5.2).

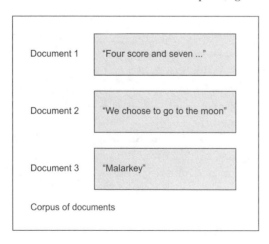

Figure 5.2   A document is a piece of text. A corpus is a collection of documents.

There are virtually limitless numbers of NLP problems because, as humans, we communicate naturally through language. We would expect our ML-driven systems to be able to parse our language and perform tasks as needed. The problem is that ML models cannot process and learn from raw strings of variable length. ML models expect data in the form of observations with fixed-length feature vectors. We will need to convert our text items into vectors of features to perform any kind of NLP, as shown in figure 5.3.

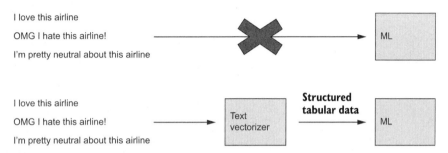

Figure 5.3   We have to convert raw variable-length text into fixed-length feature vectors before we can apply any ML algorithm.

Let's take a look at the dataset for our case study.

> **WARNING**   This chapter has some long-running code samples, particularly later on in the chapter when we get to autoencoders and BERT. Be advised that some code samples may run for over an hour on the minimum requirements for this text.

5.1   The tweet sentiment dataset

Our dataset in this case study is derived from a Kaggle competition, Twitter US Airline Sentiment (https://www.kaggle.com/crowdflower/twitter-airline-sentiment). We have further modified the data slightly to make the classes more balanced in the following listing.

Listing 5.1   Ingesting the data

```
import pandas as pd       Import packages.                      Show the first
import numpy as np                                              five rows. See
tweet_df = pd.read_csv('../data/cleaned_airline_tweets.csv')  ◁─  figure 5.4.
tweet_df.head()   #Bp
```

Like in other chapters, we will make the assumption that we have very little control over our predictive model. In fact, every time we test out a new feature engineering technique, we will test the technique against a logistic regression, and we will grid-search a single logistic regression parameter. To remind ourselves of why we are doing this, our goal is to find the best way to represent our text as structured data, and we want to be

	text	sentiment
0	@VirginAmerica What @dhepburn said.	neutral
1	@VirginAmerica it was amazing, and arrived an ...	positive
2	@VirginAmerica I <3 pretty graphics. so muc...	positive
3	@VirginAmerica So excited for my first cross c...	positive
4	I ♥ flying @VirginAmerica. ☺	positive

Figure 5.4   **Our Twitter sentiment dataset consists of only two columns: text and sentiment. Our goal is to predict the sentiment of the text using only signals available in the text.**

sure that if we see an increase in our ML pipeline's performance, it is due to our feature engineering efforts and not that we are relying on an ML model's learning ability.

There isn't much exploration to do of our dataset, but it is a good idea to take a look around to get a sense for our text column and our response label. To do this, let's introduce a new package called *pandas profiling*. The pandas profiling package provides a report for cursory data descriptions and exploration to expedite the analysis phase of our ML efforts. It can give us a description of each column, both quantitative and qualitative, as well as including other information, like a report on missing data, histograms of text length, and much more. Let's take a look at the report the profiling tool gives us in the following listing.

Listing 5.2   Using the profiler to learn about our data

```
from pandas_profiling import ProfileReport
profile = ProfileReport(tweet_df, title="Tweets Report", explorative=True)

profile   ⊲——— Inspect the profile object.
```

Running this code will generate a report of our data with some key ideas. For example, under Toggle Details of the text column in the Categories tab, we have a histogram of text length that reveals a somewhat normal distribution of text length with a spike around 140 characters (figure 5.5).

We can also see the distribution of our response label, *sentiment.* It reveals that our data are fairly well balanced in terms of sentiment and that our null accuracy—the baseline metric for classification we'd achieve by guessing the most common category— makes up only 34.9% of the data (figure 5.6). That should be easy to beat. Our goal is to create an ML system that can take in a tweet and predict one of these three categories.

The profile has many graphs and tables with more information about our dataset, but really, when it comes to it, we have text, and we have a label. Before moving on, let's take the time to split up our dataset into training and testing sets, so we can use them to confidently compare our feature engineering efforts.

> **NOTE**   We will always train our feature engineering systems on the training set and apply them to the testing set as if the testing set were brand-new data the pipeline has never seen before.

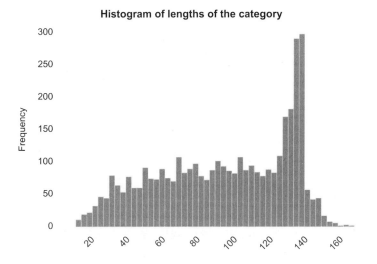

Figure 5.5   Pie chart for our response label *sentiment*, showing a fairly even distribution of the sentiment classes

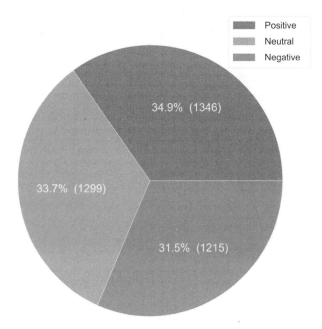

Figure 5.6   Text length histogram, as provided by the pandas profiling tool

As a reminder, we will be splitting our data into an 80/20 train/test split as we do in virtually every case study. We will also be setting a `random_state` for reproducibility (so you will get the same splits) and stratify on our class label *sentiment*, so the train and test sets have the same distribution of class labels as the overall data. Let's see this all coded up in the following listing.

Listing 5.3   Splitting our data into training and testing sets

```
from sklearn.model_selection import train_test_split

train, test = train_test_split(
    tweet_df, test_size=0.2, random_state=0,
    stratify=tweet_df['sentiment']
)

print(f'Count of tweets in training set: {train.shape[0]:,}')
print(f'Count of tweets in testing set: {test.shape[0]:,}')

Count of tweets in training set: 3,088
Count of tweets in testing set: 772
```

Now that we have our training and testing sets, it's time to discuss how to transform our text into something that ML algorithms can process through a process known as vectorization.

5.1.1   The problem statement and defining success

We are performing another classification here. The goal of our model can be summarized by the following question: Given the text of a tweet, can we find ways to represent the text and classify the sentiment of the tweet accurately?

The goal of this case study is to find different ways to convert our tweets into machine-readable features and use those features to train a model. In order to better identify which of our feature engineering techniques are helping us the most, we will stick to using a simple logistic regression classifier. By doing this, we can be more confident that boosts in our pipeline performance are due mostly to our feature engineering efforts.

5.2   Text vectorization

Every feature engineering technique in this chapter will be a kind of text vectorization procedure. *Text vectorization* is the process of converting raw, variable-length text into a fixed-length vector of quantitative features (figure 5.7). It is how we convert unstructured text into structured data. We cannot perform any kind of machine learning on text without first structuring the raw text into some structured format.

When we vectorize text, how do we know what the features are? Well, that depends on what kind of vectorization we implement. We will see many vectorization options in this chapter, and they will range from being highly interpretable to virtually uninterpretable. They will also range in complexity from very simple word counts to deep learning–based algorithms.

The main takeaway is that our goal in this chapter will always be the same: converting unstructured text into structured features to maximize predictive signal for our ML model.

	Feature 1	Feature 2	...	Feature *n*
	0.324	0	0.453	0.43543
I love this airline				
OMG I hate this airline!	1	0.23	1.761	0.34
I'm pretty neutral about this airline	0.938	1.638	1.5	0

Figure 5.7 Text vectorization is the process of converting unstructured text into a structured tabular representation. Depending on how we vectorize text, the features will have different meanings and significance. In our figure here, features 1, 2, ... *n* could represent the occurrence of a particular word or phrase or they may represent a latent feature learned by a deep learning model. This chapter will cover many ways of vectorizing text, and each method will result in a different set of features.

5.2.1 Feature construction: Bag of words

Our first attempt to vectorize our text will be to apply a bag-of-words approach. *Bag-of-words* models (figure 5.8) are ones that treat text as a *bag* (sometimes referred to as a multiset) of words.

Sinan loves his pet bearded dragon and also his pet dog and also his pet cat.

Sinan	pet	his	cat	...	dragon
1	3	3	1	...	1

Figure 5.8 A bag-of-words approach would convert text into a vector of word occurrences that does not take into account word ordering or grammar.

This approach disregards basic grammar and word order and simply relies on the number of occurrences of words.

The term *word* here is also being used a bit loosely. We can also consider phrases to be words. We can refer to phrases as n-*grams* of words (unigrams are one-word phrases—i.e., words—bigrams are two-word phrases, trigrams are three-word phrases, etc.). Because of this, bag-of-words models are sometimes referred to as *bag-of-*n-*grams* models (figure 5.9). When considering *n*-grams of 2 or higher, we start to consider grammar a bit. In the example in figure 5.8, there's more meaning in the bigram *bearded dragon* than in the word *bearded* alone. From now on, we will use the term *token* to mean any *n*-gram (including unigrams) of words in a piece of text, and *tokenizing* will refer to the act of transforming text into tokens.

Scikit-learn has built-in bag-of-words text vectorizers we can utilize for our first foray into text vectorization. So let's get to it!

Sinan loves
his pet
bearded
dragon and
also his pet
dog and also
his pet cat.

Sinan	bearded	bearded dragon	cat	...	dragon
1	1	1	1	...	1

Figure 5.9   A bag-of-words approach considering both unigrams and bigrams would consider *bearded dragon* **as a token, as well as** *bearded* **and** *dragon* **individually. By considering multiword tokens, we are able to teach the model about word co-occurrences at the same time as teaching the model about the word.**

5.2.2   *Count vectorization*

As the name suggests, scikit-learn's `CountVectorizer` module converts text samples into vectors of simple token counts. Using the module is quick and painless and can be done in a few lines of code (listing 5.4). We can *fit* the module to our training set, and it will learn the vocabulary of tokens from the training corpus and *transform* the corpus to be a matrix of fixed-length vectors.

Listing 5.4   Count vectorizing our training set

```
from sklearn.feature_extraction.text import CountVectorizer

cv = CountVectorizer()      ◁── Instantiate the CountVectorizer.
single_word = cv.fit_transform(train['text'])      ◁───

print(single_word.shape)
(3088, 6018)      ◁── 6,018 features!
```

In one line, fit the CountVectorizer to our training set, and transform it into a matrix.

The output of the scikit-learn vectorizer object is a *sparse matrix object*, which is a representation of a row-and-column matrix but optimized for matrices with large dimensions and that have most of their values as blank or 0. Why do we need the concept of a sparse matrix? When we print out the shape of our training matrix, we have 3,088 rows, which matches the number of tweets we have in our training set, but we have over 6,000 features (figure 5.10). Each feature is a unigram (single-word token) that occurs at least once in the training corpus. Let's take a look at this matrix to see what kinds of tokens are being included:

```
pd.DataFrame(single_word.todense(), columns=cv.get_feature_names())      ◁──
```

CountVectorizer feature matrix

The `CountVectorizer` has over a dozen hyperparameters at our disposal, one of which is the `max_features` parameter, which will only select the most common tokens to help us limit the number of features and, therefore, reduce the complexity of our pipeline. Of course we have to be careful when using this parameter because every token we throw away is a potential signal we are removing from the ML model, potentially making it harder to learn to model sentiment properly.

	00	000	000114	000ft	00pm	0167560070877	02
0	0	0	0	0	0	0	0
1	0	0	0	0	0	0	0
2	0	0	0	0	0	0	0
3	0	0	0	0	0	0	0
4	0	0	0	0	0	0	0
...	...	...	...	...	...	...	...
3083	0	0	0	0	0	0	0
3084	0	0	0	0	0	0	0
3085	0	0	0	0	0	0	0
3086	0	0	0	0	0	0	0
3087	0	0	0	0	0	0	0

3088 rows × 6018 columns

Figure 5.10 Our count-vectorized training corpus has one row per tweet and one column or feature for every unigram that exists in our training corpus. These seemingly gibberish tokens belong to condensed Twitter URLs within the tweets.

Let's see what it looks like to vectorize our text with the 20 most common tokens in our corpus, using the following listing. We can see the resulting DataFrame in figure 5.11.

Listing 5.5   Count vectorizing with a limited vocabulary

```
cv = CountVectorizer(max_features=20)          ⊲———  Setting max_features chooses
limited_vocab = cv.fit_transform(train['text'])       the most common words.
pd.DataFrame(limited_vocab.toarray(), index = train['text'], columns =
cv.get_feature_names())
```

Another parameter is `ngram_range`, which allows the vectorizer to consider more than just unigrams. This allows our model to learn the significance of phrases as well as single words. For example the word *group* may not be very useful, but the phrase *boarding group* now has more meaning. The con of upping our `ngram_range` to look at longer tokens is that it tends to explode the number of features to consider because now we have to consider so many more tokens in our vocabulary. Let's fit and transform our training corpus, while considering 1-, 2-, and 3-gram words as tokens in the following listing.

Listing 5.6   Count vectorizing with 1-, 2-, and 3-gram tokens

```
cv = CountVectorizer(ngram_range=(1, 3))      ⊲———  Consider unigrams,
more_ngrams = cv.fit_transform(train['text'])        bigrams, and trigrams.
print(larger_ngrams.shape)
(3088, 70613)          ⊲———  70,613 features!

pd.DataFrame(more_ngrams.toarray(), index = train['text'], columns =
➥ cv.get_feature_names()).head()
```

text	americanair	and	flight	for	in	is	it	jetblue	me	my	of	on	southwestair
@JetBlue Maybe I'll just go to Cleveland instead.	0	0	0	0	0	0	0	1	0	0	0	0	0
smh RT @JetBlue: Our fleet's on fleek. http://t.co/lRiXalfJJX	0	0	0	0	0	0	0	1	0	0	0	1	0
@SouthwestAir I would.	0	0	0	0	0	0	0	0	0	0	0	0	1
@USAirways trying to Cancelled Flight a flight urgently...get hung up on twice??? Sweet refund policy	0	0	2	0	0	0	0	0	0	0	0	1	0
@AmericanAir you are beyond redemption. Jfk. Baggage claim looks like a luggage warehouse	1	0	0	0	0	0	0	0	0	0	0	0	0
...	...	...	...	...	...	...	...	...	...	...	...	...	...
"@JetBlue: Our fleet's on fleek. http://t.co/b5ttno68xu" I just 🔫	0	0	0	0	0	0	0	1	0	0	0	1	0
@united caught earlier flight to ORD. Gate checked bag, and you've lost it at O'Hare. original flight lands in 20minutes. #frustrating!	0	1	2	0	1	0	1	0	0	0	0	0	0
@AmericanAir hi when will your next set of flights be out for next year from Dublin???	1	0	0	1	0	0	0	0	0	0	1	0	0
@SouthwestAir Finally! Integration w/ passbook is a great Valentine gift - better then chocoLate Flight. You do heart me.	0	0	1	0	0	1	0	0	1	0	0	0	1
@JetBlue @cflanagian she's on to something	0	0	0	0	0	0	0	1	0	0	0	1	0

Figure 5.11   Setting the `max_features` parameter limits the available vocabulary of our `CountVectorizer`, reducing the number of features and, therefore, limiting potential valuable signals for the ML pipeline.

The resulting matrix (figure 5.12) shows the trigrams that the `CountVectorizer` is considering and also shows that we have over 70,000 tokens and, therefore, over 70,000 features in our matrix! That is a lot of tokens, most of which likely hold little to no significance for our sentiment analysis purposes.

text	00	00 phone	00 phone hold	00 pm	00 pm that	000	000 air	000 air miles	000 crewmembers	000 crewmembers embody	...
@JetBlue Maybe I'll just go to Cleveland instead.	0	0	0	0	0	0	0	0	0	0	...
smh RT @JetBlue: Our fleet's on fleek. http://t.co/IRiXalfJJX	0	0	0	0	0	0	0	0	0	0	...
@SouthwestAir I would.	0	0	0	0	0	0	0	0	0	0	...
@USAirways trying to Cancelled Flight a flight urgently...get hung up on twice??? Sweet refund policy	0	0	0	0	0	0	0	0	0	0	...
@AmericanAir you are beyond redemption. Jfk. Baggage claim looks like a luggage warehouse	0	0	0	0	0	0	0	0	0	0	...

5 rows × 70613 columns

Figure 5.12 A sample of a matrix of vectorized tweets with unigrams, bigrams, and trigrams all being considered as possible vocabulary. There are 70,613 unique 1-, 2-, and 3-gram tokens in our training set of only 3,000 tweets.

Let's go back to looking at unigrams only for now, and let's see what our most common tokens are by setting our `max_features` to `10` and printing out the feature names.

Listing 5.7 Most common unigrams in our training corpus

```
cv = CountVectorizer(max_features=10)
cv.fit(train['text'])
cv.get_feature_names()                                          The most
['and', 'flight', 'for', 'jetblue', 'on', 'southwestair',       common words in
'the', 'to', 'united', 'you']                                ◁ our training set
```

One thing that stands out is that the majority of our most common tokens are really basic words like *to* and *the*. These are called *stopwords,* and they are tokens that generally do not hold much signal for text classification or regression. `CountVectorization` in scikit-learn has an option to remove known English stop words and take in a prewritten list of stop words as well. Let's remove English stop words, using the code in the following listing.

Listing 5.8   Most common non-stopword unigrams in our training corpus

```
cv = CountVectorizer(stop_words='english', max_features=10)
cv.fit(train['text'])
cv.get_feature_names()
```
⟵── **Don't consider common words as tokens like "A," "the," "an."**

```
['americanair', 'flight', 'http', 'jetblue', 'service',
 'southwestair', 'thank', 'thanks', 'united', 'usairways']
```
⟵── **The most common non-stopwords in our training set.**

This list makes much more sense of the most common words!

One downside of the `CountVectorizer` is that it will only learn the tokens that exist in the training corpus, and if a token exists in the testing set that doesn't exist in the training set, then the vectorizer will simply throw it away. One of the major upsides to using a bag-of-words vectorizer like the `CountVectorizer` is that the features that we end up with are more interpretable. This means that every feature represents the existence of a specific token in a document. It creates data at the ordinal level where higher numbers represent a larger number of occurrences of a token. These features are easy to explain and difficult to misinterpret. For example, if a tree-based model puts importance on a certain subset of tokens, we can directly interpret that to mean that the presence of those tokens holds importance in our ML application.

Let's run our first test of the `CountVectorizer` on our ML pipeline in listing 5.9 (figure 5.13). Throughout this chapter, we will rely on a method we are calling `advanced_grid_search`, which will

1 Take in a pipeline that has both the feature engineering pipeline and the model in it.
2 Run a cross-validated grid search on the pipeline as a whole, tuning parameters for the model and the feature engineering algorithms at the same time. This is run on the training set.
3 Pick the set of parameters that maximizes accuracy.
4 Print a classification report on the test set.

Listing 5.9   Using the `CountVectorizer`'s features in our ML pipeline

```
from sklearn.pipeline import Pipeline
from sklearn.linear_model import LogisticRegression

clf = LogisticRegression(max_iter=10000)   ⟵── Very simple classifier
ml_pipeline = Pipeline([
    ('vectorizer', CountVectorizer()),   ⟵── Our count vectorizer
    ('classifier', clf)
])

params = {
    'vectorizer__lowercase': [True, False],   ⟵┐ Lowercase is another parameter
    'vectorizer__stop_words': [None, 'english']     that, if true, will lowercase all text
                                                     before tokenizing.
```

```
    'vectorizer__max_features': [100, 1000, 5000],
    'vectorizer__ngram_range': [(1, 1), (1, 3)],          The only parameter we will fine-
    'classifier__C': [1e-1, 1e0, 1e1]          ◁——————     tune on our logistic regression
}
print("Count Vectorizer + Log Reg\n=====================")
advanced_grid_search(                                                      ◁——————┐
    train['text'], train['sentiment'], test['text'], test['sentiment'],          │
    ml_pipeline, params                     Function from our base notebook that will train
)                                             our pipeline on the training set and calculate a
                                              classification report from the testing set
```

```
Count Vectorizer + Log Reg
=====================
               precision    recall   f1-score   support

    negative       0.79      0.77       0.78       243
     neutral       0.75      0.78       0.77       260
    positive       0.84      0.83       0.84       269


    accuracy                            0.79       772
   macro avg       0.79      0.79       0.79       772
weighted avg       0.79      0.79       0.79       772

Best params: {'classifier_c':1.0, 'vectorizer_lowercase': True, 'vectorizer_max_features': 5000,
'vectorizer_ngram_range': (1,1), 'vectorizer_stop_words': None}
Overall took 59.29 seconds
```

Figure 5.13 Our results from our first-pass attempt at text vectorization. Taking a look at our overall accuracy shows that our baseline NLP model gives us a 79% accuracy on our test set. The number to beat in our future models will be 79%.

> **NOTE** Fitting models in this chapter may take some time to run. For my 2021 MacBook Pro, some of these code segments took over an hour to complete the grid search.

Our best `CountVectorizer` parameters yielded a 79% accuracy in our test set, which is much better than our null accuracy and will be our baseline text vectorization accuracy to beat. In our next section, we will see another bag-of-words text vectorizer that will add some complexity and, hopefully, some predictive power to our pipeline.

5.2.3 *TF-IDF vectorization*

The `CountVectorizer` provided a simple and easy-to-use vectorizer as a baseline feature engineering technique. To expand on its capabilities, we will introduce the *term-frequency inverse document-frequency (TF-IDF)* vectorizer (figure 5.14). The TD-IDF vectorizer is nearly identical to the `CountVectorizer`, except that, instead of just counting the number of times each token appears in a document, we will normalize the value by multiplying it by an inverse document frequency (IDF) term.

The motivation for this is that simply counting how often the word *usairways* appears in a tweet may not be that interesting because that token likely appears often throughout our corpus and, therefore, doesn't carry much weight on its own. However, if a tweet contained the word *abysmal*, then we may want to put more weight on that token, as it is likely much less common, and therefore, its presence is unique. The TF-IDF calculation, therefore, is a measure of the *originality, uniqueness,* or *interesting-ness* of tokens in a document by comparing how often it appears in the document to how often it appears in the corpus overall.

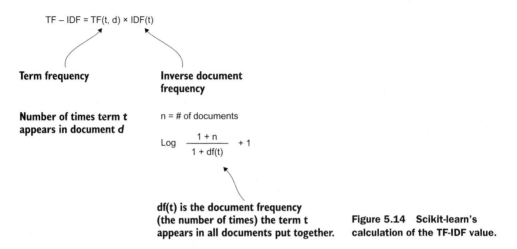

Figure 5.14   Scikit-learn's calculation of the TF-IDF value.

By calculating the TD-IDF measure, our goal is to assign more meaningful—and therefore useful—values to each token for our ML pipeline. Let's take a look at the most *unique* tokens in our training corpus in the following listing.

Listing 5.10   Listing the most unique tokens per TF-IDF

```
tfidf_vectorizer = TfidfVectorizer()     ⟵── Vanilla TF-IDF vectorizer

tfidf_vectorizer.fit(train['text'])

idf = pd.DataFrame({'feature_name':tfidf_vectorizer.get_feature_names(),
'idf_weights':tfidf_vectorizer.idf_})
idf.sort_values('idf_weights', ascending=True)
```

The resulting DataFrame (figure 5.15) will showcase the IDF value for each token, where lower values indicate less interesting tokens, and higher values indicate more interesting tokens.

> **EXERCISE 5.1**   Calculate the IDF weights by hand, using pure Python (using NumPy is OK), for a token that appears once in a given document and once in our training set overall.

Of course there's a downside here in that tokens at the end will simply be tokens that only appear once in the corpus, but that doesn't mean that they are meaningful at all.

	feature_name	idf_weights
5401	to	1.932281
5316	the	2.163475
5983	you	2.288016
2419	for	2.375028
5608	united	2.497463
...	...	...
3460	lucas	8.342456
3461	lucia	8.342456
1320	cbv7f3kbkx	8.342456
3450	lowstandards	8.342456
6017	zv2pt6trk9	8.342456

6018 rows × 2 columns

Figure 5.15   TF-IDF claims that the tokens *to* and *the* are not very interesting, which makes sense, and tokens like *lucia*, *lucas*, and *cbv7f3kbkx* are very interesting, which may or may not be that useful to us. Remember that *importance* here is based on frequency of occurrence in our corpus. The less frequently a token appears in a corpus, the more *interesting* TF-IDF will think it is.

Let's try out our new vectorizer on our pipeline in the following listing to see if these calculations will pay off.

Listing 5.11   Using TF-IDF in our ML pipeline

```
ml_pipeline = Pipeline([
    ('vectorizer', TfidfVectorizer()),    ◁——— Our TF-IDF vectorizer
    ('classifier', clf)
])
print("TF-IDF Vectorizer + Log Reg\n=====================")
advanced_grid_search(
    train['text'], train['sentiment'], test['text'], test['sentiment'],
    ml_pipeline, params            ◁——┐ The same parameters as before
)
```

Our results (figure 5.16) improve pretty dramatically, based on our overall accuracy breaking 80%! It looks like normalizing token counts to extract originality in tokens helps our model understand sentiment a bit better.

Now that we have a basis for performing simple text vectorization with the Count-Vectorizer and TfidfVectorizer, let's focus on some feature improvement techniques we can try to improve our pipeline's performance.

```
TF-IDF Vectorizer + Log Reg
=======================
                precision    recall    f1-score    support

    negative       0.80       0.84       0.82        243
     neutral       0.82       0.80       0.81        260
    positive       0.89       0.87       0.88        269


    accuracy                             0.84        772
   macro avg       0.84       0.84       0.84        772
weighted avg       0.84       0.84       0.84        772
```

Best params: {'classifier_c':1.0, 'vectorizer_lowercase': True, 'vectorizer_max_features': 5000,
'vectorizer_ngram_range': (1,3), 'vectorizer_stop_words': None}
Overall took 57.20 seconds

Figure 5.16 **The TF-IDF vectorizer provides a boost in overall model accuracy of 84% compared to the 79% accuracy from using the basic `CountVectorizer`. We can attribute this boost in performance to the TFIDF vectorizer's ability to take token importance across a corpus into consideration.**

5.3   Feature improvement

Both of our vectorizers so far take in raw text and output fixed-length feature vectors. We have also seen how many of our tokens are likely not providing a lot of signal, including random sets of characters from URLs and mentions of the airlines themselves. Setting the `max_feastures` parameter is usually enough to strip the rare useless characters, but we can do more.

In this section, we will focus on some feature improvement techniques for text. Text cleaning is not always helpful when it comes to predictive power, but it is generally always worth trying. Depending on the kind of text we are working with, we have options for how we want to improve our text.

5.3.1   Cleaning noise from text

Our first improvement technique is a simple cleaner that will take in raw text and output a cleaner version of that text. Usually, this entails stripping away known *bad regexes* and patterns the data scientist thinks ahead of time won't be useful. Figure 5.17 shows that our cleaning mechanism set the text in lowercase, removed the trailing whitespace, and removed the punctuation at the end.

"I love this restaurant! "   ⟶   "i love this restaurant"

Figure 5.17   Text cleaning is simply altering text in place to remove any potential noise that will distract the ML pipeline from the signal in the text.

Listing 5.12 sets a few parameters to clean our tweets. It will

1   Remove any hashtags from our tweets entirely (any tokens with a pound sign as the first character)
2   Remove URLs entirely

3 Remove mentions of people entirely (any tokens with an at-sign as the first character)
4 Remove numbers entirely
5 Remove emojis entirely

Listing 5.12 Cleaning tweets using `tweet-preprocessor`

Clean tweets, using https://pypi.org/project/tweet-preprocessor.

```
import preprocessor as tweet_preprocessor

tweet_preprocessor.set_options(
    tweet_preprocessor.OPT.URL, tweet_preprocessor.OPT.MENTION,
    tweet_preprocessor.OPT.HASHTAG, tweet_preprocessor.OPT.EMOJI,
     tweet_preprocessor.OPT.NUMBER
)
tweet_preprocessor.clean(
    '@United is #awesome 👍 https://a.link/s/redirect 100%'
)
```

> We can set what we want to strip from our original tweet here.

> Remove URLs and mentions.

The resulting string would be

```
'is %'
```

This is a radically shorter string with a lot of content filtered out. This is the downside of any cleaning task. We must be very careful to not strip away too much so as to remove any and all signal from the text, especially when we are working with pieces of text as short as tweets.

We can plug in this cleaning function directly into our pipeline in listing 5.13 by cleaning both the training and testing sets before running our ML on it. We will also loosen our cleaning code to only remove URLs and numbers.

Listing 5.13 Grid-searching on cleaned text using TF-IDF

```
tweet_preprocessor.set_options(
    tweet_preprocessor.OPT.URL, tweet_preprocessor.OPT.NUMBER
)
ml_pipeline = Pipeline([
    ('vectorizer', TfidfVectorizer()),
    ('classifier', clf)
])
params = {
    'vectorizer__lowercase': [True, False],
    'vectorizer__stop_words': [None, 'english'],
    'vectorizer__max_features': [100, 1000, 5000],
    'vectorizer__ngram_range': [(1, 1), (1, 3)],

    'classifier__C': [1e-1, 1e0, 1e1]
```

> Only remove URLs and mentions.

> TfidfVectorizer gave us better results.

```
    }

    print("Tweet Cleaning + Log Reg\n=====================")
    advanced_grid_search(

        train['text'].apply(tweet_preprocessor.clean), train['sentiment'],
        test['text'].apply(tweet_preprocessor.clean), test['sentiment'],
        ml_pipeline, params
    )
```
Apply cleaning here because the transformation is not dependent on the training data.

When we run our pipeline using the `TfidfVectorizer` on our cleaned tweet data, we see a steep decline in performance (figure 5.18). This is likely an indication that, because our tweets are so short, removing signals like hashtags and mentions is removing real signal from the tweets! If removing tokens won't help us, perhaps, we can standardize the tokens in place.

```
Tweet Cleaning + Log Reg
=====================
                precision     recall    f1-score    support

    negative       0.79        0.81        0.80        243
     neutral       0.78        0.78        0.78        260
    positive       0.86        0.85        0.85        269


    accuracy                               0.81        772
   macro avg       0.81        0.81        0.81        772
weighted avg       0.81        0.81        0.81        772

Best params: {'classifier_c':1.0, 'vectorizer_lowercase': True, 'vectorizer_max_features': 5000,
'vectorizer_ngram_range': (1,1), 'vectorizer_stop_words': None}
Overall took 49.63 seconds
```

Figure 5.18 Results from cleaning the text show that the cleaning has caused our performance to decline quite significantly. This signifies that our cleaning was actually removing useful signal from our model. This is common with short documents, like tweets, because every token we remove is likely a significant percentage of the overall text.

5.3.2 Standardizing tokens

In the last section, we tried to remove tokens from the corpus in hopes of removing noise to help our models. That didn't work out so well. In this section, we will focus not on removing tokens but, rather, on cleaning them. *Stemming* and *lemmatization* are two text preprocessing techniques used to standardize documents in a corpus.

The goal of both stemming and lemmatization is to reduce a word to its *root* form. When we perform this reduction, a stemmed word is called a *stem*, and a word that's gone through lemmatization is called a *lemma*.

Each method works a bit differently. Stemming, the faster technique, works by chopping off characters from a word until the root is found. There are multiple rule-sets out there for how to chop off characters, and for our case study, we will try just one that is quite common, called the *Snowball Stemmer*. Let's import it from the `nltk` package and see how it works in the following listing.

Listing 5.14 Trying out the Snowball Stemmer

```
from nltk.stem import SnowballStemmer                        ◁——— Import our stemmer.
snowball_stemmer = SnowballStemmer(language='english')      ◁—
                                                                  Instantiate our stemmer.
snowball_stemmer.stem('waiting')
"wait"
```

Stemming the word *waiting* yields the root word *wait*, which makes sense, but there is a downside. Because stemming can only remove characters from a word, it will sometimes miss the *true* grammatical root word. For example, the stemmed version of *ran* is still just *ran*, when we might expect the root word to be *run*.

Lemmatization can pick up the slack there by relying on an in-memory dictionary of words for a given language to return a more contextually reliable root word. The lemma of *ran* would be *run*, and the lemma of *teeth* would be *tooth*.

Let's try using our stemmer in our pipeline in listing 5.15. Before we do, we will need to generate a list of stemmed stopwords by stemming the words in the Natural Language Toolkit (NLTK) stopwords database. We will then use those stemmed stopwords as our input into our custom tokenizer function.

Listing 5.15 Creating a custom tokenizer

```
import re
import nltk                       ◁——— Import NLTK.
nltk.download('stopwords')
from nltk.corpus import stopwords
                                                          Custom tokenizer that
stemmed_stopwords = list(map(snowball_stemmer.stem,       stems words and filters
     stopwords.words('english')))                         out stopwords
def stem_tokenizer(_input):                         ◁—
   tokenized_words = re.sub(r"[^A-Za-z0-9\-]", " ", _input).lower().split()
   return [snowball_stemmer.stem(word) for word in tokenized_words if
      snowball_stemmer.stem(word) not in stemmed_stopwords]
                                                              Lowercases the string,
stem_tokenizer('waiting for the plane')             ◁—       stems the words, and
                                                              removes stop words
```

Stem stop words from NLTK.

Our custom tokenizer will take in raw text and output a list of tokens that have been

- Lowercased
- Stemmed
- Removed of any stop words

And in this case our resulting list of tokens is

```
['wait', 'plane']
```

We can now use this custom tokenizer by setting our `TfidfVectorizer`'s `tokenizer` parameter, as seen in listing 5.16. Note that because our tokenizer will lowercase and remove stop words for us, we won't need to grid search for these parameters.

Listing 5.16   Using our custom tokenizer

```
ml_pipeline = Pipeline([
    ('vectorizer', TfidfVectorizer(tokenizer=stem_tokenizer)),  ◁─── Using a custom
    ('classifier', clf)                                              tokenizer
])

params = {
#       'vectorizer__lowercase': [True, False],
#       'vectorizer__stop_words': [],                ◁───

        'vectorizer__max_features': [100, 1000, 5000],
        'vectorizer__ngram_range': [(1, 1), (1, 3)],

        'classifier__C': [1e-1, 1e0, 1e1]

}

print("Stemming + Log Reg\n=====================")
advanced_grid_search(
    # remove cleaning
    train['text'], train['sentiment'],
    test['text'], test['sentiment'],
    ml_pipeline, params
)
```

Not needed anymore, as our tokenizer is removing stop words and is lowercasing

Our results (figure 5.19) show a reduction in performance, like we saw with our text cleaning.

```
Stemming + Log Reg
=====================
                precision     recall    f1-score    support

    negative       0.80        0.81        0.80        243
     neutral       0.77        0.78        0.78        260
    positive       0.86        0.84        0.85        269


    accuracy                               0.81        772
   macro avg       0.81        0.81        0.81        772
weighted avg       0.81        0.81        0.81        772

Best params: {'classifier_c':1.0, 'vectorizer_max_features': 5000, 'vectorizer_ngram_range': (1,1}
Overall took 68.18 seconds
```

Figure 5.19   Our stemmer is not showing a boost in performance, which implies that the tokens we were trying to remove had enough signal in them to lower our pipeline's performance.

It looks like both of our feature improvement techniques did not show a boost in performance, but this is OK! They were both worth trying, and it reveals a deeper truth about our data.

It's tempting when working with text data to get frustrated when basic feature engineering techniques don't work, but context seems to really matter here, and this is often true in NLP cases. In our next few chapters, we will start to move away from interpretable features that represent individual tokens in our text and more towards *latent* features—features that represent a hidden structure of data that is more complex than bag-of-words.

5.4 Feature extraction

In NLP, feature extraction techniques are used primarily to reduce dimensionality of vectorized text. The term *feature extraction* is sometimes used as a superset of feature learning (we have previously referred to feature extraction as such); however, for the purposes of this text, we will consider feature extraction and feature learning to be mutually exclusive families of algorithms. At the end of the day, whether we call an algorithm feature extraction or feature learning, we are trying to create a latent (usually uninterpretable) feature set from raw data. Let's begin by taking a look at our first feature extraction technique: singular value decomposition.

5.4.1 Singular value decomposition

Our main feature extraction algorithm will be *singular value decomposition (SVD)*, which is a linear algebra technique used to perform matrix factorization on our original dataset, breaking it down into three new matrices we can use to map our original dataset into a dataset of lower dimension (i.e., fewer columns). The idea is to project the original matrix with possibly correlated features onto a new axis system that has fewer features that should be uncorrelated. These new uncorrelated features are called *principal components*. These principal components help us generate new features, while capturing as much signal from the original dataset as possible. This process is known as *principal component analysis (PCA)*, and SVD will be the algorithm we choose to use to perform PCA.

We realize there are a lot of math terms and acronyms flying around right now. The main idea is that we are going to use linear algebra to break down our matrix of tokens to extract patterns and latent structures from our raw text to create brand-new latent features to use in place of our token features. Similar to feature selection, our goal is to start with a matrix of data of size $m \times n$, where m is the number of observations, and n is the number of original features (in our case, tokens), and end up with a new matrix of size $m \times d$, where $d < n$, as shown in figure 5.20.

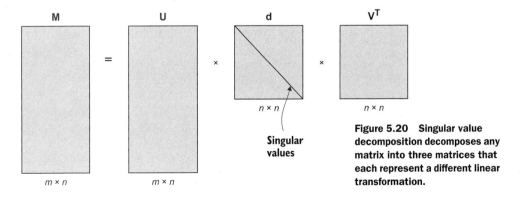

Figure 5.20 Singular value decomposition decomposes any matrix into three matrices that each represent a different linear transformation.

We can plug in scikit-learn's implementation of SVD (called `TruncatedSVD`) directly into our pipeline and place it right after our TF-IDF vectorizer (listing 5.17 and figure 5.21).

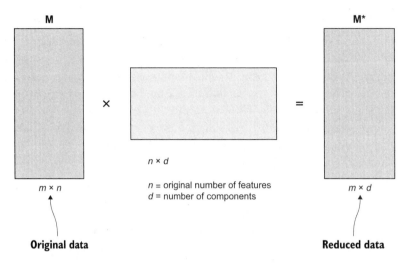

M

M*

× =

$n \times d$

$m \times n$

n = original number of features
d = number of components

$m \times d$

Original data

Reduced data

Figure 5.21   Using SVD to perform dimension reduction allows us to reduce the number of token features (n) into a latent smaller number of features (d).

Listing 5.17   Dimension reduction with SVD

```python
from sklearn.decomposition import TruncatedSVD

ml_pipeline = Pipeline([
    ('vectorizer', TfidfVectorizer()),
    ('reducer', TruncatedSVD()),
    ('classifier', clf)
])

params = {
    'vectorizer__lowercase': [True, False],
    'vectorizer__stop_words': [None, 'english'],
    'vectorizer__max_features': [5000],
    'vectorizer__ngram_range': [(1, 3)],

    'reducer__n_components': [500, 1000, 1500, 2000],
    'classifier__C': [1e-1, 1e0, 1e1]
}

print("SVD + Log Reg\n=====================")
advanced_grid_search(
    train['text'], train['sentiment'],
    test['text'], test['sentiment'],
    ml_pipeline, params
)
```

Feature extraction/dimension reduction with SVD

Our custom tokenizer didn't work out so well, so we will remove it.

Number of components to reduce to

When we run the preceding code, we see that we have achieved our second-best result in terms of overall accuracy (figure 5.22)!

```
SVD + Log Reg
=====================
                precision    recall    f1-score    support

    negative        0.79      0.84        0.82         243
     neutral        0.82      0.80        0.81         260
    positive        0.89      0.86        0.87         269


    accuracy                             0.83         772
   macro avg        0.83      0.83        0.83         772
weighted avg        0.83      0.83        0.83         772
```

Best params: {'classifier_c':1.0, 'reducer_n_components': 2000, 'vectorizer_lowercase': True, 'vectorizer_max_features': 5000, 'vectorizer_ngram_range': (1,3), 'vectorizer_stop_words': None}
Overall took 583.53 seconds

Figure 5.22   Dimension reduction via SVD yields great predictive power at a lower dimensional space (2,000 components extracted from 5,000 tokens).

Using singular value decomposition to reduce dimension in our ML pipeline was able to reduce 5,000 dimensions into 2,000, while only losing a single percentage point in predictive power. This is great because it implies that we are able to map our high-dimension bag-of-words vectors into a smaller latent space, while still retaining predictive power.

This is also evidence that underneath the surface-level bag-of-words representation of our text, we now have a good sense there is a deeper, latent structure waiting to be discovered. The SVD transformation we just did barely lost us any predictive performance, which implies there may be other ways to learn more complicated feature sets. Let's see some of these by moving on to some more complex feature learning techniques.

5.5   *Feature learning*

The main difference between feature extraction and feature learning techniques is that feature extraction techniques are generally considered to be *parametric*, which means we make assumptions about the shape of the data. In the previous section, we learned that the end result of the SVD algorithm produced components that we could use to transform data through matrix multiplication of the original data and its components. Our main assumption was that the matrix as created by text vectorization has meaningful components to be extracted through our linear algebra formula.

What if SVD is unable to extract useful features from our corpus? Algorithms such as SVD (and related algorithms, like PCA and linear discriminant analysis [LDA]) will always be able to end up extracting features, but those features will not always be useful.

Feature learning techniques, on the other hand, are considered to be *nonparametric*, which means these algorithms will attempt to *learn* latent features by looking at the data points over and over again (in epochs) and converge onto a solution (potentially different ones at run time). Learning by iterating over a dataset multiple times and updating the model's parameters consistently is a kind of *stochastic learning*. Being nonparametric has many benefits and means that feature learning algorithms can ignore any assumption on the shape of the original data. Because we are relying on an algorithm to learn the best features for us, complex neural networks or deep learning algorithms are often used to perform feature learning. In the following section, we will be building a deep neural network to learn features by trying to deconstruct and reconstruct our text, until the model understands how tokens are supposed to be used together.

5.5.1 Introduction to autoencoders

Our first feature learning algorithm is called an autoencoder. *Autoencoders* are neural networks such that the input and output layers have the same dimensionality. They are networks that are trained on the specific task of replicating the *identity function* that is the network is trying to approximate the function:

$$A: A(x) = x$$

The autoencoder is trained on the *self-supervised* task of approximating the identity function. To accomplish this, autoencoders learn to sift through noisy data to deconstruct and then reconstruct data as efficiently as possible.

An autoencoder consists of three parts, visualized in figure 5.23:

1 The *encoder* takes in data from the input layer and learns how to ignore noise and represent the input data.
2 The *code/bottleneck* is the part of the network that represents the latent representation of the input, which is then fed into the decoder. This layer is used as the final latent representation of the input data.
3 The *decoder* takes the latent representation of the code and attempts to reconstruct the input in the output layer.

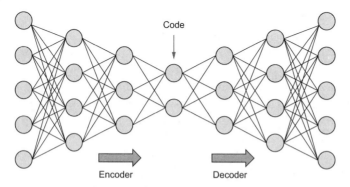

Figure 5.23   Autoencoders are neural networks that deconstruct and reconstruct data through a series of layers, with the middle layer called the "code" or the "bottleneck." The code/bottleneck layer is often used as a reduced-size latent compression of the input data.

Depending on the data type, the encoder and decoder can vary in structure. Classically, they are fully connected feedforward layers, but they can also be LSTMs or CNNs for text and images, respectively. We will build a traditional autoencoder that will attempt to learn a latent representation of our bag-of-words vectors to try to begin to learn some grammar and context.

5.5.2 Training an autoencoder to learn features

We will build an autoencoder to try to learn a brand-new feature set (figure 5.24). We will rely on *Tensorflow* and *Keras* to build and train our autoencoder network in listing 5.18. To do so, we will first vectorize our training corpus using a `TfidfVectorizer`. We will generate a 5,000-length bag-of-words representation of each document in our corpus.

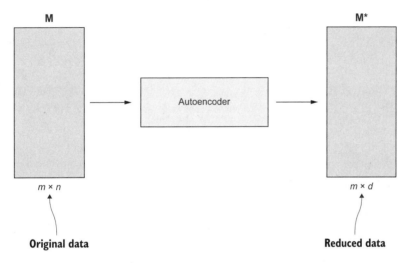

Figure 5.24 Our autoencoder, like SVD, will reduce the dimension of our original data to have fewer features.

Listing 5.18 Vectorizing our training corpus for the autoencoder

```
vectorizer = TfidfVectorizer(**{
    'lowercase': True, 'max_features': 5000,
    'ngram_range': (1, 3), 'stop_words': None
})
vectorized_X_train = vectorizer.fit_transform(
    train['text']).toarray()
vectorized_X_test = vectorizer.transform(
    test['text']).toarray()
```

Fit a vectorizer on training data, and transform training and test data.

Our goal now is to design an autoencoder to deconstruct and reconstruct the bag-of-words representation created by the `TfidfVectorizer`. By doing so, we want our autoencoder to sift through noise and learn meaningful latent representations of our text data.

We will build our autoencoder to have an encoder to take in our 5,000-length vectors and compress them into a bottleneck size of 2,000 dimensions. We chose 2,000 features by trying out a few dimension sizes and choosing the one with the best reconstruction accuracy. Our decoder will, then, take this bottlenecked latent representation and attempt to reconstruct it back into the original TF-IDF vector. If our model succeeds in this task, we should be able to take the bottleneck representation in lieu of our 5,000-length vectors and derive a pipeline of similar performance with smaller dimension. Let's build and compile our autoencoder in the following listing.

Listing 5.19 Building and compiling our autoencoder

```
from keras.layers import Input, Dense        Imports for the
from keras.models import Model, Sequential   autoencoder
import tensorflow as tf

n_inputs = vectorized_X_train.shape[1]    We will attempt to compress 5,000 tokens
n_bottleneck = 2000                       into a latent dimension of size 2,000.

visible = Input(shape=(n_inputs,), name='input')           Code/bottleneck
e = Dense(n_inputs//2, activation='relu', name='encoder')(visible)
bottleneck = Dense(n_bottleneck, name='bottleneck')(e)

                                                           Decoder
d = Dense(n_inputs//2, activation='relu', name='decoder')(bottleneck)
output = Dense(n_inputs, activation='relu', name='output')(d)
                                                     Output layer

autoencoder = Model(inputs=visible, outputs=output)
                                             Define autoencoder model.

autoencoder.compile(optimizer='adam', loss='mse')
                                      Compile autoencoder model.
```

Next, we will train our autoencoder (listing 5.20) by fitting it to our vectorized training set. To explain some of the values we are about to set:

1   We will set batch_size to 512, but this can be set to whatever size your machine is capable of handling.
2   We have 100 epochs set because our model is learning this data from scratch.
3   We will set shuffle to True, so the training loop sees a variety of data at once, rather than seeing homogenous labels in batches.

Listing 5.20 Fitting our autoencoder

Stop training when the loss stops decreasing so much.

```
import matplotlib.pyplot as plt

early_stopping_callback = tf.keras.callbacks.EarlyStopping
(monitor='loss', patience=3)
                              Training our autoencoder network

autoencoder_history = autoencoder.fit(vectorized_X_train, vectorized_X_train,
```

```
              batch_size = 512, epochs = 100,
      callbacks=[early_stopping_callback],
              shuffle = True, validation_split = 0.10)


plt.plot(autoencoder_history.history['loss'], label='Loss')
plt.plot(autoencoder_history.history['val_loss'], label='Val Loss')

plt.title('Autoencoder Loss')
plt.legend()
```

The result loss graph (figure 5.25) shows us that our autoencoder is, indeed, learning to deconstruct and reconstruct our original input but only to a degree.

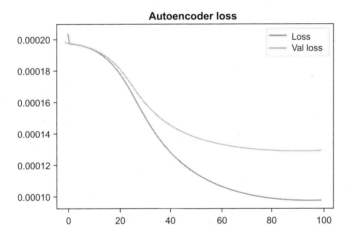

Figure 5.25   Our autoencoder is able to deconstruct and reconstruct TF-IDF features based on the dropping loss! Our hope is that, by doing so, the autoencoder has learned a latent set of features that will prove valuable to our ML pipeline.

EXERCISE 5.2   Use Keras to construct another autoencoder that would take in 1,024 length token vectors and compresses them into a bottleneck layer of 256 dimensions. For an extra challenge, add a layer directly before and after the bottleneck of size 512.

Our final step is to encode our training and testing corpora with our autoencoder and plug the model into our logistic regression in the following listing.

Listing 5.21   Using our autoencoder for classification

```
latent_representation = Model(inputs=visible,        Create our latent
outputs=bottleneck)                              ◄─── representation encoder.
encoded_X_train = latent_representation.predict
(vectorized_X_train)                             ◄───
encoded_X_test = latent_representation.predict       Encode our training and testing corpora
(vectorized_X_test)                              ◄─── into our latent representation.

ml_pipeline = Pipeline([
    ('classifier', clf)
])

params = {
```

```
    'classifier__C': [1e-1, 1e0, 1e1]
}
print("Autoencoder + Log Reg\n=====================")
advanced_grid_search(
    encoded_X_train, train['sentiment'], encoded_X_test, test['sentiment'],
    ml_pipeline, params
)
```

Our results (figure 5.26) indicate a performance that underperforms our SVD and still doesn't beat our current best results of a plain `TfidfVectorizer`.

```
Autoencoder + Log Reg
=====================
              precision    recall  f1-score   support

    negative       0.77      0.83      0.80       243
     neutral       0.80      0.79      0.79       260
    positive       0.87      0.83      0.85       269

    accuracy                           0.81       772
   macro avg       0.81      0.81      0.81       772
weighted avg       0.82      0.81      0.82       772

Best params: {'classifier__C': 1.0}
Overall took 9.20 seconds
```

Figure 5.26
Our autoencoder underperformed our SVD, suggesting we are reaching our limits of signal from bag-of-words vectors.

It seems like we are hitting a wall with our logistic regression model. We are stuck in the low 80s in terms of overall accuracy, and it is time to bring in the big guns.

Up until now, we have been working with bag-of-words models that don't take into account any sense of context and grammar. Even our SVD and Autoencoders rely on these bag-of-words vectors as inputs, and even though they are trying to learn some latent representations underneath the superficial token counts and count normalizations (TF-IDF) they still don't have access to real context and grammatical structure. Let's turn our attention now to state-of-the-art NLP, through transfer learning.

5.5.3 *Introduction to transfer learning*

Transfer learning (figure 5.27) is a branch of AI in which we train complex, usually large, learning algorithms (usually deep learning models) on a huge dataset to gain some base understanding of a domain through some unsupervised or self-supervised task in a phase called *pretraining* and then *transfer* those learnings to a smaller, related supervised task in the *fine-tuning* phase.

In the field of NLP, this usually comes in the form of having a model read over billions of words in a corpus in context and asking it to perform some relatively basic tasks over and over again, at a huge scale, and then, once the model has a grasp of language as a whole, we ask the model to turn its attention to a smaller focused dataset, pertaining to a specific NLP task like classification. The theory is that the knowledge gained, while reading the large corpus will transfer over into the more focused task and lead to a higher accuracy out of the gate.

Traditional ML   vs.   Transfer learning

Isolated, single-task learning:

• **Knowledge is not retained or accumulated. Learning is performed without considering past learned knowledge from other tasks.**

Learning of a new task relies on the previous learned tasks:

• **The learning process can be faster, more accurate and/or need less training data.**

Figure 5.27   Transfer learning aims to preteach an ML model the basics of a task before giving it a second smaller dataset to fine-tune its knowledge.

5.5.4   *Transfer learning with BERT*

One of the hottest transfer learning modules out there is *bidirectional encoder representations from transformers (BERT)*. Transformers are algorithms that, much like autoencoders, have encoders, decoders, and an intermediary latent representation of input data in between. Transformers, however, were built to input sequences of data and output another sequence of data (figure 5.28). They generally rely on a matrix representation of input sequence data, rather than a flat vector representation like autoencoders do.

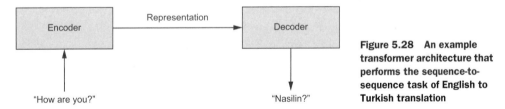

Figure 5.28   An example transformer architecture that performs the sequence-to-sequence task of English to Turkish translation

BERT is a transfer learning algorithm developed by Google in 2018 that relies only on the encoder of the transformer and has learned grammar, context, and tokens from several gigabytes of unstructured data from 2.5 billion words from Wikipedia and another 800 million words from the BookCorpus. It can transform text into a fixed-length vectors of size 768 (for the base BERT, sizes can vary).

BERT is especially great at performing *few-shot learning*, which is a type of ML in which we have very little training data (sometimes only in the 10s of examples) to learn from (figure 5.29). Our dataset has too much data for it to be considered a good example of few-shot learning.

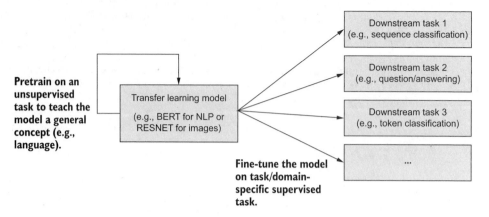

Figure 5.29   BERT is a language model that has been pretrained to understand language and can transfer that knowledge to a variety of downstream supervised tasks.

BERT is pretrained on two tasks (figure 5.30):

- The *masked language model (MLM)* task shows BERT a sentence with 15% of the words removed. BERT is then asked to fill in the blank. This teaches BERT how words are used in context in a larger sentence structure.
- The *next sentence prediction (NSP)* task shows BERT two sentences and asks, "Sentence B came directly after sentence A in the document—true or false?" This task teaches BERT how sentences align in a larger document.

Neither of these tasks may seem particularly useful, and that's because they aren't meant to be. They are tasks meant to teach BERT the basics of language modeling with context. This same concept of pretraining can be applied to images too, as we will see in the next chapter.

At the end of the day, BERT is a language model that, simply put, can take in raw, variable-length text and output a fixed-length representation of that text. It is yet

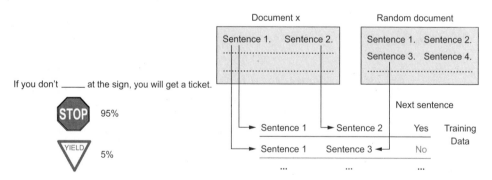

Figure 5.30   The masked language model pretraining task (on the left) teaches BERT what individual tokens mean in the context of a larger sentence. The next sentence prediction task teaches BERT how to align sentences in a larger document.

another way to vectorize text. It is among the current state-of-the-art methods for vectorizing text.

> **NOTE** Logistic regression is not the model of choice to use to take full advantage of BERT's features. Ideally, we would be training a new feedforward layer on top of the already-large BERT architecture. We are relying on logistic regression here as part of our experiment to optimize performance of a simple model using complex feature engineering.

5.5.5 Using BERT's pretrained features

We will use a package called `transformers` in listing 5.22 to load a pretrained BERT model. We will use its pretrained vector representations to try and get a boost in our logistic regression model's performance.

> **NOTE** We will be using the basic form of BERT called *BERT-base*. There are many different *flavors* of BERT, including BERT-large, DistilBERT, and AlBERT that have been pretrained on different or more data.

We are also going to make a switch from Tensorflow and Keras to PyTorch. We find that PyTorch libraries are excellent for loading these models and running training loops, and we think it will be great to have exposure to the two most common deep learning libraries out there for Python!

Listing 5.22 Getting started with BERT

**Load a vanilla BERT-base uncased
(all lowercased) model.**

```
from transformers import BertTokenizer, BertModel    ◄─── Imports for BERT
import torch
                                                      We also need to load
                                                      the BERT tokenizer.
bert_model = BertModel.from_pretrained('bert-base-uncased')
bert_tokenizer = BertTokenizer.from_pretrained('bert-base-uncased')   ◄─

tweet = 'I hate this airline'                Run a tokenized input through BERT.
token_ids = torch.tensor(bert_tokenizer.encode(tweet)).unsqueeze(0)   ◄─
bert_model(token_ids)[1].shape
```
**The base BERT model outputs fixed-
length vectors of length 768.**

The above code block loads up a BERT-base-uncased model, which is the standard BERT model (which is still quite large in memory) with a vocabulary of uncased (i.e., lowercased/case doesn't matter) tokens. These tokens have all been pretrained via the MLM and NSP tasks. Listing 5.23 has a helper function called `batch_embed_text`, which has the job of batch encoding a corpus of text into the 768-length vectors that BERT outputs.

Listing 5.23 Vectorizing our text with BERT

```
from tqdm import tqdm
import numpy as np

def batch_embed_text(bert_model, tokenizer, text_iterable, batch_size=256):
    ''' This helper method will batch embed an iterable
        of text using a given tokenizer and bert model '''
    encoding = tokenizer.batch_encode_plus(text_iterable, padding=True)
    input_ids = np.vstack(encoding['input_ids'])
    attention_mask = np.vstack(encoding['attention_mask'])

    def batch_array_idx(np_array, batch_size):
        for i in tqdm(range(0, np_array.shape[0], batch_size)):
            yield i, i + batch_size

    embedded = None

    for start_idx, end_idx in batch_array_idx(
        input_ids, batch_size=batch_size):
        batch_bert = bert_model(
            torch.tensor(input_ids[start_idx:end_idx]),
            attention_mask=torch.tensor(attention_mask[start_idx:end_idx])
        )[1].detach().numpy()
        if embedded is None:
            embedded = batch_bert
        else:
            embedded = np.vstack([embedded, batch_bert])

    return embedded

bert_X_train = batch_embed_text(
    bert_model, bert_tokenizer, train['text'])
bert_X_test = batch_embed_text(
    bert_model, bert_tokenizer, test['text'])
```

Now, we can use our helper function to batch embed our text.

Now that we have our matrices of BERT-embedded text, all that's left is to run the matrices through our classification pipeline, as in the following listing.

Listing 5.24 Classification with BERT

```
ml_pipeline = Pipeline([
    ('classifier', clf)
])

params = {
    'classifier__C': [1e-1, 1e0, 1e1]
}

print("BERT + Log Reg\n=====================")
advanced_grid_search(
    bert_X_train, train['sentiment'], bert_X_test, test['sentiment'],
    ml_pipeline, params
)
```

And our results (figure 5.31) show an immediate increase in performance! Not a huge one albeit, but it is already better than tuning countless bag-of-words vectorizers.

```
BERT + Log Reg
======================
              precision    recall  f1-score   support

    negative       0.85      0.86      0.85       243
     neutral       0.81      0.82      0.82       260
    positive       0.88      0.86      0.87       269

    accuracy                           0.85       772
   macro avg       0.85      0.85      0.85       772
weighted avg       0.85      0.85      0.85       772

Best params: {'classifier__C': 1.0}
Overall took 34.47 seconds
```

Figure 5.31   BERT's pretraining has already beaten any previous vectorizer we've seen in this chapter.

Our pipeline's seemingly stalled performance around 85% is more likely due to the simplicity of our logistic regression model. When we are using BERT, we really should be using deep learning to perform our classification if we really want state-of-the-art results. Our goal was to highlight the power of transfer learning as a language model that doesn't require constant hyperparameter tuning because it has already learned how language works from its pretraining. For now, let's wrap up our trip down text vectorization lane with a recap of what we have seen in this chapter.

5.6   *Text vectorization recap*

When performing machine learning on raw text, most of our feature engineering work goes into text vectorization: turning variable-length text into fixed-length feature vectors. We have seen at least four different methods for transforming text into features in this chapter alone, and they barely scratch the surface of what is possible.

We imposed a huge constraint on ourselves right out of the gate and only let ourselves use a logistic regression as our classifier. We did this to focus on the feature engineering techniques, but that in no way is the same as saying "autoencoders must not be as good as SVD because SVD outperformed the autoencoder in this case study." The text vectorization method you choose should be based on context and experimentation on your data and your domain.

Is transfer learning simply the answer? Did I waste your time by explaining everything else before BERT? Absolutely not! Our survey of text vectorization and journey from bag-of-words, to text cleaning, through feature extraction/feature learning, and landing on transfer learning was all to showcase that there are so many different ways of vectorizing text, each with pros and cons, as summarized in table 5.1.

Table 5.1   Summary of results for our NLP case study

	Count vectorization	TF-IDF vectorization	SVD (or similar parametric algorithms)	Autoencoders	Transfer learning (e.g., BERT)
Easily inter-pretable features?	Yes	Yes	No	No	No
Easy to use?	Yes	Yes	Yes	No	Not at first
Easy to describe to a lay person?	Yes	Yes	No	Not really	No
Likely to create huge sparse matrices?	Yes	Yes	No	No	No
In general, when to use for NLP	To form a baseline NLP model	To keep NLP pipeline complexity low	To reduce the number of dimensions of a dataset	To reduce the number of dimensions of a dataset and parametric techniques, like SVD, that didn't work well	To perform few-shot learning or to take advantage of pretrained features

5.7   Answers to exercises

EXERCISE 5.1

Calculate the IDF weights by hand, using pure Python (using NumPy is OK), for a token that appears once in a given document and once in our training set overall.

ANSWER:

```
np.log((1 + train.shape[0]) / (1 + 1)) + 1
8.342455512358637
```

EXERCISE 5.2

Use Keras to construct another autoencoder that would take in 1,024-length token vectors and compress them into a bottleneck layer of 256 dimensions. For an extra challenge, add a layer directly before and after the bottleneck of size 512.

ANSWER:

```
visible = Input(shape=(1024,), name='input')
hidden_layer_one = Dense(512, activation='relu', name='encoder')(visible)
bottleneck = Dense(256, name='bottleneck')(hidden_layer_one)
hidden_layer_two = Dense(512, activation='relu', name='encoder')(bottleneck)
output = Dense(1024, activation='relu', name='output')(hidden_layer_two)

autoencoder = Model(inputs=visible, outputs=output)

autoencoder.compile(optimizer='adam', loss='mse')
```

Summary

- Text vectorization is crucial to NLP and forms the basis of doing ML on text data.
- There are many ways to vectorize text:
  - Bag-of-words models count the number of tokens and text and use these counts as features. Counts can be normalized, such as in TF-IDF.
  - Transfer learning models can generate features by pretraining on huge amounts of data beforehand.
- Dimension reduction with SVDs and autoencoders can reduce the number of features we are working with, while retaining signal from the original dataset.
- Cleaning data can cut through noise in text data, but only when there is a sufficient amount of noise that is mutually exclusive from the predictive signal.
- There is no one right way to vectorize text, and there is no perfect NLP pipeline. NLP engineers should be ready to experiment and deduce which techniques are appropriate, based on context.

Computer vision: Object recognition

This chapter covers

- Vectorizing images into quantitative features for ML
- Using pixel values as features
- Extracting edge information from images
- Fine-tuning deep learning models to learn optimal image representations

Continuing our journey through dealing with unstructured data leads us to our image case study. Just as it was an issue with our NLP case study, the big question of this chapter is, how do we represent images in a machine-readable format? Throughout this chapter, we will take a look at ways to construct, extract, and learn feature representations of images for the purpose of solving an *object recognition* problem.

Object recognition simply means we are going to work with labeled images, where each image contains a single object, and the purpose of the model is to classify the image as a category that specifies what object is in the image. Object recognition is considered a relatively simple computer vision problem, as we don't have to worry about finding the object or objects within an image using bounding boxes, nor do we have to do anything beyond pure classification into (usually) mutually exclusive categories. Let's jump right into taking a look at the dataset for this case study—the CIFAR-10 dataset.

> **WARNING** This chapter also has some long-running code samples throughout the chapter. Working with images can be cumbersome due to file sizes and the memory required to keep them in memory. Be advised that some code samples may run for over an hour on the minimum requirements for this book.

6.1 The CIFAR-10 dataset

The *CIFAR-10* dataset is used widely for training object recognition architectures. According to the website dedicated to hosting the data, it consists of 60,000 32 × 32 color images, which are split up into 10 classes, each with 6,000 images. There are 50,000 training images and 10,000 test images. There are instructions on the site for how to parse the data, so let's use that to load up the data ourselves in the following listing.

Listing 6.1 Ingesting the CIFAR-10 data

```
def unpickle(file):                      ◁────────  Function to load the files
    with open(file, 'rb') as fo:                    from the main CIFAR site
        d = pickle.load(fo, encoding='bytes')
    return d

def load_cifar(filenames):
    training_images = []
    training_labels = []
                                                          Grab the images and
                                                          labels from the files.
    for file_name in filenames:
        unpickled_images = unpickle(file_name)
        images, labels = unpickled_images[b'data'], unpickled_images[b'labels']  ◁┘
        images = np.reshape(images,(-1, 3, 32, 32))  ┐  Reshape and transpose, so our
        images = np.transpose(images, (0, 2, 3, 1))  │  shape is (number_of_images,
        training_images.append(images)               │  height, width, channels [RGB]).
        training_labels += labels

    return np.vstack(training_images), training_labels

print("Loading the training set")
training_files = [f'../data/cifar-10/data_batch_{i}'
                  for i in range(1, 6)]  # D
training_images, int_training_labels = load_cifar(
    training_files)

print("Loading the testing set")                ┐  Load up the training
training_files = ['../data/cifar-10/test_batch']  ◁─┘  and testing images.
testing_images, int_testing_labels = load_cifar(
    training_files)

print("Loading the labels")
label_names = unpickle(                                    ┐  Load up the labels.
    '../data/cifar-10/batches.meta')[b'label_names']  ◁─┘
training_labels = [str(label_names[_]) for _ in int_training_labels]
testing_labels = [str(label_names[_]) for _ in int_testing_labels]
```

Now, we can try taking a look at our images:

```
import matplotlib.pyplot as plt
print(training_labels[0])
plt.imshow(training_images[0])
```

Each image is a 32 x 32 image with each pixel containing values for RGB. These three values are also known as *channels*. Note that if an image only has one channel, that image will be black and white. Each image, therefore, has the shape (32, 32, 3): 32 pixels high, 32 pixels wide, with each pixel containing 3 values for RGB between 0 and 255. So each image is being represented by 3,072 values.

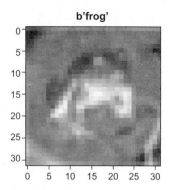

Figure 6.1   The first training image in the CIFAR-10 dataset is a frog. The CIFAR-10 dataset has 10 classes: airplane, automobile, bird, cat, deer, dog, frog, horse, ship, and truck.

6.1.1   *The problem statement and defining success*

We are performing yet another classification here, but this time we are classifying 10 classes (figure 6.1). The goal of our model can be summarized by the following question: given a raw image, can we find ways to represent the image and classify the object in the image accurately?

The goal of this case study is to find different ways to convert our images into machine-readable features and use those features to train a model. Just like in the last case, the NLP study, we will stick to using a simple logistic regression classifier to ensure that boosts in our ML pipeline performance are due mostly to our feature engineering efforts.

6.2   *Feature construction: Pixels as features*

Our first attempt to represent our images in a machine-readable format will be to use the pixel values directly as our features. To do this, we will take the *mean pixel value (MPV)* of the channels and then realign the values to be one-dimensional, rather than two-dimensional. A visualization of this method can be found in the following figure.

Using the mean pixel value happens in two steps:

1   Take the mean value of the final dimension/axis in our images.
2   Reshape each image to be a flat array.

This simple process will give us a 1,024-length (32 x 32) vector of features we can feed into our model (figure 6.2).

We can now test these features against our ML pipeline. Just as we did in the last case study, we will be testing each of our image vectorization techniques against a simple grid search of a logistic regression. Our goal, once again, is to provide a semiconsistent ML model pipeline, where the changing element is our feature engineering efforts. This will give us a sense of how our efforts are paying off.

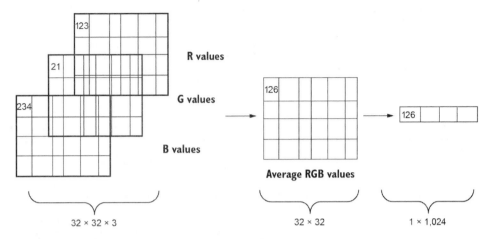

Figure 6.2 The MPV approach converts images into arrays by averaging the red, green, and blue pixel matrices into a single matrix of averaged color values and then realigning the average-color matrix to be a single dimension per image.

Let's run some code to calculate our mean pixel value features. The following code snippet will do just that!

Listing 6.2 Calculating mean pixel values

```
avg_training_images = training_images.mean(
    axis=3).reshape(50000,-1)
avg_testing_images = testing_images.mean(
    axis=3).reshape(10000,-1)

print(avg_training_images.shape)
```

> Average the RGB values together, and reshape them to make a 1D vector for each image.

We now have a training matrix of size (50,000, 1,024) and a testing matrix of size (10,000, 1,024). Let's run our grid search code (listing 6.3) to train our logistic regression on our mean pixel values. Remember that the goal of this case study is to find the best representation of an image, and our methodology is to grid search a few parameter options on a logistic regression and use the resulting accuracy on the test set as a metric for how well our feature engineering efforts have done.

NOTE Fitting models in this chapter may take some time to run. For my 2021 MacBook Pro, some of these code segments took over an hour to complete the grid search.

Listing 6.3 Baseline model: using average pixel values as features

```
from sklearn.pipeline import Pipeline
from sklearn.linear_model import LogisticRegression

clf = LogisticRegression(max_iter=100, solver='saga')
```

> Import ML packages.

> Instantiate our simple LogisticRegression model.

```
ml_pipeline = Pipeline([
    ('classifier', clf)
])

params = {  # C
    'classifier__C': [1e-1, 1e0, 1e1]
}

print("Average Pixel Value + LogReg\n==========================")
advanced_grid_search(
    avg_training_images, training_labels, avg_testing_images, testing_labels,
    ml_pipeline, params
)
```

Set up our simple grid-search pipeline to try three different values for the logistic regression model.

Run our grid search to get an accuracy value for our pipeline.

The result is that it took the machine running the code (a 2021 MacBook Pro with 16 GB RAM and no GPU) about 20 minutes in total to run a grid search of only three parameters, and the best accuracy it could come up with is 26% (figure 6.3). This is not so great, but this gives us a good baseline model to beat. At the end of this chapter, we will recap all of the image vectorization methods we saw and how they compared to each other.

	precision	recall	f1-score	support
b'airplane'	0.23	0.27	0.25	1000
b'automobile'	0.34	0.35	0.35	1000
b'bird'	0.23	0.19	0.20	1000
b'cat'	0.19	0.15	0.17	1000
b'deer'	0.20	0.13	0.16	1000
b'dog'	0.26	0.30	0.28	1000
b'frog'	0.25	0.22	0.23	1000
b'horse'	0.26	0.23	0.25	1000
b'ship'	0.28	0.38	0.32	1000
b'truck'	0.36	0.41	0.38	1000
accuracy			0.26	10000
macro avg	0.26	0.26	0.26	10000
weighted avg	0.26	0.26	0.26	10000

```
Best params: {'classifier__C': 10.0}
Overall took 1148.33 seconds
```

Figure 6.3   Just like in our last case study, we will focus on the overall accuracy of our test set as our metric of choice. Our MPV approach is not that predictively powerful but will provide a baseline accuracy to beat of 26%. We could look at the individual precision and recall scores of each class if we believed single classes were more important than others, but we will assume the overall accuracy of the model is what we value the most.

Taking raw pixel values as direct features is unstable and will likely never be the best representation of images for modern computer vision problems. Let's move on now to a more industry-standard approach to extracting features from images: histograms of oriented gradients.

6.3   *Feature extraction: Histogram of oriented gradients*

In our last section, we were using raw pixel values as features, and that did not lead to great results. In this section, we will see how *histograms of oriented gradients (HOGs)* will fare. HOG is a feature extraction technique that is used most commonly for object recognition tasks. HOG focuses on the shape of the object in the image by attempting to quantify the *gradient* (or magnitude) as well as the *orientation* (or direction) of the edges of the object.

HOG will calculate gradients and orientations in broken-down, localized regions of the image and calculate a histogram of gradients and orientations to determine the final feature values. This is why the process is known as HOGs.

The process works in five steps:

1   (*Optional*) Apply a global image normalization. This can come in the form of a gamma compression by taking the square root or log of each color channel. This step provides protection from illumination effects (having different lighting in the images could add noise to the model, for example) and can also help reduce the effects of local shadowing.

2   Compute image gradients in the *x* and *y* directions, and use the gradient to compute the magnitude—how quickly the image is changing—and orientation—in which direction the image is changing most rapidly. Gradients capture texture information, contour/edge information, and more. We use the locally dominant color channel (whichever color is the most intense in the region) to help reduce color variance effects. We can set the size of the localized regions using a parameter called `pixels_per_cell`.

3   Calculate one-dimensional orientation histograms across the cells of the image. The number of bins is a parameter we can set called `orientations`. The minor difference between a normal histogram and HOG is that instead of counting one instance in a bin like we normally would, we use the magnitude to vote in the histogram. This gives focal points in the image more power in our final feature set.

4   (*Optional*) Calculate normalization across *blocks*. This is done by applying some function to the histogram in each block to protect even further against illuminance variation, shadowing, and edge contrasts. The size of a block can be changed by altering the `cells_per_block` parameters. The normalized block descriptors are referred to as our *HOG descriptors*.

5   Collect the HOG descriptors, and concatenate them into a final one-dimensional feature vector to represent the entire image.

We can perform these five steps quickly using the *scikit-image* package. Let's see an example of HOGs on our training images. To do this, we will set a few parameters:

- `orientations=8` to compute histograms of 8 bins in each cell
- `pixels_per_cell=(4, 4)` to set our cell size to be 4 pixels by 4 pixels

- `cells_per_block=(2, 2)` to set our block size to be 2 cells by 2 cells or 8 pixels by 8 pixels
- `transform_sqrt=True` to apply a global preprocessing step to normalize the image values
- `block_norm='L2-Hys'` as our block normalization function

A quick note about the values for orientations, pixels per cell, and cells per block: we choose these values fairly arbitrarily as a baseline. We could have done more work to find optimal values for each of these parameters, but we will quickly move on to more state-of-the-art techniques. We wanted to highlight HOG features as a great baseline for image vectors, and in some simpler computer vision cases they can be optimal for speed and efficiency. We can think of HOG features similarly to the bag-of-words (BOW) vectorizers in the last chapter. HOG and BOW are both older ways to vectorize images and text, respectively, and we use them as starting points.

More information about these parameters can be found on the main page for the HOG featurizer on scikit-image's documentation: https://scikit-image.org/docs/0.15.x/api/skimage.feature.html. For now, let's move on to the following listing, where we can visualize HOG features for our CIFAR data.

Listing 6.4   Visualizing HOGs in CIFAR-10

```
from skimage.feature import hog          Import functions
from skimage import data, exposure       from scikit-image.
from skimage.transform import resize

for image in training_images[:3]:
                                         Calculate HOG for three
    hog_features, hog_image = hog(   ◁─  of our training images.
        image,
        orientations=8, pixels_per_cell=(4, 4), cells_per_block=(2, 2),
        channel_axis=-1, transform_sqrt=True,
        block_norm='L2-Hys', visualize=True)

    fig, (ax1, ax2) = plt.subplots(
        1, 2, figsize=(4, 4), sharex=True, sharey=True)

    ax1.axis('off')
    ax1.imshow(image, cmap=plt.cm.gray)
    ax1.set_title('Input image')
                                         Plot the HOG next to
    ax2.axis('off')                      the original images.
    ax2.imshow(hog_image, cmap=plt.cm.gray)
    ax2.set_title('Histogram of Oriented Gradients')

print(hog_features.shape)   ◁──── The size of the feature vector
plt.show()
```

Figure 6.4 shows a list of a few CIFAR images, with the original image on the left and a visualized HOG image on the right. We can see the outlines and movement in the HOG images without much of the background noise (pun intended).

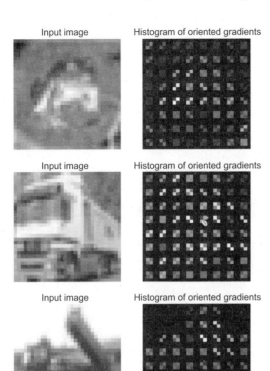

Figure 6.4 A sample of CIFAR-10 images with their accompanying HOG visualizations. Each cell shows us the most dramatic directions of movement to highlight edges in the image. The HOG visualizations are a lower-fidelity representation of their original raw images that will provide the input to our ML model.

NOTE When calculating HOGs, it is generally best practice to resize images to be of a scale 1:2 (e.g., 32 x 64), but because our images are so small already, we chose not to do this to not lose any valuable information. The HOG calculation will still work just fine!

Let's now create a helper function (listing 6.5) to batch convert our training and testing images into HOG features, using the parameters we set in listing 6.4. If we wanted to, we could set up a custom scikit-learn transformer to accomplish the same effect; however, because this conversion to HOG features is independent of anything else in our ML pipeline, it's quicker to simply convert the entire training and testing matrices into HOG matrices before running any ML. The following code snippet will do that for us.

Listing 6.5   Calculating HOGs for CIFAR-10

```
from tqdm import tqdm
def calculate_hogs(images):
    hog_descriptors = []
    for image in tqdm(images):
        hog_descriptors.append(hog(
            image, orientations=8, pixels_per_cell=(4, 4),
            cells_per_block=(2, 2), transform_sqrt=True,
```

tqdm will give us a progress bar, so we can see how long it takes to calculate our HOGs.

Function to calculate HOGs for a set of images

```
        channel_axis=-1, block_norm='L2-Hys',
        visualize=False
    ))

    return np.squeeze(hog_descriptors)

hog_training = calculate_hogs(training_images)
hog_testing = calculate_hogs(testing_images)
```

Now that we have our HOG features, let's test how well those features represent our images by training our ML pipeline on them in the following listing.

Listing 6.6   Using HOGs as features

```
print("HOG + LogReg\n=====================")
advanced_grid_search(
    hog_training, training_labels, hog_testing, testing_labels,
    ml_pipeline, params
)
```

Taking a look at the following figure, we see an immediate improvement in performance, using HOG features over raw pixel values, from 26% to 56% overall accuracy. Of course, we will not be satisfied with 56% accuracy (figure 6.5), but it's definitely an improvement! One minor drawback is that the time it takes to run our grid search code has gone up, implying that our model will likely run a bit slower. This is partly due to the fact that we are working with a larger number of overall features. Utilizing the raw pixel values yielded 1,024 features, while HOG produced over 1,500 features.

	precision	recall	f1-score	support
b'airplane'	0.61	0.61	0.61	1000
b'automobile'	0.68	0.69	0.69	1000
b'bird'	0.43	0.37	0.40	1000
b'cat'	0.42	0.36	0.39	1000
b'deer'	0.47	0.50	0.49	1000
b'dog'	0.47	0.44	0.46	1000
b'frog'	0.56	0.69	0.62	1000
b'horse'	0.58	0.60	0.59	1000
b'ship'	0.64	0.64	0.64	1000
b'truck'	0.68	0.70	0.69	1000
accuracy			0.56	10000
macro avg	0.55	0.56	0.56	10000
weighted avg	0.55	0.56	0.56	10000

```
Best params: {'classifier__C': 0.1}
Overall took 1480.04 seconds
```

Figure 6.5   Results from using HOG features show an increase in performance to 56% accuracy from our previous 26%. While 56% is not an incredible accuracy score, it's worth noting that we are asking our model to pick between 10 categories. We can also see an overall slowdown in the model due to the increase in number of features being learned from.

If only there was a way to capture the representation from HOG features, while reducing the feature complexity. Oh wait, we saw an example of this in the last chapter! Let's see if we can use dimension reduction techniques to reduce the complexity of our pipeline.

6.3.1   *Optimizing dimension reduction with PCA*

We've seen dimension reduction in action in the last chapter when we were working with the truncated SVD module in scikit-learn. We can bring the same idea here in an effort to reduce the number of features our logistic regression model needs to learn from, while retaining the representation we have from HOG.

Let's take a different approach from the last chapter. Instead of grid searching to find an optimal value, let's run a principal component analysis (PCA) on the HOG representation before running any ML code. Then, let's find the optimal number of components to use and then reduce the dimensions before running our logistic regression model on it. The following listing will run a PCA on the HOG features and output the amount of cumulative explained variance for every additional principal component used.

Listing 6.7   Dimension reduction with PCA

**Import our principal
component analysis module.**
```
from sklearn.decomposition import PCA

num_hog_features = hog_training.shape[1]
```
**Number of features from the
original HOG transformation**

```
p = PCA(n_components=num_hog_features)
p.fit(hog_training)
```
**Fit the PCA module
to the HOG matrix.**

```
plt.plot(p.explained_variance_ratio_.cumsum())
plt.title('Explained Variance vs # of PCA Components')
plt.xlabel('Number of Components')
plt.ylabel('% of Explained Variance')
```
**Visualize the cumulative
explained variance.**

The resulting graph (figure 6.6) will show us how much of the variance in the original data is being captured with every additional dimension. Our job is now to pick a number of components we believe will satisfactorily represent the original HOG features. From the graph, it seems that 600 components is likely a reasonable choice. The percent of explained variance is near 100%, and 600 is over 60% fewer features than our original HOG feature set. It feels like a great idea to choose 600 as our optimal component size, then!

> **EXERCISE 6.1**   Find the cumulative percent of explained variance, using 10, 100, 200, and 400 principal components.

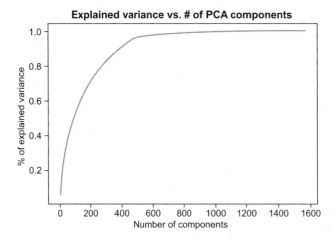

Figure 6.6   The PCA graph reveals that around 600 components should be enough to capture the information from the HOG features, while cutting down on features by 60%.

Now that we've chosen 600 as the number of features we wish to reduce down to, let's reduce our HOG features to 600 dimensions and rerun our grid search function in the following listing.

Listing 6.8   Using reduced HOG dimensions as features

```
p = PCA(n_components=600)      ◁──── Choose to extract 600 new features.

hog_training_pca = p.fit_transform(hog_training)    │ Transform the original HOG
hog_testing_pca = p.transform(hog_testing)          │ features to the reduced space.

print("HOG + PCA + LogReg\n=====================")
advanced_grid_search(                               ◁────┘ Get accuracy for reduced HOG features.
    hog_training_pca, training_labels, hog_testing_pca, testing_labels,
    ml_pipeline, params
)
```

The results are promising in figure 6.7! We did not lose any overall predictive power by looking at the model's accuracy on the test set, and the code ran over 75% faster (the last run took over 1,480 seconds to run, while this run took just under 390 seconds), implying our model is learning and predicting much more quickly. This is an excellent example of dimension reduction techniques like PCA and SVD working well!

So far every technique we have tried has led to better results in either bolstering predictive power or reducing model and feature complexity. In our last chapter, we saw the best results coming from state-of-the-art feature learning by way of transfer learning. Let's now turn our sights to our final section of the study, where we introduce another transfer learning–based model to see if the same will hold true here.

Both the mean pixel feature approach and the HOG extractor are excellent quick transformations of images with extensive histories of working relatively well in certain situations. Let's move on into more state-of-the-art feature learning techniques with our newest transfer learning model.

	precision	recall	f1-score	support
b'airplane'	0.60	0.60	0.60	1000
b'automobile'	0.68	0.69	0.68	1000
b'bird'	0.44	0.37	0.40	1000
b'cat'	0.42	0.35	0.38	1000
b'deer'	0.46	0.50	0.48	1000
b'dog'	0.48	0.45	0.46	1000
b'frog'	0.56	0.69	0.62	1000
b'horse'	0.58	0.59	0.58	1000
b'ship'	0.63	0.63	0.63	1000
b'truck'	0.68	0.70	0.69	1000
accuracy			0.56	10000
macro avg	0.55	0.56	0.55	10000
weighted avg	0.55	0.56	0.55	10000

```
Best params: {'classifier__C': 0.1}
Overall took 389.02 seconds
```

Figure 6.7 Applying PCA to our HOG features yields the same accuracy, but the pipeline complexity has dramatically been reduced, as evidenced by the amount of time it takes to run our grid search decreasing by 75%. It is safe to say that this model is faster and just as accurate.

6.4   *Feature learning with VGG-11*

As we mentioned previously, HOG features and BOW features for NLP datasets are still used by many folks in the field but are rapidly being replaced by more state-of-the-art, deep learning, feature learning and extraction techniques. For our NLP case study, we relied on the mighty BERT, and for images, we will turn our attention to the transfer learning model called the VGG-11 model from the VGG family of models.

VGG stands for a group at Oxford called the *Visual Geometry Group* (https://www.robots.ox.ac.uk/~vgg), which originally architected this family in 2014 and used it to participate in an object recognition task that focused around the *ImageNet* dataset, another object recognition dataset like CIFAR-10. VGG models are Convolutional Neural Networks (ConvNets) and rely heavily on *convolutional and pooling layers* to represent images in the network. Convolutional layers will apply some *filter/kernel,* which is a function applied to localized regions of the 3D input, and output another set of 3D results. Figure 6.8 shows a high-level view of a ConvNet compared to a traditional feedforward neural network. Pooling layers periodically reduce the size of the representation to promote faster learning and prevent overfitting. These filters are considered learnable parameters, so the goal of the ConvNet is to learn what filters (functions) are best for extracting useful information about localized regions of the image for a given task. If we think back to the HOG section, we were applying a specific gradient or orientation filter to extract edge information from the image. ConvNets are trying to learn what types of filters are best for a given task without being told explicitly what filters to apply.

The VGG family of architectures have two main sections in their networks: a feature learning section and a classifier. The feature learning section of the network uses the convolutional and pooling layers to learn useful representations of images. The

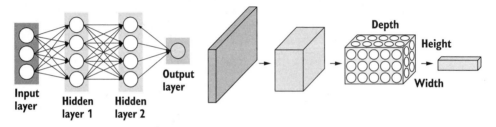

Figure 6.8   The left image shows a traditional neural network. The right image is of a convolutional network. The ConvNet will arrange neurons into three dimensions. Each subsequent layer of a ConvNet will map the 3D input to another 3D output of activations.

classifier section maps these representations to a set of labels to perform the classification. The pretrained version on ImageNet will map to one of 1,000 labels in the dataset.

VGG-11 is among the smaller of the VGG models, and its name comes from the fact that there are 11 weight layers in the model: 8 convolutional layers in the feature learning section and 3 feedforward layers in the classifier section. The 8 convolutional layers are specifically to learn functional filters that best represent the image, while the 3 feedforward layers convert that representation into a label classification task. Figure 6.9 shows a visualization of all layers of the VGG-11 model.

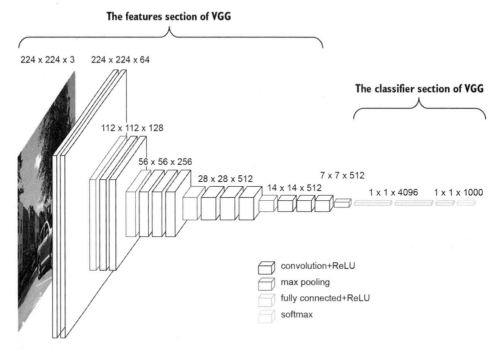

Figure 6.9   The VGG family of architectures with two main sections. The feature learning section of the network is built using convolutional and pooling layers with ReLU activations.

6.4.1 Using a pretrained VGG-11 as a feature extractor

Wait, what did he say? Feature extractor? I thought this was the feature learning section. It is, but we will be taking the feature learning section of the VGG-11 model that was trained on the ImageNet database and using it to map our images to the pretrained 512-length feature vector. Our hope is that the feature learning that happened during training will transfer over to being a good image vectorization function for our purposes.

> **NOTE** We are not using the VGG-11 to the exact specifications that its authors intended here. The authors use images that are 224 x 224 pixels to train the original model, and ours are only 32 x 32, for example. It is not imperative that we always strictly follow the author's intentions, but it is always good to know which assumptions we are explicitly breaking, so if our model tends to underperform, we have an idea of what may be going wrong.

In listing 6.9, let's load up the VGG-11 model the same way we loaded BERT in the last chapter. Let's, then, standardize our images according to a learned mean and standard deviation taken directly from the VGG paper. Recall that, by standardization, we simply mean calculating the z-score for each pixel value, where the mean and standard deviation have already been learned offline.

Listing 6.9 Loading a pretrained VGG-11 model and standardize images

Normalize the raw images, using
values from the original paper.

```
import torchvision.models as models
import torch.nn as nn
                                              Instantiate a VGG-11 model
vgg_model = models.vgg11(pretrained='imagenet')  ◁── pretrained on the imagenet corpus.

normalized_training_images = ((training_images/255) - [0.485, 0.456, 0.406])
⇒ / [0.229, 0.224, 0.225]
normalized_testing_images = ((testing_images/255) - [0.485, 0.456, 0.406]) /
⇒ [0.229, 0.224, 0.225]
```

We can take a look at the model itself and see for ourselves the 11 weight layers in the model in figure 6.10.

Now that we have our data standardized and our model loaded up, we need to do a bit more housekeeping by transforming our images into DataLoaders, which are classes in PyTorch designed to load data in batches. The model is expecting our images to also be of a different shape with the channels dimension first, rather than at the end, as we've had it so far.

```
In [185]:  vgg_model

Out[185]:  VGG(
             (features): Sequential(
               (0): Conv2d(3, 64, kernel_size=(3, 3), stride=(1, 1), padding=(1, 1))
               (1): ReLU(inplace=True)
               (2): MaxPool2d(kernel_size=2, stride=2, padding=0, dilation=1, ceil_mode=False)
               (3): Conv2d(64, 128, kernel_size=(3, 3), stride=(1, 1), padding=(1, 1))
               (4): ReLU(inplace=True)
               (5): MaxPool2d(kernel_size=2, stride=2, padding=0, dilation=1, ceil_mode=False)
               (6): Conv2d(128, 256, kernel_size=(3, 3), stride=(1, 1), padding=(1, 1))
               (7): ReLU(inplace=True)
               (8): Conv2d(256, 256, kernel_size=(3, 3), stride=(1, 1), padding=(1, 1))
               (9): ReLU(inplace=True)
               (10): MaxPool2d(kernel_size=2, stride=2, padding=0, dilation=1, ceil_mode=False)
               (11): Conv2d(256, 512, kernel_size=(3, 3), stride=(1, 1), padding=(1, 1))
               (12): ReLU(inplace=True)
               (13): Conv2d(512, 512, kernel_size=(3, 3), stride=(1, 1), padding=(1, 1))
               (14): ReLU(inplace=True)
               (15): MaxPool2d(kernel_size=2, stride=2, padding=0, dilation=1, ceil_mode=False)
               (16): Conv2d(512, 512, kernel_size=(3, 3), stride=(1, 1), padding=(1, 1))
               (17): ReLU(inplace=True)
               (18): Conv2d(512, 512, kernel_size=(3, 3), stride=(1, 1), padding=(1, 1))
               (19): ReLU(inplace=True)
               (20): MaxPool2d(kernel_size=2, stride=2, padding=0, dilation=1, ceil_mode=False)
             )
             (avgpool): AdaptiveAvgPool2d(output_size=(7, 7))
             (classifier): Sequential(
               (0): Linear(in_features=25088, out_features=4096, bias=True)
               (1): ReLU(inplace=True)
               (2): Dropout(p=0.5, inplace=False)
               (3): Linear(in_features=4096, out_features=4096, bias=True)
               (4): ReLU(inplace=True)
               (5): Dropout(p=0.5, inplace=False)
               (6): Linear(in_features=4096, out_features=1000, bias=True)
             )
           )
```

Figure 6.10   VGG-11 has 11 weight layers: 8 convolutional layers in the features section and 3 feedforward layers in the classifier section.

I promise that the results will be worth it! Let's load our data into DataLoaders in listing 6.10. The steps in general for both training and testing data are

1 Transpose the image matrices, so we have the number of images first, the channels second, and then the height and width.

2 Cast the values in the labels as a long type.

3 Load the tensor/matrix into a DataSet along with the labels.

4 Instantiate a DataLoader with our newly created DataSet, setting the shuffle parameter to true with a batch size of 2,048.

Listing 6.10   Loading the data into PyTorch DataLoaders

```
import torch
from torch.utils.data import TensorDataset, DataLoader

training_images_tensor =
torch.Tensor(normalized_training_images.transpose(0, 3, 1, 2))     ⎤  Transform the
training_labels_tensor =                                           ⎥  normalized training
torch.Tensor(int_training_labels).type(torch.LongTensor)           ⎥  image data into a
                                                                   ⎥  PyTorch DataLoader.
training_dataset = TensorDataset(training_images_tensor,           ⎦
```

```
training_labels_tensor)
training_dataloader = DataLoader(training_dataset,
shuffle=True, batch_size=2048)
```

⚠ **Transform the normalized training image data into a PyTorch DataLoader.**

```
testing_images_tensor = torch.Tensor(normalized_testing_images
.transpose(0, 3, 1, 2))
testing_labels_tensor =
torch.Tensor(int_testing_labels).type(torch.LongTensor)

testing_dataset = TensorDataset(testing_images_tensor,
testing_labels_tensor)
testing_dataloader = DataLoader(testing_dataset,
shuffle=True, batch_size=2048)
```

Transform the normalized testing image data into a PyTorch DataLoader.

We're almost ready to extract features! Let's create a helper function that will take batches of data from our DataLoaders and run them through the VGG-11 feature section of the model. Our next code listing will do just that! It will

1   Take in a feature_extractor as an input, which, itself, can take in iterables of images and output a matrix of features.
2   Iterate over batches of data from our PyTorch DataLoader.
3   For each batch, it will pass the image into the feature_extractor and then detach and convert the output to a NumPy array with only two dimensions (batch_size and feature_vector_length).
4   Run steps 2 and 3 for both the training DataLoader and the testing DataLoader.

We will aggregate them all into a final matrix in listing 6.11. Keep in mind that even though this model is among the smaller in the family, it is still over half a gigabyte large and can be a bit slow!

Listing 6.11   Helper function to aggregate training and testing matrices

```
from tqdm import tqdm

def get_vgg_features(feature_extractor):
    print("Extracting features for training set")
    extracted_training_images = []
    shuffled_training_labels = []
    for batch_idx, (data_, target_) in tqdm(enumerate(training_dataloader)):
        extracted_training_images.append(
            feature_extractor(
                data_).detach().numpy().squeeze((2, 3)))
        shuffled_training_labels += target_

    print("Extracting features for testing set")
    extracted_testing_images = []
    shuffled_testing_labels = []
    for batch_idx, (data_, target_) in tqdm(enumerate(testing_dataloader)):
        extracted_testing_images.append(
            feature_extractor(
```

```
            data_).detach().numpy().squeeze((2, 3)))
        shuffled_testing_labels += target_

    return np.vstack(extracted_training_images), \
        shuffled_training_labels, \
        np.vstack(extracted_testing_images), \
        shuffled_testing_labels
```

OK, phew! Now, we can use our same grid search helper function to extract features for our standardized images and get an accuracy score with our logistic regression in the following listing.

Listing 6.12   Using pretrained VGG-11 features

```
transformed_training_images, \
shuffled_training_labels, \
transformed_testing_images, \
shuffled_testing_labels = get_vgg_features(      ◁──  Extract features from
    vgg_model.features)                                the VGG-11 model.


print("VGG11(Imagenet) + LogReg\n=====================")
advanced_grid_search(
    transformed_training_images,          We needed to reextract the training
    shuffled_training_labels,             labels because the dataloader will
    transformed_testing_images,           shuffle the points around.
    shuffled_testing_labels,
    ml_pipeline, params
)
```

Our results are promising! A boost to nearly 70% accuracy (figure 6.11), simply by using a pretrained VGG-11 model as a feature extractor; that's not too bad, but can we do better by fine-tuning VGG-11 to the CIFAR-10 dataset?

	precision	recall	f1-score	support
0	0.72	0.74	0.73	1000
1	0.76	0.79	0.77	1000
2	0.63	0.57	0.60	1000
3	0.56	0.53	0.54	1000
4	0.63	0.66	0.64	1000
5	0.69	0.64	0.66	1000
6	0.70	0.78	0.74	1000
7	0.71	0.72	0.71	1000
8	0.76	0.76	0.76	1000
9	0.76	0.76	0.76	1000
accuracy			0.69	10000
macro avg	0.69	0.69	0.69	10000
weighted avg	0.69	0.69	0.69	10000

Figure 6.11   Using VGG-11's feature extractor with logistic regression provided the best results yet! Note that we do see an increase in training time, due to the larger set of features.

```
Best params: {'classifier__C': 0.1}
Overall took 624.69 seconds
```

6.4.2 *Fine-tuning VGG-11*

Our last section highlighted the power of transfer learning by using a pretrained VGG-11 model to vectorize images for our logistic regression pipeline. We did something in the last chapter, using BERT with text. Let's go a step further and attempt to fine-tune VGG-11 on our specific dataset to see if we can achieve even better results. We will do this in three steps:

1 Alter the classifier layer to output 10 values instead of the 1,000 in ImageNet to represent the 10 classes we wish to classify in our case study.

2 Rerandomize all weights in the classifier layer to unlearn ImageNet, but keep the pretrained feature learning.

3 Run our model over the training data, using our testing set as validation over 15 epochs, saving the best weights as we go.

Let's begin by altering the architecture to output 10 labels instead of 1,000 and rerandomizing the classification weights in the following listing. Note we have to define a device that basically tells PyTorch if we have access to a GPU or not.

Listing 6.13 Altering VGG-11 to classify 10 labels and rerandomize classification weights

```
device = torch.device(                                          Set device to
    'cuda:0' if torch.cuda.is_available() else 'cpu')      ◁──  either cuda or cpu.

fine_tuned_vgg_model = models.vgg11(      Instantiate a new
    pretrained='imagenet')          ◁──  VGG model.            Change the final classifier
                                                               layer to output 10 classes
fine_tuned_vgg_model.classifier[-1].out_features = 10  ◁──    instead of 1,000.

for layer in fine_tuned_vgg_model.classifier:
    if hasattr(layer, 'weight'):                          Randomize all
        torch.nn.init.xavier_uniform_(layer.weight)       parameters in the
    if hasattr(layer, 'bias'):                            classifier to start
        nn.init.constant_(layer.bias.data, 0)             fresh.
```

Now that our model is ready, let's set up the arguments for our training loop (listing 6.14) that will fine-tune our VGG-11 model. We will define our

- Loss function as being cross-entropy loss, which is common for multiclass classification.

- Optimizer as stochastic gradient descent, which is a popular optimizer for deep learning problems.

- The number of epochs—15 to save some time—and we shouldn't need too many epochs to fine-tune a pretrained transfer learning model. One of the main benefits of using transfer learning is that we don't need to train our models on dozens or hundreds of epochs to see great results.

Listing 6.14   Setting up training arguments for VGG-11

```
import torch.optim as optim

criterion = nn.CrossEntropyLoss()
optimizer = optim.SGD(
    fine_tuned_vgg_model.parameters(), lr=0.01, momentum=0.9)

n_epochs = 15
print_every = 10
valid_loss_min = np.Inf
total_step = len(training_dataloader)

train_loss, val_loss, \
train_acc, val_acc = [], [], [], []
```

Set our training parameters (parameter tuning happened offscreen).

Initialize lists to keep track of loss and accuracy.

OK, all systems are green. This next code block in listing 6.15 is a bit of a doozy and defines our training loop. If you are unfamiliar with PyTorch training loops, the basic idea is that we will accumulate gradients by calculating a running loss value and back-propagate through the network to update the model's weights. We, then, clear the gradients and start again. Every time we go through the training set, we set the model to evaluation mode to halt training and calculate a loss and accuracy for our 10,000 image testing set. If we detect that the network has improved, we will save the weights, so we can reinstantiate the model at a later time. Let's go!

Listing 6.15   Setting up training arguments for VGG-11

```
for epoch in range(1, n_epochs + 1):
running_loss = 0.0
correct = 0
total=0
print(f'Epoch {epoch}\n')
for batch_idx, (data_, target_) in enumerate(training_dataloader):
    data_, target_ = data_.to(device), target_.to(device)
    optimizer.zero_grad()

    outputs = fine_tuned_vgg_model(data_)
    loss = criterion(outputs, target_)
    loss.backward()
    optimizer.step()

    running_loss += loss.item()
    _, pred = torch.max(outputs, dim=1)
    correct += torch.sum(pred==target_).item()
    total += target_.size(0)
    if (batch_idx) % print_every == 0:
        print ('Epoch [{}/{}], Step [{}/{}], Loss: {:.4f}'
            .format(
                epoch, n_epochs,
                batch_idx, total_step, loss.item()))
train_acc.append(100 * correct / total)
train_loss.append(running_loss/total_step)
```

Clears the gradient to prevent accumulation

```
print(f'\ntrain-loss: {np.mean(train_loss):.4f}, \
train-acc: {(100 * correct/total):.4f}%')

batch_loss = 0
total_t=0
correct_t=0
with torch.no_grad():
    fine_tuned_vgg_model.eval()
    for data_t, target_t in (testing_dataloader):
        data_t, target_t = data_t.to(device), target_t.to(device)
        outputs_t = fine_tuned_vgg_model(data_t)
        loss_t = criterion(outputs_t, target_t)
        batch_loss += loss_t.item()
        _, pred_t = torch.max(outputs_t, dim=1)
        correct_t += torch.sum(pred_t==target_t).item()
        total_t += target_t.size(0)
    val_acc.append(100 * correct_t/total_t)
    val_loss.append(batch_loss/len(testing_dataloader))
    network_learned = batch_loss < valid_loss_min
    print(f'validation loss: {np.mean(val_loss):.4f}, \
    validation acc: {(100 * correct_t/total_t):.4f}%\n')

    if network_learned:
        valid_loss_min = batch_loss
        torch.save(fine_tuned_vgg_model.state_dict(), 'vgg_cifar10.pt')
        print('Saving Parameters')

fine_tuned_vgg_model.train()
```

Epoch 1
```
train-loss: 2.0290, train-acc: 44.4640%
validation loss: 0.9768, validation acc: 65.7600%
```
. . .
Epoch 11
```
train-loss: 0.5547, train-acc: 94.7540%
validation loss: 0.6072, validation acc: 84.2800%
```
. . .
Epoch 15
```
train-loss: 0.4310, train-acc: 98.3480%
validation loss: 0.6265, validation acc: 84.0900%
```

Alright! After 15 epochs we can see that our model definitely learned to classify our CIFAR-10 dataset and even reached an accuracy on the test set of nearly 85% (see figure 6.12)! This is wonderful news because it means we successfully fine-tuned our VGG-11 model to the CIFAR-10 dataset. One thing to note here is that on my 2018 MacBook pro, this training loop took about an hour to run.

EXERCISE 6.2 Continue training the model for another three epochs, and print out the change in testing accuracy.

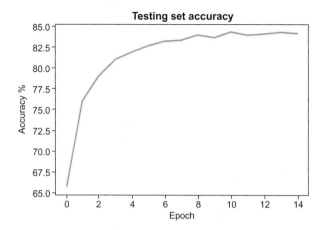

Figure 6.12   Fine-tuning VGG-11 peaked around 84% accuracy in the test set.

6.4.3   *Using fine-tuned VGG-11 features with logistic regression*

Our fine-tuning process was a great success, but we have one minor issue. We didn't use a logistic regression to do the actual classification. We relied on the final feedforward layer in the classification section of the VGG-11 model to perform the actual classification, so we don't know how much of the near-85% accuracy we achieved was due to the eight image representation layers learning better image representations and how much of it was due to the three classifier layers learning the best weights for classification. But we know how to tell!

Let's take one more step to get accuracy results from our fine-tuned VGG-11 feature extractor and use logistic regression to perform the actual classification. Put another way, we will use the features section of our fine-tuned VGG-11 model to convert our raw images to features, and instead of using the classifier on the VGG-11, we will rely on the same logistic regression model we have been using for the other models. This will give us a good sense of how much better the VGG-11 features are compared to our other image vectorizers.

To do this, let's load another VGG-11 model with the best weights from the training loop and rely on our helper function again to transform our standardized images in listing 6.16.

> **NOTE**   We could have used the model we just fine-tuned, but this is a good example of loading weights from a past training loop, and it is common practice to run accuracy metrics far after the training loop is complete.

Listing 6.16   Using a fine-tuned VGG-11 to extract features

```
cifar_fine_tuned_vgg_model = models.vgg11(
    pretrained='imagenet')                          Instantiate a new
cifar_fine_tuned_vgg_model.classifier[-1]           VGG-11 model.
.out_features = 10
```

```
cifar_fine_tuned_vgg_model.load_state_dict(
    torch.load('vgg_cifar10.pt',
map_location=device))

cifar_finetuned_training_images, \
shuffled_training_labels, \
cifar_finetuned_testing_images, \
shuffled_testing_labels = get_vgg_features(
    cifar_fine_tuned_vgg_model.features)

print("Fine-tuned VGG11 + LogReg\n=====================")
advanced_grid_search(
    cifar_finetuned_training_images, shuffled_training_labels,
    cifar_finetuned_testing_images, shuffled_testing_labels,
    ml_pipeline, params
)
```

Load up the trained parameters, and extract fine-tuned features.

Run a grid search on fine-tuned features.

Our results are nearly only 1% worse (figure 6.13) than the best testing accuracy we got during our training loop. This proves that our fine-tuning process really did lead to the VGG-11 model learning an optimal image representation for our CIFAR-10 dataset and was not simply relying on the classifier layer to achieve such a high performance.

	precision	recall	f1-score	support
0	0.84	0.87	0.85	1000
1	0.91	0.91	0.91	1000
2	0.78	0.76	0.77	1000
3	0.68	0.67	0.67	1000
4	0.79	0.81	0.80	1000
5	0.77	0.74	0.75	1000
6	0.85	0.88	0.87	1000
7	0.85	0.86	0.85	1000
8	0.91	0.90	0.90	1000
9	0.90	0.89	0.90	1000
accuracy			0.83	10000
macro avg	0.83	0.83	0.83	10000
weighted avg	0.83	0.83	0.83	10000

```
Best params: {'classifier__C': 0.1}
Overall took 607.62 seconds
```

Figure 6.13   A jump from 69% accuracy with the pretrained VGG-11 to 83% accuracy using the fine-tuned VGG-11 features proves that our fine-tuning method forced the VGG-11 model to learn an optimal representation of images for this particular object recognition task.

6.5   *Image vectorization recap*

We've seen many ways to vectorize images for ML pipelines in this chapter. Table 6.1 recaps each methodology, alongside their respective metrics. It's clear that our transfer learning approach provided the best results, just as they did in the previous chapter on NLP.

For our images, however, the boost in performance is much sharper. This is likely because, well, a picture is worth 1,000 words. There is so much more variance and noise in images than in short tweets. This is likely why the delta in performance between `CountVectorizers` and BERT was not as dramatic as the difference between HOG features and VGG-11. As always, the vectorization method we choose to use for our unstructured text and images depends on the complexity of the data and the ML task.

Table 6.1   Showcasing our image vectorization methods with accompanying statistics. Overall, using VGG-11 with the feedforward network as a classifier yielded the best accuracy on our test set.

Pipeline description	Testing accuracy	Minutes to run grid search code	Number of features
Average RGB values + LogReg	26%	19	1,024
HOG + LogReg	56%	25	1,568
HOG + PCA + LogReg	56%	**6**	600
VGG-11 + ImageNet + LogReg	69%	10	**512**
VGG-11 + ImageNet + feedforward classifier	**84%**	N/A, but fine-tuning took about an hour	**512**
VGG-11 + ImageNet + fine-tune + LogReg	83%	10	**512**

6.6   *Answers to exercises*

EXERCISE 6.1

Find the cumulative percent of explained variance, using 10, 100, 200, and 400 principal components.

ANSWER:

```
explained_variance = p.explained_variance_ratio_.cumsum()

for i in [10, 100, 200, 400]:
    print(f'The explained variance using {i} \
    components is {explained_variance[i - 1]}')
The explained variance using 10 components is 0.17027868448637712
The explained variance using 100 components is 0.5219347292907045
The explained variance using 200 components is 0.696400699801984
The explained variance using 400 components is 0.9156784465873314
```

EXERCISE 6.2

Continue training the model for another three epochs, and calculate the change in testing accuracy.

Answers may vary here, due to the randomness involved with deep learning training.

Summary

- Image vectorization and text vectorization are both ways of converting raw unstructured data into structured, fixed-length feature vectors, which are required for ML.
- Feature construction and extraction techniques, like MPV and HOG, provide a great and fast baseline method for image vectorization but will generally fall short compared to longer, more complex deep learning techniques.

Time series analysis: Day trading with machine learning

7

This chapter covers
- Working with time series data
- Constructing a custom feature set and response variable, using standard time series feature types
- Tracking intraday profits from our ML pipeline
- Adding domain-specific features to our dataset to enhance performance
- Extracting and selecting features to minimize noise and maximize latent signal

We have been through a lot together, from tabular data to bias reduction to text and image vectorization. All of these datasets had one major thing in common: they were all datasets based on a snapshot in time. All of the people represented in the COMPAS dataset had their data aggregated before we started our analysis. All of the tweets were already sent. All of the images were already taken. Another similarity is that each row in our datasets was not dependent on other rows in the dataset. If we pick a single person from the COMPAS set or a tweet from our NLP dataset, the values that are attached to each person do not depend on another data point in that dataset. We aren't, for example, tracking values for a person across time. Another similarity between datasets we have been working with up until now is that we were always given a pretty straightforward response variable to target in our ML pipelines. We always knew, for example, the sentiment of the tweet, the object in the photo, or whether the patient had COVID-19. There was never any doubt as to what we were trying to predict.

This case study will break all of these assumptions and conventions. In this chapter, we are working with *time series data*, which means each row depends on the previous row, and our dataset has a direct dependence on time. Furthermore, it will be up to us to construct our response variable because a clear one will not be given to us.

Time series data are not the most common type of data out there, but when we are faced with them, we have to shift our mindset to a whole new way of thinking about feature engineering. Time series data, in a way, are the ultimate challenge because we are not given clean features, nor are we given a clean target. Those are up to the creativeness and cleverness of the domain experts and data scientists with a stake in the data. Let's jump right in with our time series case study of intraday stock price trading.

> **WARNING** This chapter also has some long-running code samples toward the end of the chapter. Be advised that some code samples may run for over an hour on the minimum requirements for this text.

7.1 The TWLO dataset

Our dataset today is a dataset that yours truly put together via *Yahoo! Finance*. I have a hobby of making ML models predict stock price movements, and I am excited to bring the basics of the problem to this case study! We will look to predict intraday (within the same day) stock price movements of Twilio (one of my favorite tech companies). The ticker for Twilio is TWLO, so our data are called twlo_prices.csv. Let's dive in, shall we? Let's begin by ingesting our TWLO data in the following listing.

Listing 7.1 Investigating the TWLO data

```
import pandas as pd
price_df = pd.read_csv(f"../data/twlo_prices.csv")
price_df.head()
```

Our time series dataset has three columns (figure 7.1):

- *Close*, which represents the closing price at that minute
- *Volume*, which represents the number of shares traded in that minute
- A *date* column that is granular up to the minute

	close	volume	date
0	99.98	93417.0	2020-01-02 14:30:00+00:00
1	99.78	16685.0	2020-01-02 14:31:00+00:00
2	100.14	21998.0	2020-01-02 14:32:00+00:00
3	100.35	18348.0	2020-01-02 14:33:00+00:00
4	100.55	22181.0	2020-01-02 14:34:00+00:00

Figure 7.1 Each row of our time series data represents a minute's worth of trading data with associated closing price and volume of shares traded in that minute.

With only these three columns, we don't seem to have much to work with. But this is the nature of most time series data! We often have to start with a bare-bones dataset and transform our raw columns into usable and clean features, as in this case.

This is also true for our response variable—the column that we will eventually use as the ML pipeline's predictive goal. You may have noticed that, along with not really having any features to use, we don't have a clear response variable. What will our ML pipeline try to predict? We will have to construct a viable response variable as well while setting up our data.

Before we do anything though, let's fix up our DataFrame by setting our index to be our *date* column (listing 7.2). This is useful because when a pandas DataFrame has a datetime column as an index, we can perform operations that are exclusive to datetime data and also make it easier to visualize data in graphs. All datetimes are in UTC by default in our dataset, so I will also convert that datetime into a local timezone. I will use the Pacific Time Zone in the US, as that is where I was at the time of writing.

Listing 7.2 Setting a time index in pandas

```
price_df.index = pd.to_datetime(price_df['date'])      Set our index to be the date
price_df.index = price_df.index.tz_convert             column, and configure the
('US/Pacific')                                         time zone to be Pacific.

price_df.sort_index(inplace=True)  ◁──── Sort our DataFrame by the index (time).

del price_df['date']      ◁───────┐
                                  │  Delete the date column
price_df.head()  # show our work  │  because it is now our index.
```

The resulting DataFrame will have a new datetime index and will have one less column, as seen in figure 7.2.

Now that we have a datetime index, we can plot our *close* column, as follows, to get a sense of the price movement at a very high level:

```
price_df['close'].plot()
```

| | close | volume |
date		
2020-01-02 06:30:00-08:00	99.98	93417.0
2020-01-02 06:31:00-08:00	99.78	16685.0
2020-01-02 06:32:00-08:00	100.14	21998.0
2020-01-02 06:33:00-08:00	100.35	18348.0
2020-01-02 06:34:00-08:00	100.55	22181.0

Figure 7.2   After setting our DataFrame's index to be a datetime index and deleting the *date* column, this is our resulting DataFrame. Note that the *date* column is listed slightly below our columns to indicate it is now an index.

The resulting plot (figure 7.3) shows the price of TWLO over the course of nearly 2 years, starting from January 2020 to July 2021.

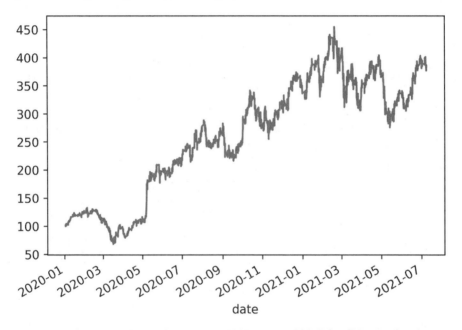

Figure 7.3   Plot of TWLO price from January 2020 to July 2021. This will be the time frame we will work in.

As mentioned previously, we don't have a real response variable yet. Let's talk about how to set up the problem we want to solve, so we can dive into time series–specific feature engineering techniques.

7.1.1   *The problem statement*

Our data are considered a *multivariate time series*, meaning we have multiple (usually scalar) variables recorded sequentially over time increments of equal size. The two variables in our case are close and volume. By contrast, a *univariate time series* problem would have a single value at each time period. If we had only `close` or had only `volume` but not the other, then we would have a univariate problem on our hands.

To keep our problem simple, let's generate a response variable using only our *close* column. This is because the more interesting question we want to solve is, can we predict the *future close value* in a given minute? The calculation will be quite simple—for every minute, calculate the percent change between the current price and the price at the end of the day. Our pipeline will then be a binary classifier; was the percent change positive or negative?

The code in listing 7.3 does the following:

1 Grabs the last price of the day and calculates the percent change between the current timestamp and the final price.
2 Transforms that percent change into a binary response variable. If the change is positive, we consider the row *bullish* (financial term for rising stock price) or *bearish* (financial term for a falling stock price).

Listing 7.3 Setting a time index in pandas

```
last_price_of_the_day = price_df.groupby(
    price_df.index.date).tail(1)['close'].rename(       Calculate the ending price
        'day_close_price')                              of TWLO for each day.
last_price_of_the_day.index = \
last_price_of_the_day.index.date

price_df['day'] = price_df.index.date      ◁───┐  Add a column to our price
                                                │  DataFrame to represent the date.
price_df = price_df.merge(
    last_price_of_the_day, left_on='day',
right_index=True)                          ◁───┐  Merge the ending prices into
                                                │  our granular DataFrame.
price_df['pct_change_eod'] = (
    price_df['day_close_price'] - price_df['close']) \
    / price_df['close']                    ◁───┐  The percent change from now
                                                │  until the end of the day
price_df['stock_price_rose'] = \
price_df['pct_change_eod'] > 0             ◁───┐  Create our response
                                                │  column—a binary response.
price_df.head()
```

Figure 7.4 shows our DataFrame as it stands with our new binary response variable.

NOTE Finally, this guy has cracked automated day trading. I can give up everything and rely on his wisdom. *Please* do not do that. Obtaining consistent gains through automated trading is extremely risky and difficult, and we would not recommend anyone get into this if they do not have the proper risk tolerance and spending capital.

date	close	volume	day	day_close_price	pct_change_eod	stock_price_rose
2020-01-02 06:30:00-08:00	99.98	93417.0	2020-01-02	103.15	0.031706	True
2020-01-02 06:31:00-08:00	99.78	16685.0	2020-01-02	103.15	0.033774	True
2020-01-02 06:32:00-08:00	100.14	21998.0	2020-01-02	103.15	0.030058	True
2020-01-02 06:33:00-08:00	100.35	18348.0	2020-01-02	103.15	0.027902	True
2020-01-02 06:34:00-08:00	100.55	22181.0	2020-01-02	103.15	0.025858	True

Figure 7.4   We now have a binary response variable, `stock_price_rose`, to give our ML pipeline something to target. All that's left is to construct some features to predict the target.

OK, we have a response variable, but we have no features to provide a signal to predict it. The same way we used our *close* column to create our response, let's also use the *close/volume* columns to create some features to give our ML pipeline something to predict with.

7.2   Feature construction

When it comes to constructing features for time series data, it usually falls into one of four categories:

- Date/time features
- Lag features
- Rolling-window features
- Expanding-window features

Each of these categories represents a different way of interpreting our initial *close/volume* columns, and each has pros and cons because ... well, because pretty much everything in life has pros and cons. We will be constructing features in each of these categories, so let's get started!

7.2.1   Date/time features

Date/time features are features that are constructed using each row's time value and, crucially, without using any other row's time value. This often takes the form of an ordinal feature or some Boolean flagging what time of day the value is occurring.

Let's create two date/time features:

- `dayofweek` will be an *ordinal* feature, representing the day of the week. We could map these to strings to make them more human readable, but it is better to keep ordinal columns as numbers to make them machine readable.
- `morning` will be a *nominal* binary feature that is true if the data point corresponds to a `datetime` before noon Pacific and false otherwise.

The following listing will create our first two features for our pipeline.

Listing 7.4 Creating date/time features

An ordinal feature representing the day of the week

```
price_df['feature__dayofweek'] = \
price_df.index.dayofweek
price_df['feature__morning'] = price_df.index.hour < 12
```

A binary feature for whether it is before noon or not

Figure 7.5 depicts two graphs:

- On the top we have the number of datapoints by the day of the week. Note that Monday and Friday (0 and 4) have fewer, mostly because most holidays on which the market is closed fall on one of those days.
- On the bottom we have the number of datapoints before and after noon. Adjusted for Pacific Time—as our DataFrame is—most datapoints are in the morning, as the market generally opens at 6:30 a.m. Pacific Time.

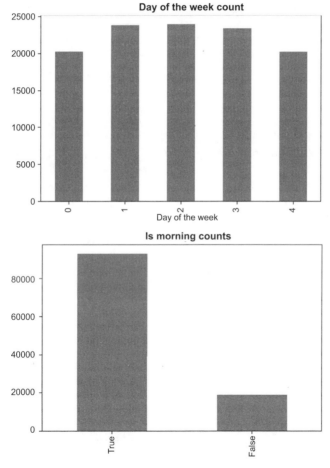

Figure 7.5 Our two date/time features give us a likely small but potentially useful signal in the way of assuming there is some relationship between stock movement and the day of the week (Monday vs. Friday) or between movement and the time of day (morning or not).

7.2.2   *Lag features*

Time series data give us a unique chance to use features from past rows as features in the present. Features that take advantage of this opportunity are called *lag features*. Put another way, at time *t*, a lag feature uses information from a previous time step (*t-1, t-2,* and so on). It is easy to construct lag features in Python using the pandas `shift` feature, which shifts a series/column forward or backward. We will also use the optional parameter `freq` to tell the `shift` method how much to move forward or backward.

Let's construct two lag features (listing 7.5):

- The features `30_min_ago_price` will be the price 30 minutes ago. We will use the freq `T`, which represents minutes.
- The features `7_day_ago_price` will be the price 7 days ago. We will use the `freq` `D`, which represents days.

Listing 7.5   Constructing lag features

```
price_df['feature__lag_30_min_ago_price'] = \
price_df['close'].shift(30, freq='T')
price_df['feature__lag_7_day_ago_price'] = \
price_df['close'].shift(7, freq='D')

price_df['feature__lag_7_day_ago_price'].plot(figsize=(20,10))
price_df['close'].plot()
```

When we plot our 30-minutes-ago lag feature (figure 7.6), we see something similar to one of those red/blue 3D glasses images. In reality, the line that is slightly to the right is simply the price 30 minutes ago, so it looks like the entire line on the left (the original price) shifted slightly forward.

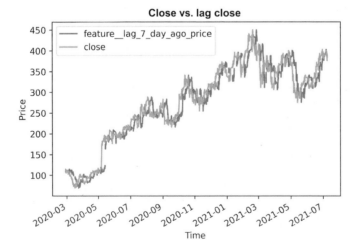

Figure 7.6   **Our lag feature is just the close price some time in the past.**

7.2.3 Rolling/expanding window features

Lag features give us insight into what is happening in the past, as do our next two types of time series features: *rolling-window features* and *expanding-window features.*

ROLLING-WINDOW FEATURES

Rolling-window features are similar to lag features in that they use values at previous timestamps as their source of information. The main difference is that rolling-window features use a chunk of data in the past in a static *window*—time frame—to calculate a statistic that is used as a feature at the current timestamp. Put another way, a 30-minute-lag feature will simply grab a value from 30 minutes ago and use it as a feature, whereas a 30-minute rolling-window feature will take all values in the last 30 minutes and apply some—generally, simple—function to the values and use the result as a feature. Oftentimes, this function is something like a mean or a median.

As we calculate a rolling-window feature for all of our timestamps, the window moves along with the timestamp (figure 7.7). This way the rolling-window feature *forgets* what happened before the fixed window size. This gives a rolling-window feature the ability to stay in the moment, but it loses the ability to remember long-term trends.

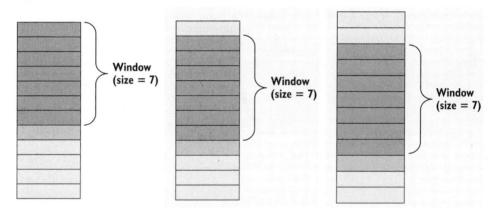

Figure 7.7   Rolling-window features use values from previous rows in a given fixed window. For any given row (just below the darkest shaded rows) we are only using the past *n* values (*n* being our windows shown in the darkest shaded rows) to calculate our rolling window feature.

In our case, we will make four rolling-window features (listing 7.6):

- `rolling_close_mean_60` is a rolling 60-minute average price. This is also known as a *moving average.*
- `rolling_close_std_60` is a rolling 60-minute standard deviation of price. This will give us some sense of volatility in the past hour.
- `rolling_volume_mean_60` is a rolling 60-minute average of volume. This will give us a sense of how much activity there has been in the past hour.
- `rolling_volume_std_60` is a rolling 60-minute standard deviation of volume. This will give us a sense of volatility in the amount of trades in the past hour.

Listing 7.6   Creating rolling-window features

```
price_df['feature__rolling_close_mean_60'] = \
price_df['close'].rolling('60min').mean()       ◁——— Rolling 60-minute average price
price_df['feature__rolling_close_std_60'] = \
price_df['close'].rolling('60min').std()    ◁——— Rolling 60-minute standard deviation of price
price_df['feature__rolling_volume_mean_60'] = \
price_df['volume'].rolling('60min').mean()  ◁——— Rolling 60-minute average volume
price_df['feature__rolling_volume_std_60'] = \
price_df['volume'].rolling('60min').std()   ◁——— Rolling 60-minute standard deviation of volume

price_df.dropna(inplace=True)

price_df['feature__rolling_close_mean_60'].plot(
    figsize=(20, 10), title='Rolling 60min Close')
plt.xlabel('Time')
plt.ylabel('Price')
```

In figure 7.8 we can see the resulting graph showing the rolling 60-minute average close price. It is common to plot the rolling average of a time series variable, as opposed to the raw value, as a rolling average tends to produce a much smoother graph and makes it more parsable for the masses.

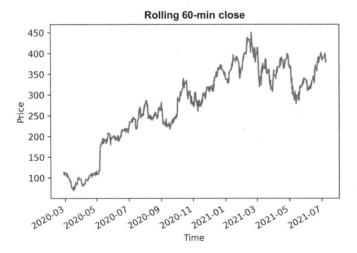

Figure 7.8   Our rolling-close feature uses a window size of 60 minutes and takes the average value in the past 60 minutes as a feature.

EXERCISE 7.1   Calculate the rolling 2.5-hour average closing price, and plot that value over the entirety of the training set.

EXPANDING-WINDOW FEATURES

Like rolling-window features, *expanding-window features* use a window in the past to calculate a statistic for the current timestamp. The main difference is that where the rolling-window feature uses a fixed window in the past and moves along with the timestamp, the expanding-window feature uses an ever-growing window from a fixed starting point. The window's expanding nature allows it to remember longer-term trends, unlike rolling-window features. Figure 7.9 shows a visualization of how windows are selected for expanding-window features.

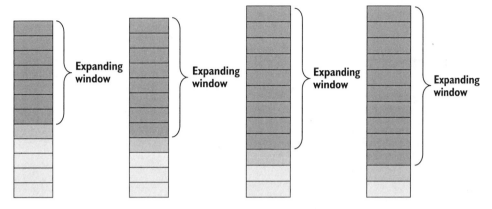

Figure 7.9   Expanding-window features use values from previous rows in an expanding window that starts from the beginning. For any given row (just below the darkest shaded rows), we use all past values (the darkest shaded rows) to calculate our expanding-window feature.

We will create two expanding-window features in listing 7.7:

- An expanding average closing price
- An expanding-average volume

Listing 7.7   Creating expanding-window features

```
price_df['feature__expanding_close_mean'] = \
price_df['close'].expanding(200).mean()
price_df['feature__expanding_volume_mean'] = \
price_df['volume'].expanding(200).mean()

price_df.dropna(inplace=True)

price_df['feature__expanding_close_mean'].plot(
    figsize=(20, 10), title='Expanding Window Close')

plt.xlabel('Time')
plt.ylabel('Price')
price_df['feature__expanding_volume_mean'].plot(
    figsize=(20, 10), title='Expanding Window Volume')

plt.xlabel('Time')
plt.ylabel('Shares')
```

Plot our expanding-window features.

Figure 7.10 shows off these two expanding-window features in a graph. The top graph depicts the expanding average for close, and the bottom graph shows the expanding average for volume. We hope that including both rolling- and expanding-window

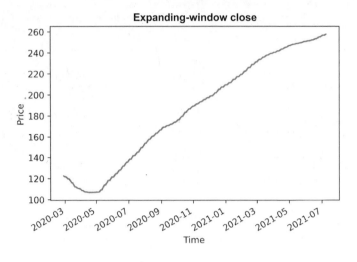

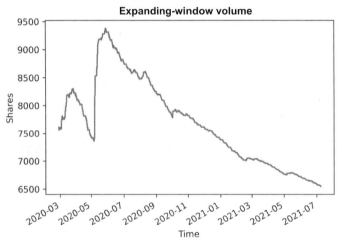

Figure 7.10   Our two
new expanding-window
features for close (top)
and volume (bottom)

features will give our pipeline a sense of short-term trends (through our rolling-window features) and long-term trends (from our expanding-window features).

CREATING OUR BASELINE MODEL

OK, we have constructed a handful of features; let's take some time to create our baseline model based on our date/time, lag, rolling-window, and expanding-window features (listing 7.8). Our pipeline shouldn't look so strange at this point. We will be grid searching a `RandomForest` on our time series data and using our `StandardScalar` to scale our data, as they are definitely on different scales. How do I know they are on different scales? For one, we used both `close` and `volume` to construct features, and `volume` is often in the thousands, while `close` is in the hundreds.

Listing 7.8   Setting up our baseline model parameters

```
from sklearn.pipeline import Pipeline            ◁────        Import the scikit-learn
from sklearn.ensemble import RandomForestClassifier          Pipeline object.
from sklearn.preprocessing import StandardScaler

clf = RandomForestClassifier(random_state=0)

ml_pipeline = Pipeline([    ◁────────        Create a pipeline with feature
    ('scale', StandardScaler()),             scaling and our classifier.
    ('classifier', clf)
])
                            │  Create the base grid search parameters.
params = {   ◁──────────────┘
    'classifier__criterion': ['gini', 'entropy'],
    'classifier__min_samples_split': [2, 3, 5],

    'classifier__max_depth': [10, None],
    'classifier__max_features': [None, 'auto']
}
```

With our baseline pipeline set up, it's time to run some cross-validated gridsearches. But before we can do that, we have to address another oddity with time series data: normal cross-validation doesn't quite make sense when data points are linked to time. Let me explain.

TIME SERIES CROSS-VALIDATION SPLITTING

Normal cross-validation involves taking random splits of data to create multiple training/testing subsets with which we can aggregate model performance. With time series, we want to alter that thinking a bit. Instead of splitting into random training and testing splits, we want to ensure the training set has data only from before the testing set. This makes the ML pipeline's metrics more believable by simulating how the training is done in the real world. We would never expect our model to train on data in the future to predict values in the past! So here is how we split data up for time series cross validation:

1 We choose a number of splits we want to make. Let's say $n = 5$.
2 We break up our data into $n + 1$ (6 in our example) equal splits.
3 Our first iteration uses the first split as the training set and the second split as the testing set. Remember, we are not shuffling our data, so we are guaranteed that the second split only has data that came after the first split.
4 Our second iteration will use the first two splits as training data and the third split as the testing set.
5 This will continue until we have five iterations worth of data to train on.

Let's instantiate an instance of the `TimeSeriesSplit` object from scikit-learn, as shown in the following listing.

Listing 7.9   Instantiating our time series CV split

```
from sklearn.model_selection import TimeSeriesSplit │ This splitter will give us train/test
tscv = TimeSeriesSplit(n_splits=2)                   │ splits optimized for time data.
```

As an example, let's create five splits on our data and check the time ranges used for the training and testing sets. This can be seen in the following listing and the resulting figure 7.11.

Listing 7.10   Example of time series CV splits

```
for i, (train_index, test_index) in enumerate(tscv.split(price_df)):
    train_times, test_times = \
    price_df.iloc[train_index].index, \
    price_df.iloc[test_index].index

    print(f'Iteration {i}\n-------------')

    print(f'''Training between {train_times.min().date()}
and {train_times.max().date()}.
Testing between {test_times.min().date()} and {test_times.max().date()}\n'''
    )

Iteration 0
-------------
Training between 2020-01-09 and 2020-07-01.
Testing between 2020-07-01 and 2020-12-22

Iteration 1
-------------
Training between 2020-01-09 and 2020-12-22.
Testing between 2020-12-22 and 2021-07-08
```

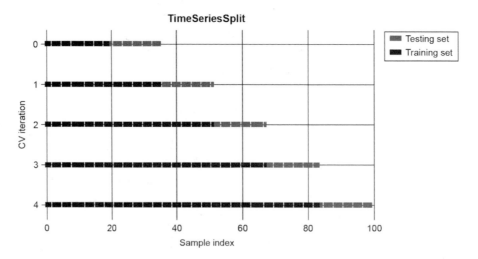

Figure 7.11   Our time series splitter visualized with five splits. The first split on the top uses a testing index in gray and a training index in black. The second split converts the first split's testing index into training and uses the next date range as a testing set.

Now that we know how to split our data into training and testing sets during cross-validation, let's create a helper function that will take in our price DataFrame and do a few things:

1. Create a smaller DataFrame by filtering out only rows on the hour (8 a.m., 9 a.m., and so on).
2. Use the data until June 2021 as our training data and data from June 1, 2021 onwards as a validation set. This means we will run our grid searches on the training set (up until June 2021) and judge our pipelines' performances on the validation set (June and July 2021).

In figure 7.12 we can see how we will be splitting our data up into a training and validation (testing) set.

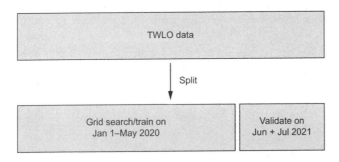

Figure 7.12 **We will split our overall data into a training and validation set. We will cross-validate on data before June 2021 and validate the pipeline (generate metrics) on the unseen validation data (June and July 2021).**

Listing 7.11 is a big one, but let's break it down step by step first. We will make a `split_data` function that will

1. Take in our price DataFrame
2. Only keep datapoints where the minute value of the `datetime` object is 0. These are points on the hour.
3. Split our price data into a training set on or before May 31, 2021, and a testing set from June 1, 2021, onward.

Listing 7.11 A helper function to filter and split our price data

```
def split_data(price_df):
    ''' This function takes in our price dataframe
        and splits it into a training and validation set
    as well as filtering our rows to only use rows that are on the hour
    '''
    downsized_price_df = price_df[(price_df
.index.minute == 0)]

    train_df, test_df = \
    downsized_price_df[:'2021-05-31'], \
    downsized_price_df['2021-06-01':]

    train_X, test_X = \
```

Limit our data to only make trades at the 0-minute mark. Usually 6–7 times a day.

Split our DataFrame into training and validation (before and after June 2021).

```
train_df.filter(
     regex='feature'), test_df.filter
(regex='feature')
```
> Use the pandas filter method to select the features based on the prefix feature__ we have been adding.

```
train_y, test_y = \
train_df['stock_price_rose'], \
test_df['stock_price_rose']
return train_df, test_df, train_X, train_y, test_X, test_y
```
> Split our target variable based on our June 2021 split.

As we add features to our DataFrame, this helper function will save us from rewriting some code to do these splits again and again. And now, let's finally run our first baseline model, using date features, time features, rolling-window features, lag features, and expanding-window features as shown in listing 7.12.

NOTE Fitting models in this chapter may take some time to run. For my 2021 MacBook Pro, some of these code segments took over an hour to complete the grid search

Listing 7.12   Running our first baseline model

```
train_df, test_df, train_X, train_y, test_X, test_y = split_data(price_df)

print("Date-time/Lag/Window features + \
Random Forest\n===========================")
best_model, test_preds, test_probas = advanced_grid_search(
     train_X, train_y,
     test_X, test_y,
     ml_pipeline, params,
     cv=tscv, include_probas=True
)
```

Let's also take a look at our classification report (figure 7.13) to see how well our model is performing.

```
Date-time/Lag/Window/Rolling features + Random Forest
===========================
                precision    recall   f1-score    support

       False        0.50       0.82       0.62         72
        True        0.41       0.13       0.20         69

    accuracy                              0.48        141
   macro avg        0.45       0.47       0.41        141
weighted avg        0.45       0.48       0.41        141
```

Figure 7.13   Results from our baseline model give us an accuracy to beat of 48%. This is not better than randomly guessing and being correct 51% of the time.

Our output, at a first glance, is not that amazing, with an accuracy of 48% on our validation data, which, remember, comprise June and July of 2021, but let's dig a bit deeper:

- Accuracy is 48%, but what is our null accuracy? We can calculate our validation null accuracy by running the following:

```
test_y.value_counts(normalize=True)
False    0.510638
True     0.489362
```

And seeing that, if we guessed that the price was going down, we'd be correct 51% of the time. We aren't beating our null accuracy yet. Not ideal.

- Our precisions and recalls are all over the place. Bearish recall (class `False`) is a high 82%, while bullish recall (class `True`) is only 13%. For this reason, let's focus on both the accuracy and the *F-1 measure* on the classification report together. Focusing on both of these metrics should give us a better overall measure of how well the pipeline is doing

Accuracy and F-1 are wonderful for measuring the performance of a classifier, but this is stock price data! It would be fantastic also to consider how much money we would have made if we had listened to the model's predictions! To do this, let's make yet another helper function (I promise this is the last one) to take in the results from our validation pipeline and do the following:

- Calculate the cumulative gains for listening to our pipeline's *first* prediction of the day
- Split out the gains by listening to
  - All predictions
  - Only bullish predictions (stock price will go up)
  - Only bearish predictions (stock price will go down)

We will focus on the total gains for all predictions, as this is the most realistic estimation of cumulative gains for our pipeline. Let's create this function in the following listing.

Listing 7.13 Plotting gains on the first prediction each day

```
def plot_gains(df, response, predictions):
    ''' A simulation of acting on the First prediction of the day '''
    df['predictions'] = predictions
    df['movement_correct_multiplier'] = \
    (predictions == response).map({True: 1, False: -1})
    df['gain'] = df['movement_correct_multiplier'] * \
    df['pct_change_eod'].abs()


    bullish = df[predictions == True]
    bullish_gains = bullish.sort_index().groupby(
        bullish.index.date).head(1)['gain']
    bullish_gains.cumsum().plot(label='Bullish Only', legend=True)
    print(f'Percantage of time with profit for bullish only: \
```

```
{(bullish_gains.cumsum() > 0).mean():.3f}')
    print(f'Total Gains for bullish is {bullish_gains.sum():.3f}')

    bearish = df[predictions == False]
    bearish_gains = bearish.sort_index(
        ).groupby(bearish.index.date).head(1)['gain']
    bearish_gains.cumsum().plot(label='Bearish Only', legend=True)
    print(f'Percantage of time with profit for bearish only: \
{(bearish_gains.cumsum() > 0).mean():.3f}')
    print(f'Total Gains for bearish is {bearish_gains.sum():.3f}')

    gains = df.sort_index().groupby(df.index.date).head(1)['gain']
    gains.cumsum().plot(label='All Predictions', legend=True)
    print(f'Percentage of time with profit for all predictions:
     {(gains.cumsum() > 0).mean():.3f}')
    print(f'Total Gains for all predictions is {gains.sum():.3f}')

    plt.title('Gains')
    plt.xlabel('Time')
    plt.ylabel('Cumulative Gains')

plot_gains(test_df.copy(), test_y, test_preds)
```

The plot_gains function will print out a few stats for us to help interpret how our model is doing. The first two print statements tell us how often we would have had profit (more money than when we started) if we only listened to the model when it predicted bullish (the price will go up) as well as the total gains from listening to the bullish predictions. The next two print statements tell us how often we would have had profit if we only listened to the model when it predicted bearish (the price will go down). The final two print statements give us the same info if we listen to all predictions (bearish and bullish):

- Percentage of time with profit for bullish only: 0.077
- Total gains for bullish: 0.043
- Percentage of time with profit for bearish only: 0.500
- Total gains for bearish: 0.004
- Percentage of time with profit for all predictions: 0.308
- Total gains for all predictions: 0.021

Our results (visually shown in figure 7.14) show that if we listened to the first prediction every day, no matter if it was bullish or bearish (in the line with an arrow pointing to it) we would have accumulated 2.1% of gains, meaning we would have lost money. Not great.

Feature-wise, we made some good progress. We have created several date/time features out of our original *close/volume* columns, such as day-of-week, expanding features, rolling features, and lag features. We could spend all day coming up with more rolling and expanding features, but at the end of the day, most day traders (who are domain experts in this case) will tell you that that isn't enough. To have even a chance of predicting stock price movements you need to bring in some domain-specific features.

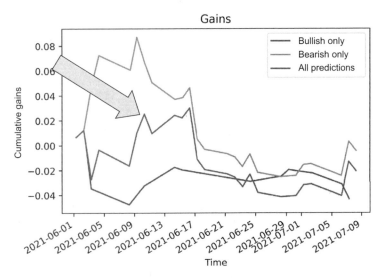

Figure 7.14 Our basic time series features are not giving profit in our validation set. This makes sense, considering we couldn't even beat our null accuracy.

7.2.4 Domain-specific features

Date/time features are an excellent start to any time series case study, but they come with a big problem: they often do not have enough signal to make predictions about future values. More often than not, when dealing with time series data, we have to bring in some *domain-specific features*, which are features that are derived from having knowledge about the specific use case of the data.

In our case, in this chapter, domain-specific features would come from having knowledge about the stock market, finance, and intraday trading. The next few sections will highlight some features that are believed to have some impact on intraday trading.

DAILY PRICE FEATURES

Our first set of domain features is based on the closing price that we have access to. Our strategy here is to calculate some statistics about the price on a larger scale:

1 The market is open for most people during specific hours of the day. But the price does move outside of this window. We will calculate `overnight_change_close` to be the percentage difference between today's opening price and the previous day's closing price.

2 We will want to know how the opening price compares to previous opening prices. We will calculate `monthly_pct_change_close` to represent the percentage change between today's opening price and last month's opening price.

3 Let's keep track of an expanding-average opening price with a feature called `expanding_average_close` to potentially give signal on the current price compared to a running-average opening price.

Let's go ahead and create these features in the following listing.

Listing 7.14   Calculating daily price features

```
daily_features = pd.DataFrame()  ◁——— Make a DataFrame to hold stats about the day itself.

daily_features['first_5_min_avg_close'] = price_df.groupby(
    price_df.index.date
)['close'].apply(lambda x: x.head().mean())
daily_features['last_5_min_avg_close'] = price_df.groupby(
    price_df.index.date
)['close'].apply(lambda x: x.tail().mean())
```

Average the first and last 5 minutes of the day to get opening and closing prices.

```
daily_features['feature__overnight_change_close'] = \
    (daily_features['first_5_min_avg_close'] -
    daily_features['last_5_min_avg_close'].shift(1)) /
    daily_features['last_5_min_avg_close'].shift(1)  ◁
daily_features['feature__monthly_pct_change_close'] =
daily_features['first_5_min_avg_close'].pct_change(
    periods=31)                                     ◁———┐
daily_features['feature__expanding_average_close'] =
daily_features['first_5_min_avg_close'].expanding(
┌——▷  31).mean()
```

The overnight change (percent change from the previous closing price to the current opening price)

A rolling-percent change of opening price (window of 31 datapoints)

An expanding-window function of average opening price (omitting the first 31 datapoints for stability)

Our first batch of features focused on smaller, short-term movements, while these new features are constructed with a larger field of view. In *conjunction with* the features we have already built, the hope is that these features will provide more signals for our pipeline.

But we aren't done! Let's look at a financial indicator often used in day trading: the moving-average convergence divergence.

MOVING-AVERAGE CONVERGENCE DIVERGENCE

The *moving-average convergence divergence (MACD)* is an indicator that highlights the relationship between two rolling averages of a security's price. To calculate MACD, we need to calculate the 26-period exponential moving average and subtract it from the 12-period EMA. The signal line we will use at the end is the 9-period EMA of the MACD line.

The *exponential moving average* (EMA) is an indicator that tracks a value (in this case, the price of TWLO) over time. The EMA gives more weight/importance to recent price data than a simple rolling average, which does not give weight to past/future values. We can calculate the MACD of daily prices with the code in the following listing.

Listing 7.15   Calculating MACD

```
def macd(ticker):                              ◁——— Function to calculate MACD
    exp1 = ticker.ewm(span=12, adjust=False).mean()
    exp2 = ticker.ewm(span=26, adjust=False).mean()
```

```
      macd = exp1 - exp2
      return macd.ewm(span=9, adjust=False).mean()
```

```
daily_features['feature__macd'] =
macd(daily_features['first_5_min_avg_close'])      ⊲┐
```
Calculate MACD, using the opening prices.

```
price_df = price_df.merge(daily_features,
left_on=price_df.index.date, right_index=True)      ⊲┐
price_df.dropna(inplace=True)
```
Merge the daily features into the main price DataFrame.

We have made six new, domain-specific features so far. Surely, these are enough domain features, right? Perhaps, but let's look at another class of features from everyone's favorite black hole: social media!

TWITTER INSIGHTS

I was a lecturer at Johns Hopkins in a past life, and one of my good friends, Dr. Jim Liew, was working on research denoting social media data, Twitter in particular, as a *sixth factor* in determining the behavior of stock on a given day (https://jpm.pm-research .com/content/43/3/102). Since then, I have adopted this mentality in my own day trading, and I believe it is interesting to talk about here. The work focused specifically on tweet sentiment. In this case study, we will take inspiration from this team and use social media statistics to help us predict stock market movements. But where will we get Twitter data?

Not to worry! I have been monitoring tweets about certain companies for years now, and I am happy to share this data with you (listing 7.16). Specifically, the following DataFrame we are about to ingest is every tweet that mentions the cashtag of Twilio. This means every tweet should have the word *$TWLO*, which signifies the tweet is meant to be about Twilio.

Listing 7.16 Ingesting Twitter data

```
tweet_df = pd.read_csv(f"../data/twlo_tweets.csv", encoding='ISO-8859-1')

tweet_df.index = pd.to_datetime(tweet_df['date_tweeted'])
tweet_df.index = tweet_df.index.tz_convert('US/Pacific')
del tweet_df['date_tweeted']

tweet_df.sort_index(inplace=True)
tweet_df.dropna(inplace=True)

tweet_df.head()
```

The DataFrame (seen in figure 7.15) has the following columns:

- Date_tweeted (DateTime)—The date that the tweet went out to the world
- Text (string)—The text of the tweet
- Tweet_unique_id (string)—The unique ID given by Twitter

- `Author_verified` (Boolean)—Whether or not the author was verified at the time of posting
- `Num_followers` (numerical)—The number of followers the author had at the time of posting

date_tweeted	text	tweet_unique_id	author_verified	num_followers
2019-12-01 00:31:34-08:00	RT @BrianFeroldi: Tech stocks I follow ranked ...	1.201056e+18	False	1557.0
2019-12-01 01:03:56-08:00	Benjamin Graham and the Power of Groth Stocks ...	1.201064e+18	False	1150.0
2019-12-01 01:25:16-08:00	RT @BrianFeroldi: Tech stocks I follow ranked ...	1.201070e+18	False	3887.0
2019-12-01 01:34:11-08:00	RT @BrianFeroldi: Tech stocks I follow ranked ...	1.201072e+18	False	881.0
2019-12-01 01:55:24-08:00	RT @BrianFeroldi: Tech stocks I follow ranked ...	1.201077e+18	False	6.0

Figure 7.15   Twitter data mentioning the cashtag $TWLO to give us a sense of what people are saying about the stock

Let's create two new features (listing 7.17):

- A rolling total count of tweets with a window of 7 days
- A rolling number of *verified* tweets

Listing 7.17   Rolling tweet count

```
rolling_7_day_total_tweets = tweet_df.resample(
    '1T')['tweet_unique_id'].count().rolling('7D').sum()

rolling_7_day_total_tweets.plot(title='Weekly Rolling Count of Tweets')
plt.xlabel('Time')
plt.ylabel('Number of Tweets')

rolling_1_day_verified_count = tweet_df.resample(
    '1T')['author_verified'].sum().rolling('1D').sum()

rolling_1_day_verified_count.plot(
    title='Daily Rolling Count of Verified Tweets')
plt.xlabel('Time')
plt.ylabel('Number of Verified Tweets')
```

Listing 7.18 will merge the statistics we calculated from our Twitter data with the original price DataFrame. To do this we will

1. Create a new DataFrame with the two features we want to incorporate: the rolling 7-day count of tweets and the rolling 1-day count of verified tweets. Figure 7.16 shows what these two new features look like when plotted over time.
2. Set the index of the new DataFrame to be a `datetime` to make merging possible.
3. Merge the two DataFrames using the `merge` method in pandas.

Listing 7.18   Merging Twitter stats into the price DataFrame

```
twitter_stats = pd.DataFrame({
    'feature__rolling_7_day_total_tweets': rolling_7_day_total_tweets,
    'feature__rolling_1_day_verified_count': rolling_1_day_verified_count
})          ◁────── Create a DataFrame with the twitter stats.

twitter_stats.index = pd.to_datetime(
    twitter_stats.index)
twitter_stats.index = twitter_stats.index.tz_convert(
    'US/Pacific')

price_df = price_df.merge(
    twitter_stats, left_index=True, right_index=True)    ◁──
```

Standardize the index to make the following merge easier.

Merge Twitter stats into our price DataFrame.

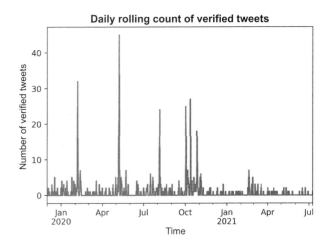

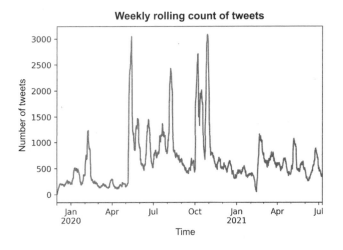

Figure 7.16   Our two Twitter-based features will help the model understand how the Twitterverse is thinking about TWLO.

OK, phew! We now have a bunch of new features. I think it's time to see how these new features work out!

EXERCISE 7.2   In preparation for running our pipeline again, find the Pearson correlation coefficient between our response variable and our two new Twitter features on the training set. Compare that to the correlation between the other features. What insights can you glean from that information?

RUNNING OUR PIPELINE AGAIN

We've spent a good amount of time creating a handful of domain-specific features based on our knowledge about the stock market and how people talk about the stock market on Twitter. Let's pause and run our pipeline again with our new features to see if we've successfully added any new signal to our pipeline in the following listing.

Listing 7.19   Running our pipeline with domain-specific features

```
train_df, test_df, train_X, train_y, test_X, test_y = split_data(price_df)

print("Add Domain Features\n==========================")
best_model, test_preds, test_probas = advanced_grid_search(
    train_X, train_y,
    test_X, test_y,
    ml_pipeline, params,
    cv=tscv, include_probas=True
)
```

Let's take another look at our resulting classification report in figure 7.17.

```
Add Domain Features
============================
```

	precision	recall	f1-score	support
False	0.53	0.92	0.67	72
True	0.62	0.14	0.24	69
accuracy			0.54	141
macro avg	0.58	0.53	0.45	141
weighted avg	0.58	0.54	0.46	141

Figure 7.17   Results from adding domain-specific features like MACD and our Twitter features gave us a bump in accuracy to 54%, which beats our null accuracy!

OK! Our accuracy and weighted F-1 score have increased from 48% to 54% and from 41% to 46%. This is a big boost! Let's see how we would have performed, listening to this pipeline on our validation data. We can do this by running our `plot_gains` function on our test data:

```
plot_gains(test_df.copy(), test_y, test_preds)
```

The results, as before, will show us how much our model has improved. We will be most concerned with the "total gains for all predictions" number, which represents the total amount of gains we could have seen had we listened to our model:

- Percentage of time with profit: 0.375 for bullish only
- Total gains for bullish: 0.036
- Percentage of time with profit: 1.000 for bearish only
- Total gains for bearish: 0.059
- Percentage of time with profit: 1.000 for all predictions
- Total gains for all predictions: 0.150

Wow! Cumulative gains of 15%! This is definitely a huge increase in quality. Let's take a look at our gains graph (figure 7.18), and our total gains line—the one with an arrow—is definitely looking positive!

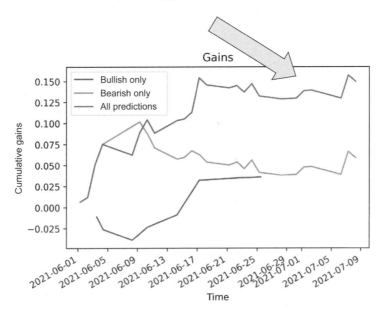

Figure 7.18   Our latest model taking MACD and Twitter features is showing massive improvement!

OK, we have made some significant progress, but let's take a step back and think about how many features we've constructed. With all of these features, it would be wise to at least test out a few feature selection techniques.

7.3   *Feature selection*

In chapter 3, we began our journey in feature selection by relying on the `SelectFrom-Model` module from scikit-learn to use ML to select features for us. Let's bring back that thinking and see if there is any noise we can remove from our dataset to boost our performance at all.

7.3.1   Selecting features using ML

SelectFromModel is a meta-transformer that requires an estimator to rank features. Any feature that falls below a given threshold, which is denoted by comparing the importance to the mean or median rank, is eliminated as potential noise. Let's use SelectFromModel as a feature selector, and let it try both logistic regression and another random forest classifier as the estimator.

The main parameter we have to be concerned with is threshold. Features with importance determined by the estimator as greater than or equal to the threshold are kept, while the other features are discarded. We can set hard thresholds with floats, or we can set thresholds to be dynamic. For example, we could set the threshold value as median, then the threshold would be set to the median of the calculated feature importances. We may also introduce a scaling factor to scale dynamic values. For example, we could set the threshold to be 0.5*mean, where the threshold would be half of the average feature importance. Let's use the SelectFromModel object to try and remove noise from our dataset in the following listing.

Listing 7.20   Using SelectFromModel to restrict features

```
from sklearn.feature_selection import SelectFromModel
from sklearn.linear_model import LogisticRegression

rf = RandomForestClassifier(
    n_estimators=20, max_depth=None, random_state=0)
lr = LogisticRegression(random_state=0)

ml_pipeline = Pipeline([
    ('scale', StandardScaler()),
    ('select_from_model', SelectFromModel(estimator=rf)),
    ('classifier', clf)
])

params.update({
    'select_from_model__threshold': [
        '0.5 * mean', 'mean', '0.5 * median', 'median'
    ],
    'select_from_model__estimator':  [rf, lr]
})

print("Feature Selection (SFM) \n==========================")
best_model, test_preds, test_probas = advanced_grid_search(
    train_X, train_y,
    test_X, test_y,
    ml_pipeline, params,
    cv=tscv, include_probas=True
)
```

> The feature importances in this random forest will dictate which features to select.

> Set a few different potential thresholds, using our scaled dynamic threshold options.

Our latest classification report (figure 7.19) is not very promising. Overall accuracy dropped to below 50%.

```
Feature Selection (SFM)
===========================
                precision    recall    f1-score    support

      False        0.49       0.71       0.58          72
       True        0.43       0.23       0.30          69

   accuracy                              0.48         141
  macro avg        0.46       0.47       0.44         141
weighted avg       0.46       0.48       0.44         141
```

Figure 7.19   Our results after applying the `SelectFromModel` feature selection algorithm are showing a drop in performance to 48% accuracy. This implies that most features the algorithm tried to throw away were, in fact, useful to the pipeline.

Our performance definitely got worse. Both accuracy and weighted F-1 have decreased from our last run. Hmmm … perhaps, we can try another feature selector that is a bit pickier and deliberative in how it selects features.

7.3.2   *Recursive feature elimination*

Recursive feature elimination (RFE) is a popular feature selection technique. RFE is another meta feature selection technique, just like `SelectFromModel`. RFE similarly uses an ML algorithm to select features. Rather than ranking features like `Select-FromModel` and removing them in bulk, RFE works iteratively, removing a few columns at a time. The process can be generally described as follows:

1   The estimator (random forest in this case) fits the features to our response variable.
2   The estimator calculates the least useful features and removes them from consideration for the next round.
3   This process continues until we reach the desired number of features to select (by default scikit-learn tries to choose half of our features, but this is grid searchable).

The following listing and the resulting figure 7.20 show how we can use RFE to also try to remove noise from our features.

Listing 7.21   Using RFE to restrict features

```
from sklearn.feature_selection import RFE

ml_pipeline = Pipeline([
    ('scale', StandardScaler()),
    ('rfe', RFE(estimator=rf)),
    ('classifier', clf)
])

params.update({
    'rfe__n_features_to_select': [0.6, 0.7, 0.8, 0.9],
    'rfe__estimator':  [rf, lr]
```

```
})

print("Feature Selection (RFE) \n==========================")
best_model, test_preds, test_probas = advanced_grid_search(
    train_X, train_y,
    test_X, test_y,
    ml_pipeline, params,
    cv=tscv, include_probas=True
)
del params['rfe__n_features_to_select']
del params['rfe__estimator']
```

```
Feature Selection (RFE)
==========================
              precision    recall  f1-score   support

       False       0.45      0.58      0.51        72
        True       0.38      0.26      0.31        69

    accuracy                           0.43       141
   macro avg       0.41      0.42      0.41       141
weighted avg       0.41      0.43      0.41       141
```

Figure 7.20   Results from using recursive feature elimination show an even bigger drop in performance to 43%. This is our worst performing pipeline yet. But the night is often darkest before dawn.

```
plot_gains(test_df.copy(), test_y, test_preds)
```

Taking a look at our results reveals a not-so-bright picture:

- Percentage of time with profit: 0.000 for bullish only
- Total gains for bullish: 0.063
- Percentage of time with profit: 0.381 for bearish only
- Total gains for bearish: 0.027
- Percentage of time with profit: 0.077 for all predictions
- Total gains for all predictions: 0.100

Our gains graph (figure 7.21) confirms that our models took a serious dip in performance.

Both of our feature selectors are removing too much signal from our pipelines and really hurting our models. This is signaling two things, as follows:

- The features we constructed are quite good on their own.
- The feature set size is too small for noise to be discernible from signal.

Let's try one more thing here to see if we can put those feature selectors to work without having them get confused from a small feature set size. Let's try extracting some brand new features from the ones we've just constructed.

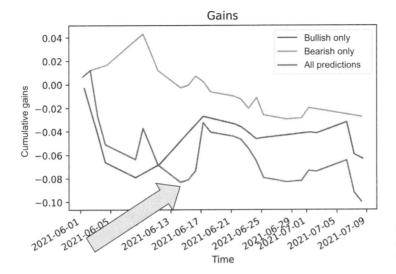

Figure 7.21 RFE is definitely removing too much signal as well.

7.4 Feature extraction

As we've been creating features, our goal has been to provide as much signal as possible for our ML pipeline to allow it to accurately predict intraday stock price movement. Our classifier (a random forest model, in this case) is tasked with using all of the available features to predict the response, and importantly, it uses multiple features at a time to make this prediction.

When it comes to ML, it is about how features interact with one another. Right now we have about a dozen features, but what if we wanted to combine them to construct even more, potentially more useful signals? For example, what if MACD multiplied by the rolling verified tweet count provides a more powerful signal than either of the original two features? I suppose we could manually try each combination, but there is an automated way to help us, and of course, it is implemented in scikit-learn.

7.4.1 Polynomial feature extraction

Scikit-learn has a module called `PolynomialFeatures`, which automatically generates interactions between our original features. For example, let's, for a minute, assume that our only features were

- `rolling_close_mean_60`
- `rolling_7_day_total_tweets`
- `morning`

As an exercise, let's extract third- or lower-degree polynomial (`PolynomialFeatures (degree=3)`) features for our three original columns. This means we would want all possible features' first-, second-, and third-order interactions (multiplications). For example, this would include the raw feature `morning` as well as `morning` cubed. A complete list of features in order would be as follows:

- A feature of all 1s (representing the constant bias in a polynomial)
- rolling_close_mean_60
- rolling_7_day_total_tweets
- morning
- rolling_close_mean_60 $^\wedge$ 2
- rolling_close_mean_60 $\times$ Rolling_7_day_total_tweets
- rolling_close_mean_60 $\times$ morning
- rolling_7_day_total_tweets $^\wedge$ 2
- rolling_7_day_total_tweets $\times$ morning
- morning $^\wedge$ 2
- rolling_close_mean_60 $^\wedge$ 3
- rolling_close_mean_60 $^\wedge$ 2 $\times$ rolling_7_day_total_tweets
- rolling_close_mean_60 $^\wedge$ 2 $\times$ morning
- rolling_close_mean_60 $\times$ rolling_7_day_total_tweets $^\wedge$ 2
- rolling_close_mean_60 $\times$ rolling_7_day_total_tweets $\times$ morning
- rolling_close_mean_60 $\times$ morning $^\wedge$ 2
- rolling_7_day_total_tweets $^\wedge$ 3
- rolling_7_day_total_tweets $^\wedge$ 2 $\times$ morning
- rolling_7_day_total_tweets $\times$ morning $^\wedge$ 2
- morning $^\wedge$ 3

The following listing contains a code sample for doing the above extraction.

Listing 7.22   Polynomial feature extraction example

```
from sklearn.preprocessing import PolynomialFeatures

p = PolynomialFeatures(3)
small_poly_features = p.fit_transform(
    price_df[['feature__rolling_close_mean_60',
    'feature__rolling_7_day_total_tweets',
    'feature__morning']])

pd.DataFrame(small_poly_features, columns=p.get_feature_names())
```

The resulting DataFrame (figure 7.22) shows a snippet of the many features created.

Now, a lot of these features are likely a lot of noise (e.g., morning $^\wedge$ 2), so let's build a final pipeline in listing 7.23 that extracts only up to second-degree features (which

		1	x0	x1	x2	x0^2	x0 x1
	0	1.0	108.297719	213.0	1.0	11728.396017	23067.414223
	1	1.0	108.330916	213.0	1.0	11735.587280	23074.485028
	2	1.0	108.358464	213.0	1.0	11741.556642	23080.352755
	3	1.0	108.384685	213.0	1.0	11747.240006	23085.937968
	4	1.0	108.405694	213.0	1.0	11751.794554	23090.412883
	...	...	...	...	...	...	...
	113257	1.0	384.732251	361.0	0.0	148018.905101	138888.342677
	113258	1.0	384.714454	361.0	0.0	148005.211319	138881.917989
	113259	1.0	384.690810	361.0	0.0	147987.019194	138873.382361
	113260	1.0	384.676488	361.0	0.0	147976.000273	138868.212099
	113261	1.0	384.656996	362.0	0.0	147961.004870	139245.832692

113262 rows × 20 columns

Figure 7.22 Polynomial features extract automatic interactions between features to generate more signals hidden in the combination of our originally constructed features.

will generate 152 new features), excluding the bias (the all 1s feature) and relies on the SelectFromModel module to filter out the noise. Fingers crossed.

Listing 7.23 Polynomial features + SelectFromModel

```
from sklearn.preprocessing import PolynomialFeatures

ml_pipeline = Pipeline([
    ('poly', PolynomialFeatures(1, include_bias=False)),
    ('scale', StandardScaler()),
    ('select_from_model', SelectFromModel
(estimator=rf)),          ⟵         Adding in SelectFromModel
    ('classifier', clf)                 into our pipeline
])

params.update({
    'select_from_model__threshold': [
        '0.5 * mean', 'mean', '0.5 * median', 'median'],
    'select_from_model__estimator': [rf, lr],
    'poly__degree': [2],
})
```

```
print("Polynomial Features \n==========================")
best_model, test_preds, test_probas = advanced_grid_search(
    train_X, train_y,
    test_X, test_y,
    ml_pipeline, params,
    cv=tscv, include_probas=True
)
```

The classification report (figure 7.23) reveals a model with an accuracy on par with where we'd want it to be with the highest weighted F-1-score of any model so far.

```
Polynomial Features
===========================

                precision    recall   f1-score   support

        False        0.53      0.68       0.59        72
         True        0.52      0.36       0.43        69

     accuracy                             0.52       141
    macro avg        0.52      0.52       0.51       141
 weighted avg        0.52      0.52       0.51       141
```

Figure 7.23   Introducing polynomial features and relying on the `SelectFromModel` feature selector has put us back to an accuracy above our null accuracy, but it is not the strongest accuracy we have seen. However, it does have the highest weighted F-1 score of any of our pipelines.

OK! Now we are talking. Let's take a look at our estimated gains, using this new pipeline:

```
plot_gains(test_df.copy(), test_y, test_preds)
```

- Percentage of time with profit: 0.737 for bullish only
- Total gains for bullish: 0.028
- Percentage of time with profit: 1.000 for bearish only
- Total gains for bearish: 0.095
- Percentage of time with profit: 1.000 for all predictions
- Total gains for all predictions: 0.158

This is excellent! It may only be a small boost in gains, but our model is performing much better. Once again, the line with the arrow pointing to it represents our overall model's performance by way of cumulative gains in our latest gains graph (figure 7.24).

It looks like we were able to boost our trading performance after all! All it took was coupling a feature extraction technique with a feature selection technique. Let's take a step back and look at the final feature engineering pipeline we've constructed to perform this tricky task. Figure 7.25 visualizes the pipeline from our latest run, showing how we manipulated our raw data and merged them with Twitter and the MACD. It then shows how we took our features and ran them through an automatic feature extractor and, finally, a feature selector to filter out any noise.

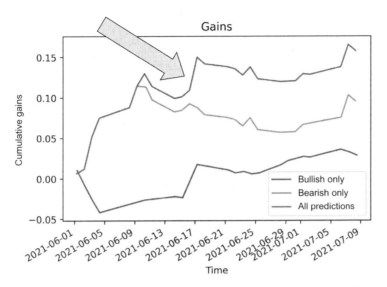

Figure 7.24   Our best pipeline yet extracts a large set of features and relies on `SelectFromModel` to remove the noise for us.

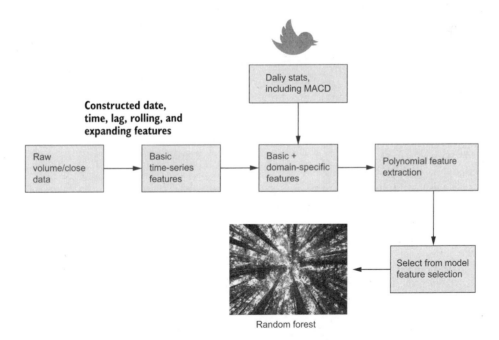

Random forest

Figure 7.25   Our best pipeline represented as a series of steps from our initial date/time feature construction to the introduction of domain features from Twitter all the way to our feature extraction and selection modules

7.5   Conclusion

Time series data present a whole new world of options for data scientists. We can generate our own response variables, construct our features from scratch, and interpret our results in a more creative way! Let's take a look in table 7.1 at what we did in this chapter.

Table 7.1   **An overview of the many attempts we've made to predict stock price movement**

Description of pipeline	Accuracy	Weighted F-1	Cumulative gains on validation set
Date/time, rolling, expanding window, and lag features	48%	0.41	-2.1%
Adding domain features	**54%**	0.46	15%
All features + `SelectFromModel`	48%	0.44	0.4%
All features + RFE	43%	0.41	-10%
All features + polynomial extraction + SFM	52%	**0.51**	**15.8%**

When dealing with your time series dataset, it can be very ephemeral. We don't have clear features, and we, often, don't have a clear response variable. We can, however, think about five key considerations:

- What is the response variable going to be? What will our ML pipeline be trying to predict? This is usually some variation of trying to predict a future value of a system like the stock market.
- How can we construct basic date/time features from our raw data, using techniques like expanding windows and lag features?
- What domain-specific features can we construct? MACD is an example of a feature that is specific to day trading.
- Are there any other sources of data we could bring in? In our case, we brought in Twitter data to augment our pipeline.
- Can we automatically extract feature interactions and select the ones that improve our model the most?

These five thoughts should be at the forefront of our mind when dealing with time series data, and if we can answer all five of them, then we have a great chance of being successful with our time series data.

7.6   Answers to exercises

EXERCISE 7.1

Calculate the rolling 2.5-hour average closing price, and plot that value over the entirety of the training set.

ANSWER:

```
price_df['feature__rolling_close_mean_150'] =
➥ price_df['close'].rolling('150min').mean()
price_df['feature__rolling_close_mean_150'].plot(
    figsize=(20, 10), title='Rolling 150min Close')

plt.xlabel('Time')
plt.ylabel('Price')
```

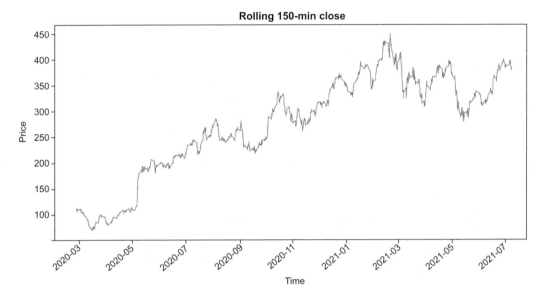

EXERCISE 7.2

In preparation of running our pipeline again, find the Pearson correlation coefficient between our response variable and our two new Twitter features on the training set. Compare that to the correlation between the other features. What insights can you glean from that information?

ANSWER:

If we run the following code, we can get the correlation coefficients between the response and the current set of features:

```
price_df.filter(
    regex='feature__'
).corrwith(
    price_df['stock_price_rose']
).sort_values()

feature__rolling_7_day_total_tweets        -0.030404
feature__dayofweek                         -0.002365
feature__expanding_volume_mean             -0.000644
feature__monthly_pct_change_close           0.001672
feature__rolling_1_day_verified_count       0.005921
```

```
feature__rolling_volume_mean_60          0.007773
feature__rolling_volume_std_60           0.010038
feature__expanding_close_mean            0.024770
feature__expanding_average_close         0.024801
feature__morning                         0.025106
feature__rolling_close_mean_60           0.030839
feature__lag_30_min_ago_price            0.030878
feature__lag_7_day_ago_price             0.031859
feature__macd                            0.037216
feature__overnight_change_close          0.045098
feature__rolling_close_std_60            0.051801
```

Our rolling verified count (`feature__rolling_1_day_verified_count`) has a pretty weak correlation coefficient of .005, but the rolling count of tweets (`feature__ rolling_7_day_ total_tweets`) has a pretty high value of .03. This implies that these features—at least the rolling 7-day tweet count—have a pretty good chance of adding some signal to our model.

Summary

- Time series data allow us to be creative and construct both features and response variables for our ML pipeline.
- All time series data can have constructed date, time, lag, rolling-window, and expanding-window features to provide insight on past periods.
- Domain-specific features, like MACD or social media statistics, tend to enhance ML pipeline performance over just using basic time series features.
- Feature selection does not always lead to a performance boost, especially when all of our features are hand-constructed thoughtfully.
- Feature extraction techniques like polynomial feature extraction can add a boost to overall performance—but not always!
- Combining extraction and selection techniques can be the best of both worlds; the extraction technique will give us potential new signals, while the selection criteria will help prune the noise from the pipeline.

Feature stores

This chapter covers

- Discovering the importance of MLOps to scalable data science and machine learning
- Learning how feature stores help data teams collaborate and store data
- Setting up our own feature store for day trading
- Investigating feature store features that help machine learning engineers and data scientists

So far, in this book, we've been doing solo work, in which you and I are independently running code in a notebook to test different feature engineering algorithms and techniques to try and make the best pipeline we can. At the end of each case study, we've gotten to a place where we are generally happy with our results. Let's say you are working on a project and are on to something. You want to see what it would take to get your ML pipeline and your feature engineering work into a production-ready state. You also want to bring in a trusted partner to help you continue the work, and you want to know how to enable them in any way you can, but all you have is a notebook with code that looks promising.

The next step in pushing your project forward is to consider modern data science and engineering practices to help you collaborate with new team members and to keep your data consistent and easy to use outside of your local development environments and notebooks. In this chapter we look at modern MLOps practices and, specifically, how to deploy and use a cloud-enabled feature store to store, handle, and distribute data.

8.1   MLOps and feature stores

The term *MLOps* builds on of the traditional DevOps principles of system-wide automation and test-driven development. Proper DevOps is meant to enable more sustainable and predictable software, while reducing the time and stress it takes to deploy new versions of software. MLOps extends the principles of automation and test-driven development to provide similar tools and ideas to test and automate ML architectures and pipelines. There are many facets to MLOps, but a few of the major pieces of a successful MLOps architecture include the following:

- *Data ingestion pipelines for data ingestion and aggregation, potentially from multiple data sources*—Data engineers may need to grab data from a MySQL database and join it with data from Apache Kafka or Amazon S3 to create a unified tabular dataset. Along the pipeline, the data may need to go through some log transformations and imputations or even feature selection improvement algorithms.
- *Model training, testing, and versioning*—Once data have been ingested and transformed, we can use the data to train and test our ML models. As we update models with new data and enhanced parameter configurations, we can version them to keep track of which models were used to make which predictions. This gives us the ability to track model performance over time and versions.
- *Ability to continually integrate and deploy pipelines*—Continuous integration and development (CI/CD) is a principle borrowed from DevOps and is concerned with constantly evaluating and deploying new versions of ML models to keep up with the latest data.

Feature stores are a large part of MLOps architectures. A *feature store* is a system or platform made specifically to automate data input, tracking, and governance for ML models. Feature stores were built to simplify the data science workflow by performing and automating many feature engineering tasks on behalf of data scientists. This, in turn, helps make ML pipelines accurate and fast at scale. Feature stores perform a variety of feature engineering–related tasks and, among other things, make sure that features are accurate, up to date, versioned, and consistent. Let's dive right into the many benefits of implementing a feature store.

8.1.1   Benefits of using a feature store

At first glance, after all of the work we have done in this book, it may not seem worthwhile to step back from the algorithms and techniques in Python and dive into feature stores. The benefits of using a feature store, however, start to become clearer and clearer as we switch from a development and research mindset to a scalable, production-ready one. As a whole, the benefits of using a feature store include these:

- Providing a centralized location where features can be used, reused, and understood by various members of a data science organization
- Reducing tedious and time-consuming feature engineering work
- Maximizing ML pipeline performance and the reliability of any deployed ML models
- Providing the ability to serve engineered features to multiple ML pipelines
- Enforcing data expectations and adherence to compliance standards and data governance best practices

Feature stores are particularly useful for data scientists, data engineers, and ML engineers on a data team, as illustrated in figure 8.1. Some of the many reasons a feature store can be useful are

- For the data engineer, feature stores provide a centralized place to enforce data governance, maintain security guidelines, and implement a permission structure to limit access to data when applicable.
- For the ML engineers on the team, they can use a feature store to grab clean data for ML experiments as well as to discover new features from other sources for projects they are already working on.
- For the data scientists on the team, they have a one-stop shop for both raw and clean data. Like the ML engineer, they can discover features for their work, but more often it is the case that a data scientist can use historical raw data to perform crucial analyses that would otherwise prove impossible without such a clean source of data.

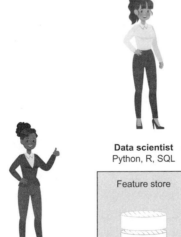

Data scientist
Python, R, SQL

Feature store

Data engineer
SQL, Spark, Flink, Python

ML engineer
Kubernetes, Cloud, Python

Figure 8.1   The feature store is an integral part of ML and data science. It enables data scientists, data engineers, and ML engineers to access the data they need to be the most effective they can be.

Let's dig into a few of these benefits a bit more to see precisely how feature stores can be helpful for us and data teams.

SINGLE SOURCE OF FEATURES

One of the main use cases of a feature store is to provide a single source of data used to train and deploy models for an entire organization. Data and ML teams use feature stores to collaborate in real time with less friction. Much like software engineers rely on Git and GitHub to structure and work on code, so too would data-minded folk use feature stores to structure and work on datasets together. The goal is to leave teams with more time to improve the quality of the features and models they work with, rather than waste time engineering features that have already been engineered by someone else at the organization.

Having a single source of data also enables more creativity across teams. The ability to browse through models and features that other groups or individuals worked on may spark inspiration for a new project, and once the project is kicked off, all know exactly where to find data!

Imagine being a data scientist working for a chatbot company, and one day you are driving on a day trip to the beach (one of my favorite ways to unwind) when you suddenly get an idea for a process that can potentially enhance the performance of the chatbot by monitoring bot conversations' emerging topics of conversation. This isn't technically the project you are working on, but you know that if you came to your team with a prototype of what you are envisioning, then you would be able to work on it.

To develop your prototype and experiment further, you would need the following:

- *User interactions with the bot and, specifically, data around when users abandon the chat*—These data live in a Cassandra database that was set up by someone not on the team anymore, and documentation is sparse on how to get data from there.
- *Historical chat transcripts from your bot*—This metadata about a conversation lives in the PostgreSQL database, while the actual transcripts live in S3. Combining them is easy enough but will take some time.
- *Information about the users chatting with the bot*—These data live in a PostgreSQL database. You have SQL experience, so getting data shouldn't be too difficult.

Even though you technically have a way to get data from all of these sources, without a feature store those ways may involve interrupting other people's work or reading up on documentation that may be outdated or nonexistent (figure 8.2). If only there was a way to have the data flow from these disparate sources to a centralized location with a single source of documentation and features at your disposal.

Well, there is! With a feature store, the data engineering team can set up pipelines to have data flow from all of these disparate sources into a single platform that is queryable by anyone at the organization, given that they have the proper permission levels. In the same scenario, if we had a feature store set up in our organization, you wouldn't have to worry about understanding four different data sources and how to query, join, and load up data from each of them, as shown in figure 8.3.

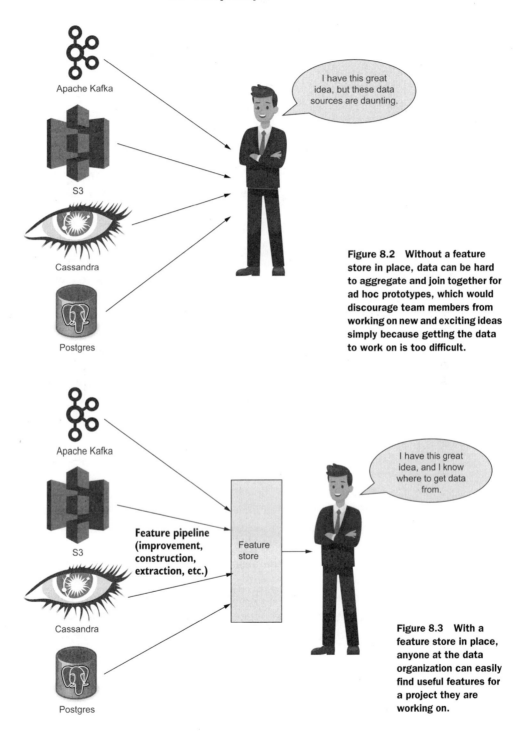

Figure 8.2 Without a feature store in place, data can be hard to aggregate and join together for ad hoc prototypes, which would discourage team members from working on new and exciting ideas simply because getting the data to work on is too difficult.

Figure 8.3 With a feature store in place, anyone at the data organization can easily find useful features for a project they are working on.

Instead of spending all that time aggregating data from your different sources and because your team implemented a feature store, you spent more time working on your prototype and were able to get some solid preliminary results to show your team. Now you are leading the project to bring your prototype to production.

REAL-TIME FEATURE SERVING

Imagine you are scrolling through your social media of choice, and suddenly you are recommended a new person to follow. You squint because you recognize that person. You check, and you are right—you already follow them! You, the ever-curious data scientist, stop to think, "Well, technically, the algorithm was right in that I'd want to follow them because I already do. But if only it told me this a few days earlier, then I could have acted on it sooner."

Unfortunately this is a classic feature engineering dilemma. The features we generated during our training phase built a very performant model, but the features the pipeline uses at prediction time may be old and stale. In the social media recommendation engine example, the data that the recommendation engine had about me was stale. The engine did not realize that I already followed that account and served up a prediction that—while technically accurate—was old and, therefore, a waste of computation time and power.

The ability to serve and read real-time features from a feature store can help alleviate this problem by versioning features and offering only the most up-to-date features built with the latest raw data. This ability to read real-time features at a moment's notice makes it more likely that the model's predictions being generated rely on only the freshest features.

COMPLIANCE AND GOVERNANCE

Data compliance is a requirement for pretty much any enterprise-grade feature store. To meet several guidelines and regulations, we have to maintain the lineage of data and algorithms that are being deployed and used. This is especially important in verticals that handle sensitive data, like financial services or healthcare. A feature store can keep track of data and algorithm lineage, so we can monitor how any given feature or feature value was computed and can provide insights, and even generate reports, that are needed for regulatory compliance.

It is often critical to adhere to many different forms of compliance and best practices in a production system. One of these best practices is maintaining proper lineage from any prediction, from an ML model down to the features used to make that prediction. Let's take a look at how Wikipedia, a nonprofit organization, uses MLOps and feature stores to bring state-of-the-art ML predictions and recommendations to their users.

8.1.2   *Wikipedia, MLOps, and feature stores*

Figure 8.4 shows how Wikipedia is building for continuous ML and feature engineering. Its system seeks to continually improve the quality of its ML models by relying solely on its own users using the platform. Its MLOps framework can be found in the figure 8.4, starting from the top left:

1 Wikipedia extracts user information, like time spent on website and articles clicked on from its website, and places them into its data lake (a database).
2 They transform that user data into usable features for their ML pipelines (using techniques found in this book) for their feature store (the main topic of this chapter).
3 They then use those engineered features from the feature store and convert them into a DataFrame to train a model to, perhaps, provide recommendations for articles to read.
4 Wikipedia compares the new model to the older version against a set of internal metrics and decides whether or not they want to replace the model with the newer version.
5 Finally, it deploys any new model and serves it for real-time predictions.

This process will then repeat itself based on the data team's requirements. Figure 8.4 shows how Wikipedia is building for continuous ML and feature engineering.

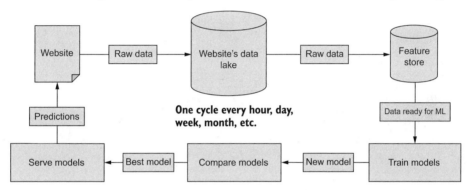

Figure 8.4 The Wikipedia roadmap explains how they are aiming for stronger MLOps to attract more users with accurate predictions, which, in turn, will generate new data to update its models with.

At the company where I currently lead the data science team, we keep to a daily schedule—updating feature values roughly every 24 hours. For some companies, they may opt for a slower cycle—once every week or month, where the age of feature values may not be of the utmost importance. A real estate company may not update values for average home values in a zip code every day, as that information is not likely to drastically change overnight.

Much of the Wikipedia MLOps process should be familiar to us. The website generates raw data, which is put in some data storage (for us, in this book, it was primarily CSVs). Data was used to generate features (the topic of this whole book), and that data is then used to train models and compare feature engineering techniques. Really, the only part of this pipeline we didn't touch at all was serving models, which, in my defense, has very little to do with feature engineering. This highlights that almost all data-driven organizations need to incorporate MLOps into their engineering infrastructure, and if you were to compare multiple organizations' MLOps structures, you would find that they have more in common than they have differences.

8.2   *Setting up a feature store with Hopsworks*

OK, enough talk; let's set up a feature store for ourselves. We have many platforms to choose from. From Uber's Michelangelo Palette to AWS SageMaker to all-in-one data platforms like Databricks. However, let's use an open source feature store and do our part to support the open source community! We will be using Hopsworks as our feature store in this chapter.

Hopsworks (hopsworks.ai) is an open source platform used to develop ML pipelines at scale. The platform has features to serve and version machine learning models; connect to a wide variety of data sources, including AWS Sagemaker and Databricks; and provide a UI to monitor data expectations and user permission levels. Hopsworks is one of the most feature-rich open source platforms out there to provide enterprise-grade feature store capabilities. Figure 8.5 is taken directly from Hopsworks's website and showcases the plethora of features they offer when building a full AI lifecycle.

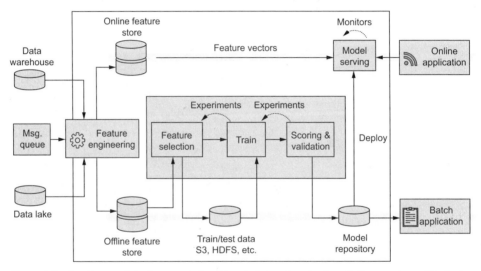

Figure 8.5   Per Hopsworks's documentation (found at docs.hopsworks.ai), Hopsworks and its feature store is an open source platform used to develop and operate ML models at scale. It offers a multitude of services, but today, we will focus on its feature store capabilities.

We will be working with the Hopsworks Feature Store portion of the platform, both through its UI and its API, known as Hopsworks Feature Store API (HSFS). The API uses DataFrames as its main data object, so we won't have to change up how we have been manipulating data to work with Hopsworks. Most modern feature store APIs, including those for Databricks, AWS SageMaker, and Feast, also use some kind of DataFrame-esque object as well, but for now, let's dive right in and start connecting with the Hopsworks Feature Store!

8.2.1   *Connecting to Hopsworks with the HSFS API*

The HSFS API has both a Python and a Scala/Java implementation available. We will stick to our tried-and-true Python implementations and use the Python API wrapper.

Most of the code snippets in this chapter can be executed as is, using either a PySpark or a regular Python environment.

To get started with your feature store, you can

1 Register for a free account on www.hopsworks.ai or install open source Hopsworks (https://github.com/logicalclocks/hopsworks) on your own machine. I went with the free account on Hopsworks.

2 Install the HSFS library: `pip3 install hsfs`.

As of writing, Hopsworks offers a 14-day free demo account, which I chose to use for this chapter. If you would rather set up your own instance on AWS, for example, the steps would be as follows:

1 Sign up for an account on hopsworks.ai.

2 Under Clusters, select your cloud provider. I went with Connect Your AWS Account (figure 8.6).

3 Follow the step-by-step instructions to connect your cloud provider.

4 Let Hopsworks spin up the resources for your feature store!

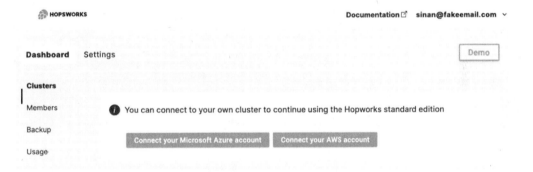

Figure 8.6 Hopsworks can create a cluster for you by connecting to either Azure or AWS as a cloud provider. If you select the AWS option, you can follow the step-by-step tutorial on connecting AWS with Hopsworks. It took me about 15–20 minutes to set it up for the first time.

Once we are set up with a feature store ready to go, whether we've installed it locally or set up a hosted version on hopsworks.ai, we are prepared to use our API wrapper to establish our first connection to the feature store, shown in the following listing.

Listing 8.1   Connecting to Hopsworks using Python

Import a new module to connect to Hopsworks.

```
import hsfs
connection = hsfs.connection(
    host="uuid_if_you_use_hosted_version.cloud.hopsworks.ai",
    project="day_trading",
    api_key_value="XX123XX"
)
fs = connection.get_feature_store(name='day_trading_featurestore')
```

The host of your instance

The API key

The name of the project. Mine is day_trading.

Connect to the feature store.

Nice! Now we have a successful connection to our feature store. Let's take a look at what it looks like on their sleek UI (figure 8.7).

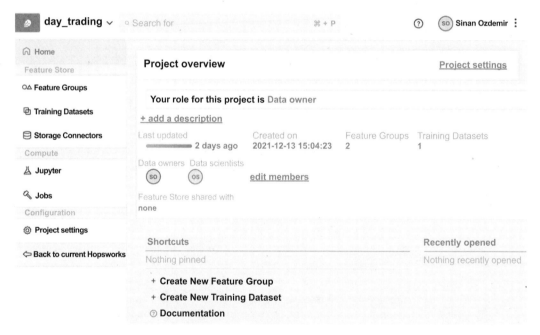

Figure 8.7   The Hopsworks UI for feature stores offers a visual way to navigate their platform. Note the name of the project is at the top left. For me this is `day_trading`.

Now, we have a connection to our feature store; it's time to upload some features! Let's look at our first concept in Hopsworks: the feature group.

8.2.2 Feature groups

After we've done the difficult work of identifying features for our ML pipelines, we can create a feature pipeline to store these feature values in our feature store. As we write our features, we want to organize them into buckets that delineate between the kinds of features we are using. For example, in our day trading use case, we had features we derived from our closing and volume and an additional set of features derived from Twitter. We can logically separate these two groups into what Hopsworks calls feature groups. A *feature group* is a set of mutable (i.e., values are editable) features and feature values that are stored and retrieved together within the feature store. Feature groups provide an easy-to-read and easy-to-digest name and description of the group's features as well as easy feature discovery by other data team members.

Let's consider a hypothetical video streaming service à la Netflix or YouTube. If an internal team is working on a new kind of recommendation engine for their videos, and they are setting up a feature store, some examples of feature groups they may create include the following:

- *User demographic info*—A feature group holding demographic features about website users (e.g., date of birth or location) to make recommendations based on user preferences
- *Recommendation engine features*—A catchall feature group that holds all relevant features for the recommendation engine under development
- *Video metadata*—A feature group that holds basic features about the video, including video length, when the video was uploaded, or location that the video was uploaded

Feature groups allow data teams to bucket features together into groups, but it is up to us how we want to separate them. When deciding how to organize which features into which feature groups, usually the following factors are considered:

- Ownership and access control. Some groups may only have access to certain types of data.
  - Perhaps we don't want all data teams to have access to a *User Demographic Info* feature group to protect user data privacy.
- Whether or not a specific ML pipeline/project uses those features.
  - The *Recommendation Engine Features* feature group in our example would be a pretty expansive feature group but could prove useful if the team has a handful of active projects. These feature groups would provide a quick and easy way to switch between features used by the different projects.
- If features share a specific relationship, including the source of the features, or they describe the same object or group of objects in our system.
  - All features in the *Video Metadata* feature group represent basic information about a video, and therefore, it makes sense that they are in the same feature group.

NOTE   I would not generally recommend creating features purely based on which ML pipelines will be using them because that would defeat one of the most useful features of a feature store—the ability to reuse features from feature groups across projects. Grouping features by pipeline/project is more useful for larger data organizations with dozens of active projects going on in tandem.

For our case today, let's separate our features based on their relationships to each other. We will have one feature group for Twitter features and another for the rest of our features. This is a logical separation based on the features' relationships (that is, their sources). When creating a feature group, we need to consider two main options. We first have to consider the type of feature group, which is either cached or on-demand. *Cached* feature groups grab data from connecting sources (e.g., PostgreSQL, Cassandra, or S3) and store the values on Hopsworks for retrieval. *On-demand* feature groups will not store features on Hopsworks but will retrieve/compute features from the connecting sources whenever a user calls for them. Cached feature groups are faster for feature value retrieval but require periodic or streaming jobs to send data from their original source to Hopsworks.

The second consideration when creating a feature group only matters if we choose the cached type. If we have a cached feature group, we can choose whether we want to enable *online feature serving* that will set up a secondary database on Hopsworks to provide a low-latency (i.e., fast) method of obtaining the most recent feature values for a given entity. Imagine our day trading use case. If we populate a feature group with values for TWLO for all of 2020 and 2021 and choose to retrieve them all at once, that would be offline retrieval. If we enable online serving, then we could grab the most recent value for TWLO to make a real-time prediction. The alternative is not enabling online serving and relying on offline retrieval, which is enabled by default. Offline feature groups are basically a tabular DataFrame in the cloud that we can access whenever we need. Figure 8.8 shows the UI in Hopsworks for creating a new feature group and the parameter fields required.

Create New Feature Group

Feature Group Name	Description optional
cached feature group	Cached feature groups store values on Hopsworks. Online serving allows for low-latency retrieval

Mode

● Cached feature group ○ On-demand feature group

■ Enable Online Feature Serving for this Feature Group

Create New Feature Group

Feature Group Name	Description optional
on-demand feature group	On-demand feature groups compute values from original sources and do not store values on Hopsworks

Mode

○ Cached feature group ● On-demand feature group

Figure 8.8   Feature groups can either be created as cached (top), which will store the feature values directly on Hopsworks or on-demand (bottom), which computes feature values in real time and does not store any values on Hopsworks.

Cached feature groups

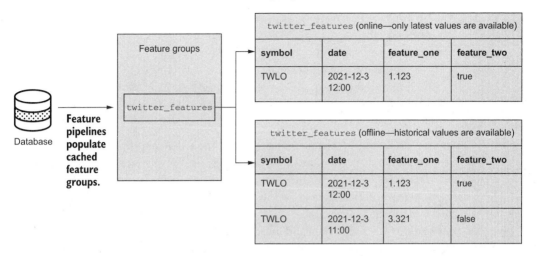

Figure 8.9 A cached feature group `twitter_features` that is available both online and offline. Only the most recent information about a stock entity is stored in the online version. In the offline version, we can see the historical values for all of our Twitter features.

Figure 8.9 depicts a feature group called `twitter_features` that we are going to make in a later section. This feature group will be cached and made to be available online. Remember that *cached* means we will store the feature values directly on Hopsworks, and *online* means that we have the option to retrieve recent values with very low latency. Figure 8.10 depicts what our feature group would look like had we decided to go with an on-demand feature group instead and had our data stored somewhere other than Hopsworks.

On-demand feature groups

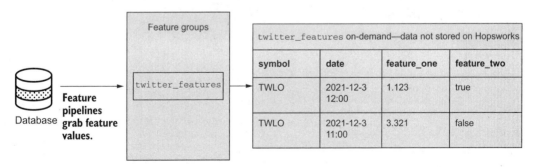

Figure 8.10 An on-demand feature group `twitter_features` will grab data from the connecting database (e.g., MySQL or S3) whenever the user requests the data and will not store any values on Hopsworks.

To recap, the options when creating a feature group are the following:

- The *type* of the feature group can either be cached, meaning it stores feature values on Hopsworks, or on-demand, meaning it will compute feature values in real time, using a connection to a database like SQL.
- If we choose a cached feature group, we can choose to retrieve values *online*, which means the feature group can be used for real-time serving of features. If a feature group is *offline*, the feature value histories are also stored for testing purposes or a cohort analysis.

On-demand sounds like online, and honestly, their definitions can be easy to mix up. Just remember that on-demand feature groups are simply pass-through entities that enable data access from multiple sources through a single point, whereas online feature groups can offer the most recent feature values by storing them on Hopsworks for faster retrieval.

Let's come back to our data and import the features from one of our best-performing day trading models from the last chapter, then make sure that our date column is formatted adequately as a datetime because this will be a crucial column for us. The steps in listing 8.2 are

1. Import a CSV file with features constructed in the last chapter.
2. We will add a new column to our DataFrame called *symbol* to signify the company we are working within in case we want to add new companies later on. In our case we will only have one symbol, but think of this column as a way to differentiate the multiple stock tickers we will eventually be adding to our feature group.
3. Format the *date* column, using Python's datetime.strptime feature to transform the values from a string to a datetime.
4. Set the index of our DataFrame to be our new datetime values, so we can localize the datetimes into Pacific Time (where I am located).

Listing 8.2   Ingesting our data from the day trading case study

```
import datetime
import pandas as pd

day_trading_features = pd.read_csv(
    '../data/fifteen_percent_gains_features.csv')
day_trading_features['symbol'] = 'TWLO'

day_trading_features['date'] = day_trading_features[
    'date'].apply(
        lambda x:datetime.datetime.strptime(
            x[:-6], '%Y-%m-%d %H:%M:%S'))

day_trading_features.set_index('date', inplace=True)

day_trading_features = day_trading_features.tz_localize(
    'US/Pacific')

day_trading_features['date'] = day_trading_features.index.astype(int)
```

Read in the feature set from one of our best-performing models from the day trading case study.

Add a feature called symbol to signal that these refer to TWLO.

format our datetime a=using Python's datetime strptime feature.

Set our index to be our date feature and localize to US/Pacific.

Once we have our data ready, we can create a feature group using the code in listing 8.3. Let's save our Twitter features into our first feature group, using the `create_feature_group` method in our feature store. This work is usually done by the data engineer of the organization or, more likely, is done as part of a larger feature pipeline. We are wearing multiple hats, so let's put on our data engineer hat and upload some data in listing 8.3.

As we prepare our data for the feature store, we have to be aware of a couple of things:

- We will need to specify which column is the `primary_key` that identifies unique entities in our data. The primary key is usually an indicator of an object for which we are tracking feature values. Oftentimes, this will be something like a user of a website, a location we are monitoring, or a stock price ticker we wish to track.
- We will need to specify which column is our `event_time` column, which allows for time-joins between feature groups and also tells the feature store which values are older or newer than others.

In our case, we will use the *symbol* column as our `primary_key` and our *date* column as our `event_time` column. The code block in listing 8.3 will

1 Create a feature group using some named parameters to identify the features and enable online usage.
2 Select only the Twitter-related features from our DataFrame as well as our *date* and *symbol* columns. Our *date* feature will be used as our `event_time` feature, which tells the feature store which feature values are earlier and later, while our *symbol* column will act as our `primary_key`.

Listing 8.3 Creating our first feature group

The primary key of our table identifies the entities in the data.

```
twitter_fg = fs.create_feature_group(
    name="twitter_features",          ← The name of our feature group
    primary_key=["symbol"],
    event_time = "date",              ← The event_time tells the feature store which data points are more recent.
    version=1,                        ←
    description="Twitter Features",       We can version features, but that won't be covered in this text.
    online_enabled=True
)
```

A brief description of the feature group

```
twitter_features = day_trading_features[
    ['symbol', 'date', 'feature__rolling_7_day_total_tweets',
    'feature__rolling_1_day_verified_count']]
twitter_fg.save(twitter_features)
```

Select the Twitter features, and save them to our feature group.

Enabling online feature groups gives us the ability to get the most recent feature values quickly.

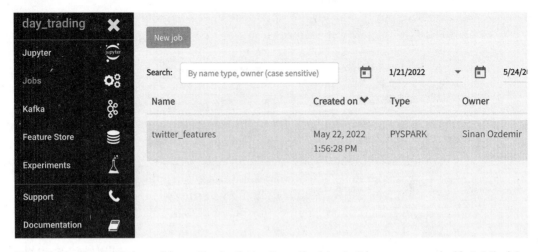

Figure 8.11   Hopsworks has a Jobs section to display the active jobs. In this case, we are looking at the job to upload our data.

Once we run this code, it should give us a URL to monitor data upload through a Job on Hopsworks (figure 8.11). Once the upload is complete, we follow the same steps to create our second feature group with every column except the two Twitter features (listing 8.4).

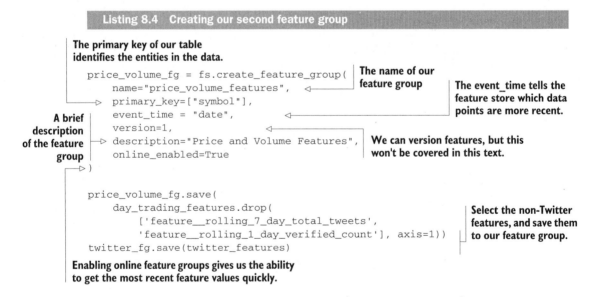

We can also see the features in the UI by navigating to the feature group in the Hops-works UI, as seen in figure 8.12.

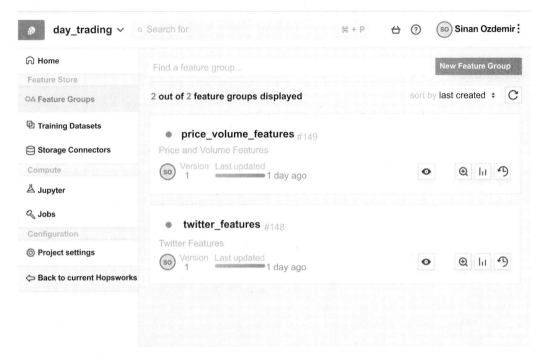

Figure 8.12   Our two feature groups, logically separated by how we created them. We have one for price, volume, and date-time-related features and another for Twitter-related features. Each feature group has the symbol and date feature in common to perform joins.

Excellent! We have done a lot in the past few sections, so let's take a minute to recap what we've done:

1   We either created a Hopsworks instance or are using the demo instance provided to us.

2   We installed the Hopsworks Python API wrapper to allow us access to our feature store using code.

3   We created two feature groups from our day trading case study:

   a   `price_volume_features` holds features related to the closing price and volume columns as well as our date/time features.

   b   `twitter_features` holds the features that we constructed from our Twitter dataset.

Now, we have our feature store set up, and we have actual data in our feature store in two feature groups. It's time to put on our data scientist hat and read the data back from our feature store into our notebooks.

8.2.3   Using feature groups to select data

We have some data in our feature store in our two feature groups. We can take a look at our data by calling the read method of our feature group.

The code in listing 8.5 will do the following:

1 Get the feature group for our Twitter features (this can be done at any time now).
2 Read the data into a pandas DataFrame, using the `read` method of the feature group instance.
3 Inspect the data.

Listing 8.5   Reading data from our Twitter feature group

```
twitter_fg = fs.get_feature_group(
    name="twitter_features", version='1')

data_from_fs_twitter = twitter_fg.read()

data_from_fs_twitter.head()
```

Get our data out of the feature store as a pandas DataFrame.

You may notice the prefixes that Hopsworks put on our columns, signifying that it is part of a feature group. This is usually done only when reading the data back as a pandas DataFrame.

We have two feature groups now, but how do we join them together to do our work? That's a great question—we have two ways of doing that. We can simply join them together, as seen in the following listing.

Listing 8.6   Joining our two feature groups together

```
query = twitter_fg.select_all().join(
    price_volume_fg.select_all(), on=['date', 'symbol'])

query.show(2)   ◁——— Show our joined data.
```

Combine our two feature groups to reconstruct our original data.

This gives back our original dataset as a pandas DataFrame (figure 8.13).

	right_fg0.symbol	right_fg0.date	right_fg0.feature__rolling_7_day_total_tweets
0	TWLO	1582815600000000000	213.0
1	TWLO	1582819200000000000	216.0

Figure 8.13   Joining our two feature groups gives us a DataFrame, just like the CSV we started with.

Hopsworks also provides basic descriptive statistics on our feature groups, as seen in figure 8.14. For the most part, it will not provide any statistics we haven't already gotten ourselves using Python in this book; however, these statistics may be useful for other folks who may not be as adept at using Python as the experienced data scientist. With our data in the feature store with online features enabled, we can also now grab our most recent features by passing a simple online flag when reading data, as in listing 8.7.

Figure 8.14   Hopsworks offers some basic statistics about features but usually nothing we wouldn't be able to get on our own.

Listing 8.7   Getting online features

```
price_volume_fg = fs.get_feature_group(
    name="price_volume_features", version='1')

price_volume_fg.read(online=True)    ⟵—— Only get the most recent datapoint.
```

This code provides a low-latency (i.e., fast—within milliseconds) way to grab the most recent features for a given entity (TWLO in this case) to power our real-time predictions. Now that we have set up our main data objects—the feature groups—let's turn our attention to how we can use feature groups to create training datasets and investigate data lineage or provenance.

8.3   Creating training data in Hopsworks

Our features currently live in two mutually exclusive feature groups. Let's imagine we have a new team member joining us in our endeavor, and we need to show them how to get data in order to start experimenting. Hopsworks and other feature groups will have features to help us expedite and simplify this process, so we can get back to the important work of ML and feature engineering. Let's start by joining our feature groups to create a reproducible training dataset.

8.3.1   Training datasets

The training dataset feature in Hopsworks provides an easy-to-use centralized location for creating and maintaining training datasets to train ML models on. Let's turn our attention to the UI to easily create a new training dataset from the two feature groups we have already created. A common use case for this would be if you had multiple people on your data team, and you all wanted to share a common training set, so you could compare results after working separately. Every person would have the same training split and testing split, and you would be able to compare everyone's work fairly.

Let's start to create our own training dataset. By clicking Create New Training Dataset on Hopsworks, we will see a screen like that in figure 8.15.

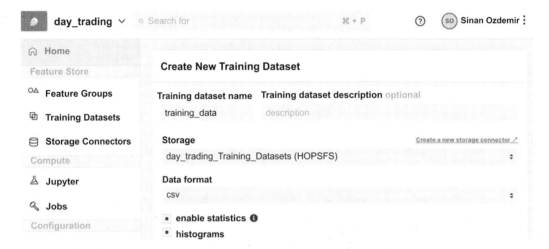

Figure 8.15   The Create New Training Dataset screen allows us to combine feature groups together to create a unified dataset.

Once we are on the page to create a new training dataset, we are presented with a few options. The first one is our data sources. The dataset needs to know which features we want to include. Luckily, it includes a handy UI (figure 8.16) for choosing features by placing them in a basket. Let's go ahead and select both our feature groups and all of the features within them.

Once we have selected our feature groups and our features for our training dataset, we need to define our join operation. This tells Hopsworks how to combine the two feature groups based on keys that they share in common. For our use case, we will join on *symbol* and *date*, as seen in figure 8.17.

Now that we have chosen our feature groups and told Hopsworks how to combine them, the last thing we will do is define our splits. We can set up splits of our data, so they remain consistent across the organization. If 50 people decide they want to use this training dataset, they will be working with the same splits as everyone else, so their results can be compared fairly.

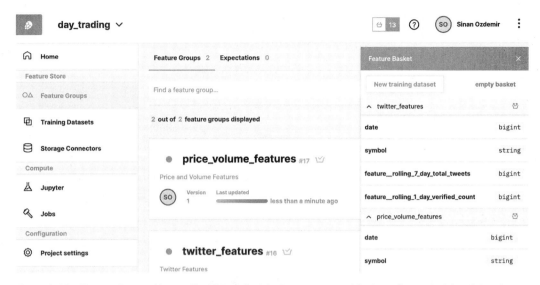

Figure 8.16   Hopsworks provides a nifty UI to select feature groups and features for our training datasets.

Feature group joins

twitter_features ↔ price_volume_features

twitter_features		inner joins	price_volume_features	
date	⇕	↔	date	⇕
symbol	⇕	↔	symbol	⇕ ×
Add join key				

Figure 8.17   We can define our feature joins, so the training dataset knows how to combine our feature groups into a single unified dataset.

Let's set up a training split, which will consist of 80% of our data, and a testing split, which will house the remaining 20%. Figure 8.18 shows what that looks like in the Hopsworks UI. Let's create our first training dataset and use some more Python code to pull it down and check it out (listing 8.8).

Splits

Name	Proportion (percent)
training	80
testing	20
Add a split	

Figure 8.18   Setting up splits in our training dataset allows for consistent and fair comparisons of model training across the organization.

EXERCISE 8.1   Create a new training dataset, using only two features from both of our feature groups. They can be any two features of your choosing.

Listing 8.8   Reading our training and testing datasets from Hopsworks

```
td = fs.get_training_dataset('training_data', version=1)
```
⟵ Select our training dataset from Hopsworks.

```
training_df = td.read(split='training')
print(training_df.shape)
```
│ Read and print the shape of our training set.

```
(1555, 18)
```

```
testing_df = td.read(split='testing')
print(testing_df.shape)
(403, 18)
```
│ Read and print the shape of our testing set.

This dataset is presplit and already contains all of the features from our feature groups. Anyone who pulls this dataset can now know that they work with the same data as everyone else (figure 8.19). This is merely one of the many features that feature stores offer that provide stability and access to data to all data team members.

Figure 8.19   Training datasets provide an easy-to-distribute training dataset so you can make sure that everyone has the same data, the same splits, so comparing work can be much easier. Training datasets are also used to train and evaluate models.

It may seem that we could have just done these joins and splits manually via Python, which is correct. However, if we decided to do this manually for a team of, say, six, then we would have to create CSVs for our training and testing data and distribute them out, which can be a real hassle. What if our dataset changes, and we have to add more data? Then, we have to do our joins again, resplit and redistribute the data, and make sure everyone is using the same version of a dataset. This sounds like a huge hassle. Feature stores give us a simpler way to do this and to make sure that our data teams are always working with the most up-to-date versions of datasets. Now that we have a training dataset set up, let's take a look at another feature provided to us by Hopsworks that helps us track the lineage of our data: the provenance.

8.3.2   Provenance

It is important to know how datasets' values are populated, and more importantly, where the data values came from. This is especially important when we are building datasets from multiple data sources, like we are in our day trading example. We have values derived from a Twitter dataset and other values derived from historical closing and volume values for the stock price.

Knowing and retrieving data provenance—a well-defined lineage of data values—is often a security requirement for compliance regulations like SOC2 or HIPAA. If we know where data values are coming from, then we have a way to track potentially problematic data points or data sources.

Training datasets can be used to track the lineage of a model back to the features that were used to train it. As we've seen in chapter 4, models can be susceptible to bias, and it is more often the case that the data is responsible for the bias and not the models themselves. *Provenance* provides a quick snapshot into how datasets are populated and gives the user a way to backtrack from the model back to the raw source data, speeding up the process of mitigating bias in the pipeline.

Figure 8.20 highlights a simple provenance for our training data, showing that it is the combination of two feature groups—`price_volume_features` and `twitter_features`. In more complicated examples, you will most likely see this tree expanding wider and deeper, as you create deep data dependencies when creating training datasets.

Provenance

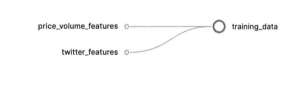

Figure 8.20   An example of a provenance (lineage) graph for our training dataset and the source feature groups in Hopsworks

Training datasets, like feature groups and feature statistics and provenance, are another feature of a feature store that can benefit a comprehensive data team or organization.

There are dozens of features across different feature stores out there, like provenance and the ability to create cloud-enabled training datasets. Even with a feature store in place, our work to discover features for our day trading application is only just beginning. With my feature store, I can now share my data with my team and enable them to come up with their own versions of models based on a shared data platform. I hope that as you continue your journey with feature engineering and grow your data team, you will keep in mind the benefits of implementing a feature store and even deploy one yourself!

8.4   *Answer to exercise*

EXERCISE 8.1

Create a new training dataset, using only two features from both of our feature groups. They can be any two features of your choosing.

ANSWER:

Answers will vary here, as you can choose whichever features you want to use! As long as you ended up with a training dataset using the procedure outlined in section 8.3.1 with four total features—two from `price_volume_features` and two from `twitter_features`—then you have succeeded!

Summary

- Feature stores provide a crucial missing link between disparate data sources, like application data and databases, and usability among data teams.
- Features are meant to be discovered and reused by data scientists.
- Real-time feature serving enables models to use the latest feature values with low latency.
- Feature stores generate consistent and reliable training data that can be shared across the data team to enforce consistency and stability.
- Feature stores provide a provenance trail to explain ML pipelines that are often a requirement for regulatory compliance.
- There are many feature store options out there, and some are open source, while others come at a financial cost. Choose the right one for your organization!

Putting it all together

This chapter covers

- A recap of the feature engineering pipeline
- The five categories of feature engineering
- Frequently asked questions about feature engineering
- Other less-common applications of feature engineering

Wow. We did it. We have been through a lot together—from trying to distinguish between COVID-19 and the flu to trying to predict the stock market and a lot of things in between. In each of our case studies, we saw ways of manipulating data for the explicit purposes of maximizing ML metrics, minimizing bias from data, and simplifying how we view data. This chapter aims to wrap up everything we've talked about in a neat bow and give you the confidence and power to use feature engineering to enhance your ML pipelines.

9.1 Revisiting the feature engineering pipeline

We've spent a long time in the weeds engineering features for all kinds of data and use cases. If we zoom back out and look at the feature engineering pipeline from our first chapter, we can see our overall goal: *transforming data into features that provide a signal to ML pipelines.*

In this book, we have mainly looked at feature engineering as a way to enhance predictive ML pipelines, but that is not the only use of feature engineering. We can also rely on these techniques to do the following:

- Clean data for business intelligence dashboards and analytics.
- Perform unsupervised ML, like topic modeling and clustering.

Feature engineering techniques can be used outside of traditional ML use cases. This text largely focused on the predictive ML use cases for feature engineering, but the techniques can be repurposed for different needs. Let's take a look at some key takeaways from our time together.

9.2 Key takeaways

This book is structured in a way in which you may have skipped around a few chapters if the case study wasn't beneficial for you. That's OK! Just in case, I want to leave you with a few takeaways:

- *Feature engineering is as crucial as ML model selection and hyperparameter tuning.* I hope this was clear. We improved ML pipeline performance drastically, and we never once touched the ML model itself. All our gains could be attributed to our feature engineering.
- *Always have a quantifiable way of telling if your features are helping or hurting.* This usually comes in training and testing a model on your features and measuring the change in predictive performance. Don't forget to split your data into training and test sets first!
- *Don't worry if some techniques you thought would help hurt pipeline performance.* Sometimes, feature engineering is an art, and it takes practice and patience to identify which techniques will work best.
- *Feature engineering is not a one-size-fits-all solution.* Just because we saw gains in one dataset using a technique doesn't mean the technique will produce similarly for another dataset. Every dataset and the domain it comes from is unique, and it is up to us to be diligent and thorough in our analysis.

Figure 9.1 outlines the train/test split paradigm in ML that we have been using to test our feature engineering techniques. You may have heard this term in a slightly different format as a *train/test/validate* split, which is similar, except with a third split. Our choice to rely on a simpler train/test split stemmed from the fact that our training set was split up many times via cross-validation, and our testing set was held constant across our feature engineering pipelines, which is what a validation set is used for. Let's zoom in on two of our main takeaways from this book to help solidify the main concepts.

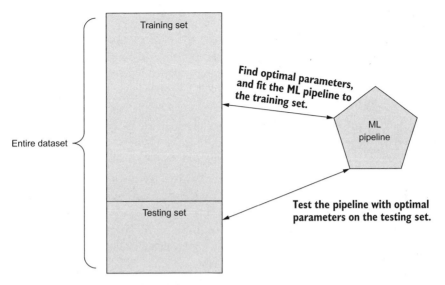

Figure 9.1   We must rely on training and testing datasets to validate our feature engineering work. We train our feature engineering techniques on the training set and apply them to the testing set to see if they work well on unseen data.

9.2.1   *Feature engineering is as crucial as ML model choice*

I hope one thing that is clear after making our way through these case studies is that feature engineering works. I realize that sounds obvious, but it truly is the one thing I hope you walk away with. *If you are a data scientist or machine learning engineer, spend thoughtful time engineering features and improving your performance.* It isn't always just about hyperparameter tuning and ML model selection.

How we choose to improve, construct, select, extract, and learn features can make all the difference in ML. What features we eventually choose to include in our pipeline will ultimately have an effect on the performance of our pipelines, as measured by classic performance metrics of the model—including accuracy and precision—as well as speed. Fewer, more efficient features generally mean faster, better performing, and sometimes even smaller models.

9.2.2   *Feature engineering isn't a one-size-fits-all solution*

We saw, in several case studies, that some techniques worked in some cases and didn't work in others. For example, when using the `SelectFromModel` object from scikit-learn in chapter 3, we saw that our results stayed about the same. In contrast, our performance plummeted when we used the same module in chapter 7 with our day trading algorithm. The same techniques will work differently for different datasets. It's up to us to be diligent, try options given our hypotheses and assumptions, and validate that we are on the right track by quantifying our performance.

9.3   Recap of feature engineering

Let's go over our five high-level categories of feature engineering and how we have applied them in our various case studies. Hopefully, this will help us recall them in the future in similar situations.

9.3.1   Feature improvement

Our feature improvement work dealt with augmenting existing features. We imputed missing data values, standardized features to force them to be on the same scale, and normalized values like *Yes* and *No* to be machine-readable Booleans. We relied on feature improvement heavily in several chapters when we needed to standardize features to be on the same scale, using the StandardScaler module from scikit-learn.

Our biggest example of feature improvement was data imputation—filling in missing data. We used many different forms of imputation, such as end-of-tail imputation and arbitrary imputation, to name two.

9.3.2   Feature construction

Feature construction is all about creating new features by hand. We did that by taking existing features and transforming them into new ones or joining our data with data from a new source. For example, we constructed Twitter-related features in our day trading case study by introducing social media data. Those Twitter features pushed our day trading model into the profitable zone. We constructed dozens of features in this book, including when we applied data transformations in chapter 4 to help our model work past the inherent bias in the data.

Examples of feature construction include the following:

- Data transformations, like Box-Cox and Yeo-Johnson, to affect the distribution/shape of our data.
- Binning data, like we did in chapter 3 to create new (usually ordinal) data from both numerical and categorical data. In chapter 3, we binned most of our numerical features to reduce the range of values that the feature could take on, hoping that it would make it easier for our ML pipeline to classify COVID-19 diagnoses.
- Domain-specific constructions, like constructing the MACD feature in chapter 7, the juv_count feature in chapter 4, or creating the FluSymptoms feature in chapter 3.

9.3.3   Feature selection

Throughout our case studies, we always asked ourselves, which of these features are just a lost cause? Not all features can be helpful, and that's OK. Feature selection techniques like mutual information, recursive feature elimination, and SelectKBest gave us easy and powerful tools to select the most useful features for our ML pipelines automatically.

Examples of feature selection include the following:

- `SelectFromModel`—We relied on ML models to rank and select features, given a threshold of importance.
- *Recursive feature elimination*—Iteratively removes features by running an estimator against the features/response, until we hit a desired number of features.

9.3.4 Feature extraction

Once we got the hang of improving, constructing, and selecting features, it was time to bring in the big guns by way of principal component analysis and polynomial feature extraction. These helped us generate a whole new set of features by applying mathematical transformations to our dataset to come up with a brand-new set of features that are oftentimes completely different than our starting features.

Feature extraction relies on mathematical transformations (usually by way of matrix math or linear algebra) to map our original data onto a new set of features that are optimal in some way. For principal component analysis, for example, our goal was to create a smaller set of features that didn't remove too much signal from our original data. Figure 9.2 shows the mathematical operation done in PCA to reduce the number of dimensions in the ML pipeline.

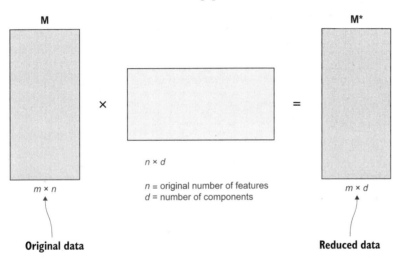

Figure 9.2   In chapter 5, we used principal component analysis to generate a new suite of features by reducing the number of dimensions to a more manageable number, while maintaining as much signal as possible from the original dataset.

Examples of feature extraction include the following:

- *Principal component analysis*—Generates a new, smaller set of features, using linear algebra. We used PCA in chapter 5 to reduce the number of features we got from our count and TFIDF vectorizers.
- *Learning fair representation*—We learned in chapter 4 that this helps us map our data to a fairer vector space to help mitigate the bias in our data.

9.3.5   *Feature learning*

If feature extraction techniques are the big guns, welcome to the gun show. Techniques like autoencoding and using deep learning feature extractors, like BERT and VGG-11, skyrocketed our performance when dealing with text and image data. We aren't limited to using feature learning techniques when working with unstructured data, but they are the most common use case. Figure 9.3 visualizes how we used the autoencoder to take in our original tabular data and reduce them down to a more compact form by learning latent representations between original features.

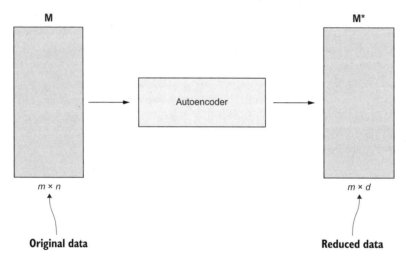

Figure 9.3   Chapter 5 also included an autoencoder that deconstructed and reconstructed our data to learn a latent representation of the underlying original feature set.

Examples of feature learning include the following:

- Autoencoders to learn latent representations from chapter 5.
- Also in chapter 5, we used a pretrained BERT to *extract* the features it had learned from its vast pretraining.
- We also relied on pretrained learned features in chapter 6 when we used the VGG-11 model to vectorize images.

9.4   *Data type–specific feature engineering techniques*

Thinking back to our first few chapters, we made a big deal around being able to identify the differences between structured and unstructured data (figure 9.4). Whether we are working with classical row/column structured data or less-organized unstructured data makes all the difference in what kinds of feature engineering techniques we are able to use.

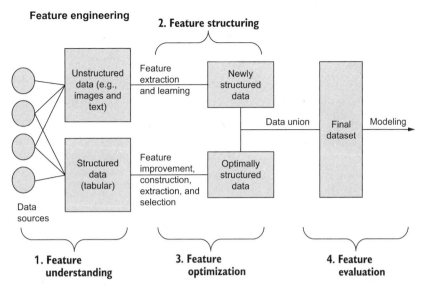

Figure 9.4   Our feature engineering pipeline from chapter 1 reminds us to treat structured and unstructured data differently to utilize both for our ML pipelines.

Thinking back to our feature engineering pipeline back in chapter 1, one of the first things we learned was how to treat structured and unstructured data differently. Let's revisit these concepts one more time after having seen them in action through many case studies. We will also revisit some of the major techniques available to us that are useful for enhancing the signal within our features.

9.4.1   *Structured data*

Much of our work in this text was on structured/tabular data. This kind of data generally comes in a CSV file, SQL query dump, and so on. When we were working with structured data, we had many tools in our arsenal.

DATA IMPUTATION

Imputing—or filling in—missing data is probably one of the most common techniques a data scientist will use when working with data. Data can be messy, especially when the data source is imperfect. We discussed multiple ways to impute data, including

- *Mean/median imputation*—We filled in missing values with either the mean or median of the rest of the column.
- *Arbitrary value imputation*—We filled in values with a static *missing* token to signify that the value was missing but still rendered the datapoint usable.

CONSTRUCTING DUMMY FEATURES FROM CATEGORICAL DATA

One of the most commonly applied feature engineering techniques for structured data is creating dummy features. This process—sometimes referred to as one-hot encoding—is performed on nominal features. We did this in chapter 3 when we were creating dummy features for the risk factors in our patient data. Creating dummy variables gives us a way to transform categorical data into something machine readable but comes at the cost of introducing many potentially harmful features that may confuse our pipelines.

In a later section, we will revisit dummy features in a bit more detail with different use cases and a helpful trick for knowing when to dummify features and, more importantly, when not to dummify data.

STANDARDIZATION AND NORMALIZATION

Standardization and normalization are both ways to transform existing features in place, meaning we aren't necessarily creating any new features so much as we are improving features that already exist. Data *standardization* is the act of altering the values of a feature to change the *scale* of the data, which would in turn change the min, max, mean, and so on without affecting the distribution or shape of the data too much or at all. We saw this in action when we applied both a min-max standardization and a z-score standardization to our data in chapter 3.

Data *normalization* has more to do with mapping features to a more machine-readable state. We also had to do some normalization in chapter 3 by mapping hardcoded values from humans, like *yes* and *no*, to Booleans that ML algorithms can understand. Normalizations are crucial when working with data from more human sources like surveys or forms.

DATA TRANSFORMS

Unlike standardization, transforms are meant to alter the distribution and shape of data physically. This can come in handy when we are trying to force our features to fit a normal distribution or we are concerned about bias in our data.

In chapter 4, upon investigating our COMPAS dataset, we learned that we had some deep correlations between race and other features that opened the door for bias to be introduced. We used the Yeo-Johnson transformation to reduce this correlation without rendering the age feature useless (figure 9.5), and we barely took a hit on our ML performance. In contrast, our measurable bias was reduced significantly.

These were only some of the many techniques we saw for dealing with structured data, and the main takeaway was that there could be a lot to do! Even after filling in missing data through imputation techniques and normalizing machine-unreadable values (the full feature engineering pipeline is shown in figure 9.6), we can apply transformations like Yeo-Johnson and standardization techniques like z-scores to make our data even more useful.

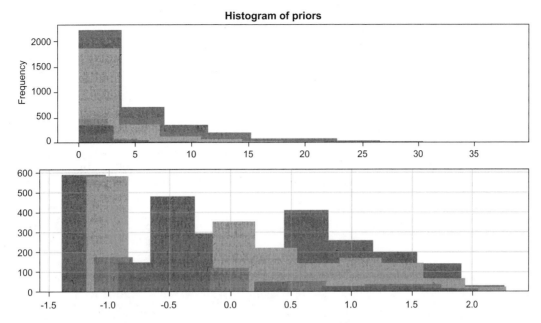

Figure 9.5   In chapter 4, we applied the Yeo-Johnson transformation to our original data (above) to create a new distribution of prior counts (below), making it difficult for our ML pipelines to draw correlations between protected features, like race, and features like priors counts. In our dataset, folks who identified as African American had more priors counts than the rest of the people in the dataset. That opened the door for bias to be introduced by reconstructing race from previous counts.

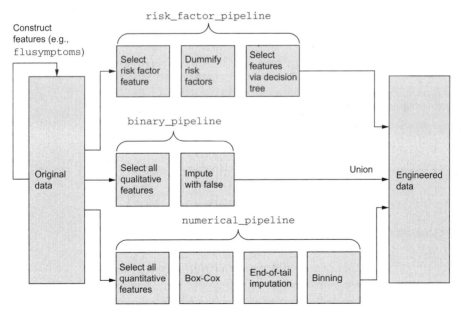

Figure 9.6   Our feature engineering pipeline from chapter 3 showed us how much work can go into transforming a raw dataset into something clean and usable by ML pipelines.

9.4.2 *Unstructured data*

The three types of unstructured data we worked on within this book are text, image, and time series. These are arguably the most difficult types of data to work with because they require the most massaging and manipulation to get to a state where the data are usable by ML pipelines.

TEXT DATA

Way back in chapter 5, we had to classify tweets with a sentiment label, and the game's name was vectorization. Our goal was to convert the raw tweet text into a vector of numbers that ML algorithms could interpret. We tried many different techniques, including bag-of-words vectorization and using learned features from BERT (figure 9.7).

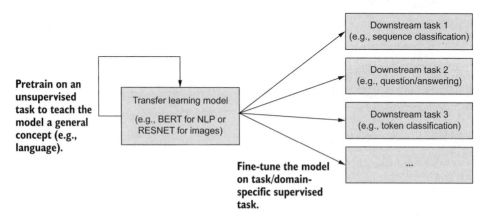

Figure 9.7   We relied on learned features from BERT in chapter 5 to obtain our best ML performance for sequence classification.

IMAGE DATA

In chapter 6, we ingested raw images and used computer vision algorithms to recognize what the images were. We saw new ways to vectorize data, just like we had to in chapter 5 with our text data. We used histograms of oriented gradients to extract features, and we used the VGG-11 deep learning architecture to learn features for our images. Unlike in chapter 5, using BERT, we went a step further and fine-tuned the VGG-11 model (shown in figure 9.8) on our data to obtain even more meaningful learned features. When working with text and image data, the most important thing is vectorizing the data in a meaningful way to our ML pipeline.

TIME-SERIES DATA

Time-series data are a bit odd in that they are structured in a row/column format, but at the same time they are primarily unstructured. By *unstructured* I mean we have to do a fair amount of feature engineering work to create a set of usable features for our ML pipelines, as seen in figure 9.9.

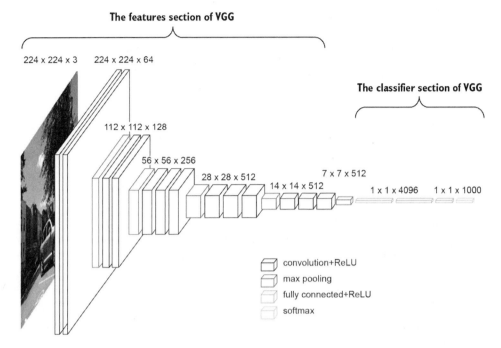

Figure 9.8 In chapter 6, we fine-tuned the VGG-11 model to obtain state-of-the-art object detection performance, using learned features.

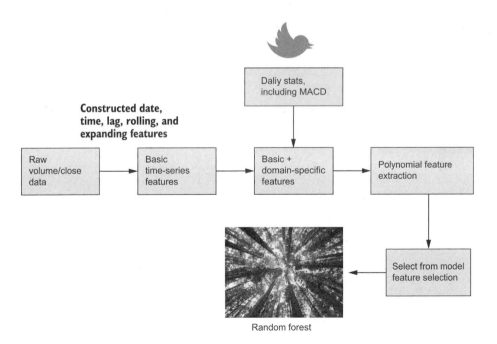

Figure 9.9 Our time series pipeline from chapter 6

Text, image, and time series data all had their unique ways of transforming the data into something meaningful. Still, it was up to us, the data scientists, to measure the effectiveness of our work by applying the features we engineered to our testing dataset and measuring the delta in performance.

9.5   *Frequently asked questions*

In this section, I'd like to take some time to walk through some common questions I get while I'm talking about my book or giving a lecture on feature engineering. These aren't the only questions I get, but they're definitely in the top 10 by volume.

9.5.1   *When should I dummify categorical variables vs. leaving them as a single column?*

Thinking back to one of our first feature engineering techniques, we sometimes need to convert qualitative variables into a feature that is machine readable as an integer or a floating-point decimal. In chapter 3, we dummified our risk factors into a large matrix with dozens of binary features like `chronic liver disorder`, `lung disease`, and others. In chapter 7, we created a column called `dayofweek` to signify the day of the week we were considering while day trading but did not dummify that column. Why did we dummify one qualitative column but leave the other alone? It comes down to our levels of data!

WHY NOT DUMMIFY EVERYTHING?

It's tempting to simply say, "Well, just dummify everything." But this will inevitably cause more harm than good. Dummifying any column comes with more cons than pros:

- Pros:
  - It makes a qualitative column machine readable.
- Cons:
  - It creates features that are guaranteed to be dependent on one another. If one dummy feature is 0, we can make a good guess that one of the other dummy features will be 1.
  - Each feature is unlikely to carry a massive amount of signal, and therefore, it is likely that the addition of all of these dummy features will add noise to our system. If we do not mitigate this noise, it will lead to a degradation of pipeline performance.

Really, our only pro is that it makes the feature machine readable, and everything else is a con. For nominal features (where there is no order—there are simply categories), dummifying the feature is pretty much our only option to use it. It is possible to convert the nominal feature into encoded integers (0 is the first category, 1 is the second category, etc.), but this will be confusing to the pipeline because it looks like an ordinal column, where 1 somehow is after/better than 0, which is not true.

WARNING You should never encode nominal features into a single feature of integers like you would ordinal features.

Say we have a dataset with two columns:

- *Month*—An ordinal column with time being our order
- *City*—A nominal column

Because `Month` is ordinal, I would encode it in place, using `sklearn.preprocessing.LabelEncoder`, and because *City* is nominal, I'd rely on `pandas.get_dummies` or `sklearn.preprocessing.OneHotEncoder` to create one-hot encodings (dummy features) for each known category. This can be seen in figure 9.10.

Index	Month (ordinal column)	City (nominal column)
0	December	San Francisco
1	January	Istanbul
2	March	Karachi

Index	Month (encoded ordinal)	San Francisco (dummy)	Istanbul (dummy)	Karachi (dummy)
0	12	1	0	0
1	1	0	1	0
2	3	0	0	1

Figure 9.10 Nominal features should become dummy variables, while ordinal features should stay as single, encoded features.

With ordinal features, we don't need to dummify the values because by simply encoding the categories as integers (0, 1, 2, etc.), we maintain order in our system (literally and figuratively), and we don't need to add new noisy dummy features into our system.

TAKEAWAY

We've learned the following:

- If your feature is nominal, dummify it (using `pandas.get_dummies`, `sklearn.preprocessing.OneHotEncoder`, or `sklearn.preprocessing.MultiLabelBinarizer`, like we used in chapter 3).
- If your feature is ordinal, do not dummify it; rather, encode it in place as integers.

9.5.2 *How do I know if I need to deal with bias in my data?*

OK, this is a tough one, but there are a few rules of thumb to consider right out of the gate. Remember that bias is often thought about in a human context, but really, it is a disproportionate prejudice for or against *something* that may or may not be human:

- Do your data points directly represent human beings like the COMPAS dataset in chapter 4?
  - If yes, do your data have any protected variables in it? This would include sex, gender, race, and age.
- Is the response of your data subjective? Our airline sentiment data in chapter 5 could be considered subjective if people disagree on what is positive or negative.
- Is the data source nonrepresentative of the population you will eventually use your model on? Put another way, do your training data not look like the data you will be eventually applying your model on?

If you answered yes to any of the preceding questions, then bias is likely to be present in your dataset. Bias, as a topic, requires a much longer discussion than what we were able to discuss in our single chapter dedicated to the topic. In the final section of this book, you will find resources to learn more about bias in AI/ML.

TAKEAWAY

Bias isn't always as obvious as it was in the COMPAS dataset. I encourage you to think hard about your data and pipeline's ability to affect real people and their lives and use your judgment as a barometer of whether or not you feel the need to dive deeper into bias detection.

9.6 *Other feature engineering techniques*

We didn't have time to cover every single feature engineering technique in this book, but we can briefly cover three more that often come up for my students. Of course, even then we won't have covered everything, but my first and foremost goal is to give you the ability to self-diagnose and analyze your own data, so you can continue to do research or learn on your own.

9.6.1 *Categorical dummy bucketing*

Thinking back to our previous FAQ regarding when to dummify qualitative features, we have another less common technique that, if applicable, can be quite helpful. It's called *categorical dummy bucketing*, and it is a combination of bucketing feature values and dummifying the buckets. This is similar to the idea of *binning* that we saw in chapter 3 when we introduced the KBinsDiscretizer class in scikit-learn.

Say we have a dataset with a *City* column, like in our last example in the last section. Each value is a string that represents a city in the world. There are a lot of those, in my experience, so perhaps we don't want to create a dummy variable for each city. Why? Because as we mentioned earlier, this can cause an explosion in the number of features in our dataset with a likely burst of noise being introduced. So instead, let's take the following approach:

1   We will bucket the nominal feature (city) into larger categories. In our case let's make two categories: Western Hemisphere and Eastern Hemisphere.
2   Once we have buckets, we can create dummy variables of the larger categories, rather than the original feature values.

This process can be visualized in figure 9.11, showing how we went from a *City* column filled with a bunch of cities around the world to two larger dummy buckets, Western or Eastern Hemisphere.

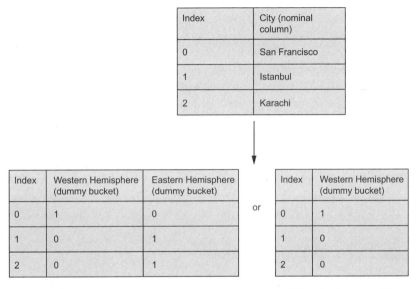

Figure 9.11   Nominal features should end up as dummy variables. In the case of two categories, I'd recommend removing one of the dummy variables because they are 100% correlated in this case. A 0 in one feature means the other feature is 1.

NOTE   When dummifying a nominal feature, we have the option of omitting one of the dummy features. This is because if the pipeline had the values of the other dummy features, it can, with 100% accuracy, predict the one we omitted. We are, in theory, losing little to no information. For a large amount of features (say $x > 10$) this will likely not cause a huge difference, but if we have fewer than 10 categories, it may be worth it.

We can't always perform dummy bucketing on nominal features, and this should be a decision by the data scientist or ML engineer in charge of the project. The main consideration is that, by the nature of bucketing, we are intentionally losing granularity in the feature values. *San Francisco* becomes the exact same thing as *Rio de Janeiro* because they are both in the Western Hemisphere. Is this OK for your ML problem? Do we need to make more granular buckets to give the pipeline more signal? I cannot answer that question without knowing your unique problem, but I encourage you to think about it.

TAKEAWAY

Categorical dummy bucketing is a great way to encode nominal features while mitigating the number of features that can be created when blindly dummifying features. Be aware, however, of the data you lose when squashing granular values into larger buckets or categories.

9.6.2   *Combining learned features with conventional features*

In chapters 5 and 6 we dealt with images and raw text as our main sources of data, and we eventually relied on state-of-the-art transfer learning techniques and deep learning models, like BERT and VGG-11, to *vectorize* our raw text and images into fixed-length vectors. Both case studies made a pretty big assumption in that the text and images alone were all the information you needed to perform our task. In both cases this was likely true, but what if in chapter 5 we wanted to combine vectorized text with other features about the tweet, like the number of mentions in the tweet or whether the tweet was a retweet?

We have two basic options (seen in figure 9.12):

- We can concatenate the vectorized text with a vector of the conventional features to make a longer vector of information to pass into our ML pipeline.
- Combine the text and features into a *feature-rich* text that we can vectorize and use in our pipeline.

Option 1 is more popular when our other features are at the ratio/interval levels, whereas option 2 is more popular when our other features are nominal/ordinal.

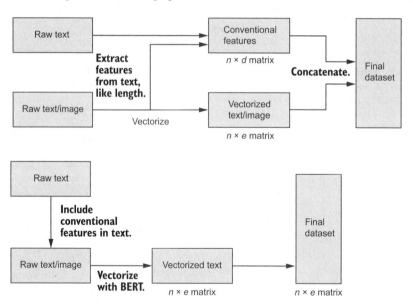

Figure 9.12   Option 1 (top) to incorporate conventional features with text is to concatenate the vectorized text. Option 1 can also work with image data. Option 2 (bottom) to incorporate conventional features with text is to create a single *feature-rich* text to vectorize and use in our ML pipeline. This option only works with text, as we don't really have a way to incorporate features into a single feature-rich image.

Concatenating data like this is easy using the `FeatureUnion` class in scikit-learn or by simply concatenating them using pandas, like we did in past chapters. The second option can be a bit difficult as a concept, so let's take a look at some code to create sample feature-rich texts, using the same Twitter data from chapter 5. Let's begin by importing our tweet data from the previous chapter in the following listing. The dataset can be seen in figure 9.13.

Listing 9.1 Ingesting tweets from chapter 5

```python
import pandas as pd

tweet_df = pd.read_csv(
    '../data/cleaned_airline_tweets.csv')      Import our tweets
                                                from chapter 5.
tweet_df.head()
```

	text	sentiment
0	@VirginAmerica What @dhepburn said.	neutral
1	@VirginAmerica it was amazing, and arrived an ...	positive
2	@VirginAmerica I <3 pretty graphics. so muc...	positive
3	@VirginAmerica So excited for my first cross c...	positive
4	I ♥ flying @VirginAmerica. ☺	positive

Figure 9.13 Our original tweet dataset from chapter 5

Now that we have our tweets, let's begin by adding a few new features we didn't construct in chapter 5. First, let's isolate the emojis in the tweet as a list, as shown in the following listing.

Listing 9.2 Counting the number of emojis

```python
import emoji                                    Use a package called emoji. To
                                                install, run pip3 install emoji.
english_emojis = emoji.UNICODE_EMOJI['en']

def extract_emojis(s):
    return [english_emojis[c] for c in s if c in english_emojis]
                                                                    Convert emojis to
tweet_df['emojis'] = tweet_df['text'].map(                          English words.
    lambda x: extract_emojis(x))

tweet_df['num_emojis'] = tweet_df['emojis'].map(len)     Count the number of
                                                         emojis used in the tweet.
```

With `num_emojis` as a new feature, let's create a few more (listing 9.3):

- `mention_count`—This is a ratio-level integer that counts the number of mentions in the tweet.
- `retweet`—A nominal Boolean will track whether the tweet was a retweet.

Listing 9.3   Counting mentions and retweets

```
tweet_df['mention_count'] = tweet_df['text'].map(
    lambda x: x.count('@'))

tweet_df['retweet'] = tweet_df['text'].map(
    lambda x: x.startswith('RT '))

tweet_df.head()
```

Count the number of
mentions in the tweet.

Boolean, whether or not
the tweet is a retweet

Now that we have three new features, listing 9.4 will show us how to create a feature-rich text object that includes the original tweet text as well as the three features we just created. By creating this feature-rich text, we are letting the deep learning algorithms read and learn from the features without specifically calling them out as columnar features.

> **NOTE**   I am not claiming that these features are definitely going to be signals for our use case. I am simply creating these features as an example of creating feature-rich text.

Listing 9.4   Creating feature-rich text

```
import preprocessor as tweet_preprocessor

# remove urls and mentions
tweet_preprocessor.set_options(
    tweet_preprocessor.OPT.URL, tweet_preprocessor.OPT.NUMBER
)

def combine_text(row):
    return f'tweet: {tweet_preprocessor.clean(row.text)}. \
mention_count: {row.mention_count}. \
emojis: {" ".join(row.emojis)}. \
retweet: {row.retweet}'


tweet_df['combined_text'] = tweet_df.apply(
    combine_text, axis=1)

print(tweet_df.iloc[4]['combined_text'])

tweet_df.head()
```

Use the same tweet preprocessor
we used in chapter 5.

A function that takes in a row of data and creates a
single piece of text with all of our features in them.

Vectorize this feature-rich text
instead of the original text.

The output of this is a feature-rich piece of text (see the combined_text feature in figure 9.14) that has

- The tweet text
- The mention count
- An itemized list of emojis in English
- Retweet

```
tweet: I 💜 flying @VirginAmerica. 😊👍. mention_count: 1. emojis:
:red_heart: :smiling_face: :thumbs_up:. retweet: False
```

	text	sentiment	length	emojis	num_emojis	combined_text	mention_
0	@VirginAmerica What @dhepburn said.	neutral	35	[]	0	tweet: @VirginAmerica What @dhepburn said.. me...	
1	@VirginAmerica it was amazing, and arrived an ...	positive	80	[]	0	tweet: @VirginAmerica it was amazing, and arri...	
2	@VirginAmerica I <3 pretty graphics. so muc...	positive	83	[]	0	tweet: @VirginAmerica I <3 pretty graphics....	
3	@VirginAmerica So excited for my first cross c...	positive	140	[]	0	tweet: @VirginAmerica So excited for my first ...	
4	I 💜 flying @VirginAmerica. 😊👍	positive	31	[:red_heart:, :smiling_face:, :thumbs_up:]	3	tweet: I 💜 flying @VirginAmerica. 😊👍. mentio...	

Figure 9.14   An example of our feature-rich text along with our final DataFrame

Now, we can vectorize our new feature-rich text using BERT or some other text vectorizer and use that instead of simply vectorizing the text. Newer deep learning models like BERT are better at recognizing the different features in feature-rich text, but vectorizers like `TfidfVectorizer` and `CountVectorizer` can still work.

TAKEAWAY

Combining traditional tabular features with raw text features can be troublesome. One way to invoke the power of transfer learning is to combine them into one large, feature-rich text feature and let our deep learning algorithm (e.g., BERT) learn the feature interaction for us.

9.6.3   *Other raw data vectorizers*

We've looked at base BERT and VGG-11 in chapters 5 and 6 for vectorizing text and images, respectively, but these are far from our only options for text and images, and we never even covered vectorizers for other forms of raw data, like audio. On Hugging Face—an AI community—there is a repository of models that we can use for our ML pipelines. To check them, head to https://huggingface.co/models (shown in figure 9.15), and filter by Feature Extractors.

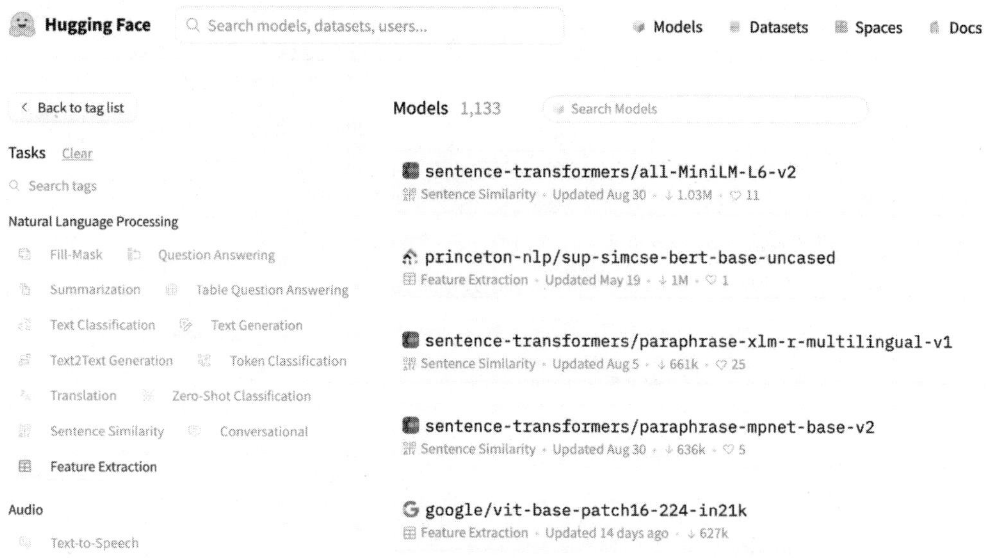

Figure 9.15   Hugging Face has a repository of models and feature extractors that we can use.

Some alternative feature extractors we could use that I personally find useful are

- https://huggingface.co/sentence-transformers/all-MiniLM-L6-v2—Maps text to a 384-dimensional vector space. This model is excellent for applications like clustering or semantic search.
- https://huggingface.co/google/vit-base-patch16-224-in21k—The Vision Transformer, by Google, is a transformer encoder model (like BERT but for images) pretrained on a large collection of images called ImageNet-21k, at a resolution of 224 × 224 pixels.
- https://huggingface.co/roberta-base—RoBERTa is a model pretrained on a large corpus of English data in a self-supervised fashion. It is like BERT in that it is for text, except RoBERTa is larger and trained on more data.

TAKEAWAY

Explore different ways of vectorizing text, images, and other forms of raw data to find what works for you and your use cases! Repositories like Hugging Face are great centralized locations.

9.7   *Further reading material*

Of course, your learning experience isn't over just because you've successfully finished this book! Here are some other resources to help you on your journey to becoming the most aware and well-rounded data scientist/ML engineer you can be!

- *The Principles of Data Science* (2nd ed.) by yours truly is my introductory text to data science to help you learn the techniques and math you need to start making sense of your data. See https://www.oreilly.com/library/view/principles-of-data/9781789804546/.
- *MLOps Engineering at Scale* by Carl Osipov is a guide to bringing your experimental ML code to production, using serverless capabilities from major cloud providers. See https://www.manning.com/books/mlops-engineering-at-scale.
- *Machine Learning Bookcamp* by Alexey Grigorev presents realistic, practical ML scenarios, along with crystal-clear coverage of key concepts for those who are looking to get started with ML. See https://www.manning.com/books/machine-learning-bookcamp.
- Some live projects for more practice dealing with bias include
  - *Mitigating Bias with Preprocessing*—https://www.manning.com/liveproject/mitigating-bias-with-preprocessing
  - *Mitigating Bias with Postprocessing*—https://www.manning.com/liveproject/mitigating-bias-with-postprocessing
  - *Measuring Bias in a Dataset*—https://www.manning.com/liveproject/measuring-bias-in-a-dataset

Summary

- Feature engineering is a broad field of study, and there isn't always a single technique to use to tackle each situation. Achieving a sense of proficiency in feature engineering comes with constant practice, patience, and researching about new techniques.
- The base trajectory of feature engineering is to
  - Gather available data from one or more sources.
  - Combine and convert data into structured quantitative features.
  - Fill in as many missing values as possible.
  - Drop any features that are missing too many values.
  - Apply transformations to features to create a dataset with as much signal as possible for ML pipelines.
  - Fit a model to measure performance of the pipeline, and repeat previous steps as needed.
- More data are not always better, and smaller datasets are not always more efficient. Every ML situation calls for something different, and every data scientist may have their own metrics to optimize for. Always measure metrics that matter, and throw away any techniques that do not optimize those metrics.
- Feature engineering is a creative practice. Often, what makes a great engineer is someone who can sit with the data for a while and construct/learn interesting signals/features based on their domain knowledge of the problem.

index

A new online reading experience

liveBook, our online reading platform, adds a new dimension to your Manning books, with features that make reading, learning, and sharing easier than ever. A liveBook version of your book is included FREE with every Manning book.

This next generation book platform is more than an online reader. It's packed with unique features to upgrade and enhance your learning experience.

- Add your own notes and bookmarks
- One-click code copy
- Learn from other readers in the discussion forum
- Audio recordings and interactive exercises
- Read all your purchased Manning content in any browser, anytime, anywhere

As an added bonus, you can search every Manning book and video in liveBook—even ones you don't yet own. Open any liveBook, and you'll be able to browse the content and read anything you like.*

Find out more at www.manning.com/livebook-program.

*Open reading is limited to 10 minutes per book daily

RELATED MANNING TITLES

Machine Learning Bookcamp
Build a portfolio of real-life projects
by Alexey Grigorev

ISBN 9781617296819
472 pages, $49.99
October 2021

Data Science Bookcamp
Five real-world Python projects
by Leonard Apeltsin

ISBN 9781617296253
704 pages, $59.99
October 2021

For ordering information, go to www.manning.com